Lynda Lyday's
Do It Yourself

Lynda Lyday's
Do It Yourself

The Room-by-Room, Step-by-Step
Guide to the Most Popular Home Repair
and Renovation Projects

A PERIGEE BOOK

THE BERKLEY PUBLISHING GROUP
Published by the Penguin Group
Penguin Group (USA) Inc.
375 Hudson Street, New York, New York 10014, USA
Penguin Group (Canada), 10 Alcorn Avenue, Toronto, Ontario M4V 3B2, Canada
(a division of Pearson Penguin Canada Inc.)
Penguin Books Ltd., 80 Strand, London WC2R 0RL, England
Penguin Group Ireland, 25 St. Stephen's Green, Dublin 2, Ireland (a division of Penguin Books Ltd.)
Penguin Group (Australia), 250 Camberwell Road, Camberwell, Victoria 3124, Australia
(a division of Pearson Australia Group Pty. Ltd.)
Penguin Books India Pvt. Ltd., 11 Community Centre, Panchsheel Park, New Delhi—110 017, India
Penguin Group (NZ), Cnr. Airborne and Rosedale Roads, Albany, Auckland 1310, New Zealand
(a division of Pearson New Zealand Ltd.)
Penguin Books (South Africa) (Pty.) Ltd., 24 Sturdee Avenue, Rosebank, Johannesburg 2196,
South Africa
Penguin Books Ltd., Registered Offices: 80 Strand, London WC2R 0RL, England

Copyright © 2005 by Lynda Lyday
Text design by Tiffany Estreicher
Cover design by Ben Gibson
Cover photo © by Kelly Campbell

PRINTING HISTORY
Perigee trade paperback edition / April 2005

PERIGEE is a registered trademark of Penguin Group (USA) Inc.
The "P" design is a trademark belonging to Penguin Group (USA) Inc.

Library of Congress Cataloging-in-Publication Information

Lyday, Lynda.
    Lynda Lyday's do-it yourself : the illustrated, stey-by-step guide to the most popular
home renovation and repair projects / Lynda Lyday.
        p.   cm.
    ISBN 0-399-53091-6
    1. Dwellings—Maintenance and repair—Amateurs' manuals.
  2. Dwellings—Remodeling—Amateurs' manuals.   3. Do-it-yourself work.   I. Title.

TH4817.3.L96   2005
643'.7—dc22

                                                                    2004057675

PRINTED IN THE UNITED STATES OF AMERICA

10   9   8   7   6   5   4   3   2   1

To my parents, Dot and Bob Lyday,
and
to all those who thought they could do it,
were told they couldn't do it,
and went ahead and did it anyway!

ACKNOWLEDGMENTS

I could have never written this book without the support of my family and friends. First, I'd like to thank my parents, who thought I was absolutely nuts wanting to become a carpenter in the '80s and now are my biggest fans! Thanks to the rest of my family for all your many words of encouragement, which mean so much to me.

A special thanks to artist extraordinaire Rose Masterpol, who not only helped me find my illustrator and design the original concept for the cover, but also helped me believe in myself as a writer. Thank you for all your advice and support through every decision I had to make when writing this book.

Many thanks to the very talented illustrator Marcia Underwood, who put in painstaking hours and never complained once. My thanks to Peepaw (a.k.a. Kecia Quin) for the hours of combing through and editing my first draft. Thank you Don DeFranco, for counseling me through the rough times and always believing in my ability. You will always be my go-to man! Thanks to Heidi Oringer, who I can call up any time of day in a panic and ask a grammatical question and hang up the phone laughing. Thanks to Cathleen Young, for all the lunches and being of sound mind to give me advice even though you just gave birth to twins! Erica Perel, I thank you for all your professional advice, support, and helping me keep a cool head. A special thanks to Brian Santos, "The Wall Wizard," for allowing me to share his magic potions in this book.

To my agent, Alex Smithline, thank you for all your hard work and hours of advice. To the folks at Perigee Books, thank you for believing in me and giving me this opportunity to write this book. Many thanks to Christel Winkler, my editor, for your keen eye, clear mind, and making every phone call enjoyable, and I thank Katie McHugh for all the work you did early in the project. Patricia Horan, thank you for your hard work on the proposal and the many words of encouragement, which I still hold dear to my heart.

Thanks to the Discovery Channel and Bo Kaprall, for my start on the Discovery Channel. Thanks to Scripps Networks, HGTV, and the DIY Network, for the opportuntiy to co-host *The Fix* and *Talk2DIY*.

There could be no other than Kelly Campbell to shoot this cover. Kelly, you're the best! To Phyllis, Tracey, and Vikki, thank you for your generous use of your homes for the cover shoot.

And many thanks to the rest of my friends for your support: Brigette, Jack, Chris Herrmann, Chris DeFranco, Candace, Carol, Cissy and the rest of Charlie's Angels, Dorie, Laura for that last-minute proofreading, Pop, Kelley, Leslie, Donna, Lisa, Stef, Randy, and the rest of you who were there for me from the start.

I wouldn't be able to write this book if it weren't for all the carpenters I worked with over the years. Dennis Currier, my very first foreman at 75 Rockefeller Center, thank you for all your teachings and techniques, for getting me into the union, and for your friendship! My thanks to Harlow Haagensen. If it wasn't for you, the Discovery Channel would have never found me. Ray O'Kane, I owe you big time for getting me into the Carpentry School when there were only a handful of women carpenters. Thanks to all the men in Local 608 in Manhattan, who shared their trade secrets with me and helped me learn my trade. Saul at the Lumber Store on Eighth Avenue, thank you for always coming through for me.

A special thanks to our Rhodesian Ridgeback, Frankie, who laid at my feet under my desk while I wrote this book. Frankie, I could have never written this without you by my side. May you rest in peace.

Many thanks to all the viewers and readers whose courage to tackle home repairs inspired me to write this book.

CONTENTS

PROLOGUE

How does a gal like me come to write a book on home repair you may ask? Well, the journey has been a long one. A hard one. But a rewarding one.

The first thing I ever watched being built back home in Atlanta was a house. A tree house. I was watching because no one would let me help. I wasn't even allowed to walk up the three steps to the second level—way too dangerous for a little Southern girl. Okay, I was only five. I'll cut the builders—my Dad and brother—some slack.

When there was a project to be done in the house, there was a lot of prepping for it, beginning with phone calls next door to "Uncle Wallace," our neighbor. Wallace and my Dad would clean the gutters together, dig the ditch out back that divided our property from theirs so the water would drain properly, and so on. Year in and year out, I saw what had to be done to maintain a home and grounds, and how much easier it was when Dad and Uncle Wallace helped each other.

There was never a thought of wives or daughters helping with any of these outside projects. This was a man's territory, and all the women got the message . . . except for me.

When it came to painting, though, my mother rolled up her sleeves and pitched in. They were a crew, Bob and Dot, my parents. For some reason, a woman was trusted with a paint brush, and my mom was always assigned the trim while Dad tackled the walls. Not until years later did I realize the skill and steady hand it took to cut-in properly to the wall.

Once, when I was eleven years old, I found a starving kitten. After a successful covert action by my mother, I was allowed to keep her. But when winter came, my mom stuck to our agreement and wouldn't let me bring the cat inside. So I had to come up with some kind of shelter. I spotted a triangular-shaped cat house at one of the stores, and I waited until my dad had business out of town. It was then that I built my first project. I simply re-created what I saw in the store, and soon paneling, nails, and carpet made my little kitty a shelter for the cold weather. My mom eventually broke down and let "Puss" indoors, but the house remained for years.

Building that cat house felt good. So when I turned sixteen, I decided to take shop class in high school. I hardly got the plea out of my mouth before my answer was a huge laugh and an absolute "No" from Mom. So I took home ec instead and learned how to sew pleats in a halter top. (To this day I swear it's easier to use a router than to sew a good pleat!)

When I was about twenty-one and living in New York City, I began to feel called to the ministry. Don't ask me why . . . because I wasn't religious. All I knew is that it would certainly hamper my acting career, which had brought me to Manhattan in the first place, so I prayed for something else . . . anything else!

A month later, I was at a friend's home for dinner. While she was showing me her new kitchen counter and countertops, I glided my hand over the woodwork and an epiphany shot through me. That's what I've always wanted to do . . . learn carpentry! I went to the restaurant where I worked and told my manager, Fredda, about my decision. She informed me about the union. Unions! You mean the "Communists" my father used to warn me about back in Atlanta?

Yes indeed, the union. I called the closest carpenter's union, which had merged with a local in the Bronx. I got a business agent on the phone who was completely taken aback that it was a woman calling. He sputtered, "Well, come to the union hall and talk to me if you're serious!"

I was . . . so I did.

Even more baffled when I actually showed up, Business Agent Marcello Svedese picked up the phone and spoke with the Union Carpentry School. I was to go down to the school to enroll . . . and say that I was working on a job in the Bronx. I went to the union school, found the back door, and for the next four years I learned how to read a rule, form concrete, hang everything from a door to acoustical ceiling, laminate a countertop, and so on. From there, I was given a test like all fourth-year apprentices. I aced it so solidly that I was asked to be in the fourth-year apprenticeship contest. As a matter of fact, I was *told* I was going to be a contestant. Because I was the first "girl" to ever get that far, they were going to make sure I showed up for the contest. When I received a Golden Hammer Award and a cash prize, they asked me to teach carpentry. I did, and years later, I became a contractor.

Ask any groundbreaking woman, being the only gal among guys is a special challenge. All our lives we've heard stories about the lengths people will go to get what they want. You know, "I walked twenty-five miles to school barefoot in winter." Well, my sacrifice was left on the floor of a beauty parlor. I had come to the conclusion that if I were to learn this trade and be taken seriously, I needed to follow Barbra Streisand's example in *Yentl* and remove as many traces of "the little lady" as I could. So I had my hair cut. Short. Real short. Shockingly short. So short, in fact, that when I was walking home (not twenty-five miles!) from the Union Carpentry School one night, I was approached by a couple "ladies of the evening." You can imagine my surprise! They, too, were a bit caught off-guard when they heard my voice. We all broke out in a big roar of laughter. I walked away feeling a mixture of embarrassment and flattery. I had succeeded becoming "one of the guys" . . . maybe a little too well.

It worked, and so did I—harder than I ever had before, unloading trucks and carrying two-hundred-pound doors to prove I was serious about becoming a carpenter. I earned their respect . . . along with a hernia.

You see, not only did I want to be taken seriously, but I wanted to crack the code of the trade "secrets." The men believed that whoever learned the secrets would take their jobs, and many went to their graves with all their knowledge.

At the end of my apprenticeship I decided to let my hair grow again. I had won the Golden Hammer and started teaching at the Union School. By that time I had won enough respect and could hold my own in the business. It was then that I started writing and performing sketch comedy in the clubs in Manhattan after my day working as a carpenter. It was the experience of feeling comfortable in front of an audience that allowed me to make the jump in front of the camera.

My friend Harlow Haagensen gave the Discovery Channel's talent scouts my name and number for their new show *Gimme Shelter*, where I became the interior finish carpenter on the show and met Joel Schmarje. That show led me to HGTV's *The Fix*, where I worked with Joel Schmarje again, who is nice as the day is long. The DIY Network asked me to co-host *Talk2DIY* with Brad Staggs, another wonderful home improvement expert.

The rest is history, which leads me to this book. It gives me great pleasure to share with you the trade secrets and know-how that I've spent my life learning.

INTRODUCTION

Congratulations on opening this book! It means you are willing to educate yourself on home repair. Everywhere I have traveled I am approached by people of all sizes, ages, and both sexes, who proudly tell me the many repair projects that they have accomplished. I have found that tackling one's own home repairs builds confidence and self-esteem. A person is empowered when they see what their own two hands can build, fix, or demolish.

Because I have always had a hard time finding repairs in home improvement books, I have decided to divide this book into rooms. If you have a problem in a particular room, look up that room. Each room chapter is divided into the areas of construction, such as plumbing, carpentry, electrical, and in some cases, appliances. The interior chapter covers the bedroom, living room, dining room, and halls. The tool chapter gives you a better explanation of a particular tool you might need.

If you're a perfectionist, you may have a hard time starting a project. I find that many people are timid to make mistakes and then end up not tackling the project altogether. All do-it-yourselfers, please allow yourself three mistakes per project. If I could tell you how many mistakes I've made, it would take me years. (I allow myself to make mistakes because it helps me get unstuck from my fear and get started on a project.)

If you have been raised being told that you can't do home repair or that it's a man's job, remember this: ability knows no sex. I heard a voice early on that said "I can do it." It was that same voice that gave me the courage to show up every day on an all-male union construction site for fifteen years, stand in front of a camera to tell you what I learned, write this book, and design my own tool line. I encourage all women and men to listen to that inner voice. Whether it's telling you to pick up a tool, look under the hood of a car, or put on ballet slippers or a chef's hat, follow your dream. Remember, carpentry, plumbing, and electricity are very linear. There is a beginning, a middle, and an end. Knowing the correct tool for the job will help you get the job done efficiently and will help you build confidence. I encourage you to pick up those tools and enjoy what your hands can do!

Chapter One

Tools

I would have to dedicate an entire book to tools if I was to list all that are used in construction. For that reason, I have kept the tool glossary to the tools used in this book.

If you are new DIYer, I would recommend the following tools for your starter tool kit.

Starter Tool Kit

Hand Tools

- **Toolbox:** Essential to keep everything together. No longer do we use a kitchen drawer.
- **Hammer:** Also known as a persuader. Be sure you get one that fits your hand and frame.
- **Screwdrivers:** Get an assortment of flat and Phillips tips. Not all screws are the same size, so get a set, or one with removable tips.
- **Measuring tape:** Get a 25-foot tape measure. Find one that has the different measurements ($\frac{1}{16}$", $\frac{1}{8}$", $\frac{3}{16}$", $\frac{1}{4}$", etc.) spelled out for you.
- **Stud finder:** No need to make holes in your wall to find the studs!
- **Utility knife:** This is a must. Get extra blades, too.
- **Drywall keyhole saw:** Always good to have on hand if you need to get into your drywall.
- **Adjustable wrench:** You might have heard this called a Crescent® Wrench (which is a brand name). Used for tightening/loosening nuts.

- **Locking jaw pliers:** Also known as Vise-Grips® (brand name). The jaws lock together so you don't have to keep gripping and holding the handles together.
- **2-foot level:** In carpentry, everything needs to be plumb, level, and square. This will show you level and plumb.
- **Combination square:** This will give you a square line or a 45-degree line for miter cuts. A scribe also comes with this tool, which is a sharp, pointy steel rod found on the bottom and is used for marking.
- **Set of drill bits:** You will need drill bits for countless home repair projects.
- **10-point hand saw:** This is easily accessible and great for those quick cuts without the hassle of setting up a power saw.
- **Groove-joint pliers:** Perfect for gripping a bolt or pipe. Many people refer to these pliers as Channellocks®, which is a brand name.
- **Prybar:** Let leverage take the burden and not your back!
- **Five-in-one putty knife:** One of the most used tools in the toolbox for scraping, gouging, opening paint cans, and smoothing and applying spackle or wood putty.

Power Tools

- **Drill:** I suggest a battery-operated rechargeable drill. Get a lightweight 12V or 18V model.
- **Magnetic bit guide:** This is a sleeve that fits over your screw and keeps it from wobbling and falling. Pick up Phillips and flat bits.
- **Jigsaw:** If you're going to buy one power saw, get this. It's the easiest, safest, and most versatile saw to work with.

Accessories

- **Hammer hook:** Not a must, but this is great to have. I like knowing where my hammer is at all times!
- **Nail apron:** They are lightweight because they are made out of canvas. You can keep nails, screws, and tools that you are using in it, and it helps free up your hands.

Safety

- **Safety glasses:** A must for protecting your eyes.
- **Dust mask:** Have these on hand to protect your lungs.

Hand Tools

The following tools are used throughout this book:

Adjustable wrench: A smooth-jawed wrench for turning bolts, nuts, and pipe fittings. The movable jaws are adjusted with your thumb on the worm gear, which twists the jaws wider.

Allen key: A different name for a hex key or hex wrench.

Aviation snips: Needle-nose snips used for cutting sheet metal. The jaws are spring-loaded to open and are color-coded. Yellow-handled aviation snips cut straight and are what I'd recommend. The red-handled snips cut in a left-hand curve, and the green-handled snips cut a right-hand curve.

Backsaw: A stiff, crosscutting saw used for making miters and anything that requires a precision cut. The back of the saw is reinforced and stiffened by a metal ridge to keep the blade straight.

Basin wrench: An odd-looking wrench with a long, round, thin arm; a claw hook on one end; and a T-handle on the other. This is the only tool that will get in the tight area underneath the sink to remove the nut holding the sink faucet.

Bath socket wrench: A long, hexagon cylinder that fits over the bonnet nut of the stem assembly on a shower handle.

Cam tool: A specialty tool used for a ball-type faucet. This tool looks more like a flat, stubby open-end wrench with notched sides to fit in the slotted cam of the faucet.

Can opener: A steel tool with a V shape on one end for puncturing a hole in a can for pouring, and a blunt end for opening bottle caps.

Carpet cookie cutter: A round cutting tool with a center pivot to hold the tool in place while the round cutting blade cuts through the carpet. It's used for making repair patches in carpet and is usually sold in a kit.

Carpet knife: An L-shaped utility knife for cutting carpet with a square-shaped razor blade that slides into the casing.

Caulking gun: A tool to push the caulk through a tube of caulk. The tube of caulk sits in the channel of the gun, and the bar with a disc on the end pushes the caulk through the nozzle at the end of the tube when the trigger is squeezed.

Chalk line: A steel or plastic case in the shape of a diamond that is filled with powdered chalk and a reel of line. When the line is pulled from the case and held taut to a flat surface, it can be snapped to leave a perfectly straight chalked line.

Chisel: A thick, rigid blade with square sides and a long handle for making mortises and for removing stock for hinges and other hardware. Strike this tool with a mallet or the side of your hammer.

Circuit tester: A tool used to detect the stability of the wires in your wall socket. Some testers can be plugged directly into the receptacle (socket) and will have a lamp light display for verification of correct wiring, open ground, open neutral, and open hot.

Clamps: There are many types of clamps: C-clamps are in the shape of a C and have a T-handle; spring clamps open by hand; bar clamps slide on a bar with a wooden handle that screws down; and pipe clamps slide on a pipe with a T-handle. All are used for clamping various-size projects.

Closet auger: A curved end on a flexible rod allows access to a toilet's built-in trap to remove clogs. The crank handle turns the cable to grab or cut through debris.

Cold chisel: A narrow chisel made of steel used for chipping tile or cutting sheet metal, brick, or stone.

Combination square: A combination measuring tool, marking tool, level, and 45° miter angle with a sliding head on a steel ruler. This has been one of my most used carpentry tools.

Compass: An instrument with two pointed arms joined at the top by a pivot. It's used for drawing a perfect circle and for scribing material to floors and walls.

Coping saw: A C-framed saw with a long, wooden handle and a removable thin blade made for cutting curves and making a cope joint on moldings. The blade can be rotated by releasing or unscrewing the handle. This saw is used on the "pull" stroke, so be sure you insert your blade properly: with the blade teeth pointing up when the handle is held up.

Countersink bit: A stubby, wide-angled bit used to form a recess in material to allow the flat-head of a screw to sit in flush or flat to the surface.

Drywall knife: Also known as a "joint" knife for spreading and smoothing joint compound over drywall tape. The blade length varies.

Emery cloth: A sandpaper cloth used in plumbing to clean burrs from the ends of pipes before soldering.

Five-in-1 putty knife: A multifunctional tool that has a sharp scraper blade; a sharp point for opening cracks when patching; a paint roller cleaner; a dull, flat end to help you open a paint can; and a putty remover and spreader. Some even have a hole in the middle to help you remove a nail in the wall. Wait a minute! . . . that's more than five uses!

Floor nailer: A tool used to nail in hardwood flooring. The plunger on the tool is struck with a rubber mallet, sending the nail through the groove of the floorboards.

Framing square: A flat piece of steel forming a perfect right angle with inch increments marked. This is similar to a carpenter's square except it has formulas and tables for making framing calculations.

Garden sprayer: A plastic 1- to 3-gallon drum with a pump handle on top and a spray hose leading out of the drum.

Groove-joint pliers: Mostly used in plumbing to hold pipes and to turn tight plumbing nuts. The long handles allow extra leverage while the various settings of the jaws allow a better grip on the object you are holding.

Grout float: A trowel-shaped tool with a flat, thick piece of rubber with a curved handle for applying grout between tile.

Grout removal tool: A small, thin carbon saw used to remove the grout between tiles.

Hacksaw: A sturdy frame holding a thin and narrow blade for cutting metal. The blades are removable and can be rotated to cut up, down, or sideways.

Hammer: There are many different types of hammers that are weighted differently to do different tasks; however, you need a hammer that feels comfortable in your hand. Buy either a curved claw or a straight claw hammer:

> **Curved claw hammer:** Unless you plan on doing a good bit of demolition, this should be the first hammer you buy. The curved claw will give you better leverage when pulling up a nail. When nailing, hold the nail between your thumb and forefinger, place it onto the piece of wood, and lightly make a couple strikes with the hammer. Once the nail is in at least a ¼", take your hand away and use the hammer to nail the head into your material or wood. If what you're working on is a rough job, such as building a deck, you can use the hammer to strike the nail head flush to the wood. If this is a more delicate, fine work, then use a nail set to set the nail into the wood. *See* Nail set.

> **Straight claw hammer:** A straight claw or ripping claw is more efficient in prying boards apart and makes a great demolition tool when you need to hack into drywall.

Hex wrench/key or allen key: An L-shaped tool that comes in various sizes to fit in a recessed hex head of a screw. Many people call these "allen keys." They come in a holding set.

Hole saw: A hole-boring attachment that fits on your drill to cut through wood, plastic, or metal depending on the type of teeth on the saw. Most commonly used for drilling out the hole for a doorknob.

Keyhole saw: A fine-tooth tapered saw that is usually used to cut through drywall, but also cuts through wood and light metal.

Laminate cutter: A tool with a carbide tip used to cut laminate.

Level: An instrument that establishes a horizontal (level) line or vertical (plumb) line when the bubble reads in the center of a tube of liquid. Levels come in all sizes. A 2-foot level is perfect for the DIYer.

Linesman's pliers: A tool used for cutting and twisting electrical wire. The flat jaws allow a solid grip to pull electrical wire, and the sharp cutter in the joint cuts through the wire.

Locking pliers: Both pliers and clamp in one tool. Adjust the knob on one handle to control the width and tension of the jaws. When the handles close together, the pliers lock into place. This tool allows your hand to relax if needed to hold something tight.

Metal file: There are many types of metal files. Some are finer, such as a "mil file," which is used for fine finishing on metal. This is also a good file to use on laminate to smooth the edges.

Miter box: A three-sided box used to make crosscuts or miter cuts for jointing molding. A backsaw slides into the 45° angled grooves to make these cuts.

Nail set: A small, pointed, hardened steel tool with a round or square end used to drive nails below the surface level.

Needle-nose or long-nose pliers: A tool with jaws tapered to a blunt point with wire cutters in the joint of the jaws. This tool allows you to grip parts in a confined area.

Notched trowel: A flat, thin piece of steel with at least two notched edges with a handle used to apply mastic (glue) to floors and walls to hold tiles.

Paint brush: There are many different types and sizes of paint brushes depending upon the application and the paint used. Hold a paint brush at its base, letting the handle rest against the groove between your thumb and forefinger. A *chisel-edge* brush has bristles that are cut on an angle for painting clean edges. A *wall brush* will be at least 4 inches wide to cover a broad area. A *trim brush* will be smaller widths up to 2 inches. *Nylon bristles* are for latex paint, and *Chinese bristles* are natural animal hairs used for oil paint, stains, and varnish.

Paint roller: A tool for rolling paint onto a wall. Sleeves made of various sizes, naps, textures, and thicknesses depending on the application slip on the arm of the roller.

Paint roller stick: A long, round stick similar to a broom handle that sometimes can be extended and used to reach the top of walls and ceilings.

Paint tray: A rectangular tray set on a slant for easy application of paint on a wall used with a roller. The ridges on the tray help remove any excess paint from the roller.

Plane: A tool used for removing thin layers of wood with a flat steel bottom plate (sole), a handle at the back, and a knob in the front for control. The flat blade is adjusted to allow you to remove different thicknesses of stock. There are many different planes for many different uses. A block plane and a jack plane are the more common ones. I recommend the block plane for an intermediate DIYer.

Plumb bob: Basically nothing more than a line attached to the center of a weight. The weight is in the shape of elongated top, the kind that you spin. This instrument uses gravity to pull it straight down, establishing a "plumb" vertical line once it is held steady. A plumb bob is the perfect tool for hanging a doorjamb and framing up new walls in your home.

Plumber's hand snake: A disc-shaped gun with a pistol grip and a flexible, ribbed cable that extends from the end of the disc. The cable has a spiral coil on the end that grabs or plows through drain clogs when the crank handle is turned. The set key locks the cable so it doesn't go back into the disc-housing when pushing the cable while turning the handle. There are also snakes that fit onto your drill and work similarly to the hand snake except the drill turns the cable instead of a handle.

Plumber's wrench: Also known as a pipe wrench, this heavy-duty wrench has an upper jaw that is adjusted by turning the corkscrew knob and serrated teeth for gripping tight threaded pipes.

Plunger: A rubber cup on the end of a wooden dowel to form suction around a tub or sink drain to free drain clogs.

Powder actuated nail gun: A tool that uses gun powder cartridges to drive nails into cement slabs and cinderblock walls. The gun drives the nail into the concrete when the cartridge is struck.

Propane torch: A propane gas tank with a screw-on nozzle that uses the surrounding air and the gas to produce a hot flame when ignited.

Pry bar: A prying tool with two blades. One side is used for pulling nails, and the other is used for prying and gaining leverage. These come in various sizes.

Putty knife: A flexible steel blade knife that resembles a spatula more than a knife. Different size blades are available to smooth and spread spackling, joint compound, wood putty, etc. This tool is also good for scraping off paint, old glue, and various materials.

Rasp: A type of file with rough teeth used for removing wood. There are files with coarse teeth and finer teeth depending on your need. A fine-toothed rasp is what we use in finish carpentry on moldings.

Ratchet wrench: A tool with a locking device that enables you to turn a nut in one direction without picking up the tool and readjusting your position. Usually sold in a kit with adjustable sockets that attach to the square pin on the tool. The sockets allow you to cover the entire nut, giving you better leverage and less possibility of slippage.

Rubber hammer or mallet: A hammer with a big rubber head used for gently persuading stone, components, and other finish pieces of carpentry into place. This hammer will also enable you to hit something with force without leaving a mark or hurting the object.

Safety glasses: Plastic glasses worn for protecting the eyes from particles flying from grinding, chipping, and hammering.

Scoring tool for wallpaper: A tool for removing wallpaper that fits in the palm of the hand. The cutting wheels have small teeth that perforate the wallpaper, enabling the wallpaper removal liquid to penetrate the paper.

Screwdriver: A simple tool but well worth buying a really good set! I have seen what happens to cheap screwdrivers. A couple turns and the metal gives way and strips or chips, and they lay to rest in the kitchen drawer morgue. This tool has a handle and blade tip that fits into the head of a screw. Here are the kinds of tips:

> **Flat:** It's flat and fits into a slotted screw. They come in different lengths and tip sizes. The larger the number, the thicker and longer the tip is. I would recommend getting a #1, #2, and #3 tip.

> **Phillips:** This tip looks like an X. I recommend getting a #1, #2, and #3 tip.

> **Magnetic screwdriver:** A popular screwdriver that holds interchangeable tips. This screwdriver is an all-in-one screwdriver because it can be used on any type of screw head as long as you have the appropriate tip.

> **Spiral ratchet screwdriver:** In the trade, we use the term *Yankee® screwdriver*. When you push down, it will turn the screw 2½ times. When it's released, it returns to its original position. These were used prior to electric and cordless tools. They may be old-fashioned, but they're still a great tool!

Seam roller: A wheel on a handle that is used to press down seams and corners of wallpaper or wall coverings.

Seat wrench: An L-shaped tool much like a hex key but with tapered ends to reach into the compression faucet's stem socket. Turning the wrench to the left will loosen the removable seats, and turning to the right will tighten.

Seat-dressing tool: A wheel on the end of machine-threaded shank with a T-handle used to resurface and smooth non-removable seats in faucets.

Sledgehammer: A heavy-duty hammer with a thick head used for demolition of concrete, stone, or brick, or driving stakes into the ground. Weight varies from 2 pounds to 20 pounds, depending on the job.

Slip-joint pliers: A gripping tool with two settings and coarse teeth in the jaws for extra control.

Smoothing brush: A flat, long-bristle brush used to flatten wallpaper. Shorter bristles are used for vinyl wall coverings.

Spade bit: This bit fits into a drill and has two sharp cutting points or edges with a very pointy middle. This bit is also known as a paddle bit because it's flat. This is the bit to use when drilling out for the deadbolt in a door.

Spark lighter: A tool used to safely light a propane torch without using matches. When the handles are squeezed together, the flint is dragged across the bottom of a cup, producing a spark.

Sponges: Usually sponges used in home improvement are bigger than your average kitchen sponge. Sponges come in various shapes for faux painting, and thicker sponges are used for grouting a tile floor.

Stud finder: A tool used to locate the stud in the wall. Various battery-powered stud finders are on the market and can locate the stud, electricity, and metal such as a plumbing pipe. Most stud finders turn on a light when the edge of the stud is detected.

Tape measure: A retractable metal rule in a plastic or metal case with inches and fractions marked on the tape. This spring-loaded measuring tool comes in various lengths of metal tape up to 30 feet, with the most common at 25 feet. One side will have a belt clip so you can always have it on you.

Tile cutter: A tiny, replaceable carbide cutting-wheel underneath a handle that scores tile as the handle is pulled down the track. The throat of the tool is usually made of black foam and accepts up to 12-inch tiles.

Tile nippers: A sturdy and strong tool for cutting, trimming, or shaping tile. These nippers are used mostly to cut tile around plumbing fixtures.

Toilet auger: Same as a closet auger.

Tubing cutter: A tool used to cut copper and plastic pipe for plumbing. The pipe is held between a roller wheel and a cutting wheel. Tighten the handle and spin the wheel around the pipe, and repeat until the pipe has been cut through.

Utility knife: A knife with a retractable razor-sharp disposable blade. The blade retracts in the handle, and the replacement blades are stored in the handle itself.

Wire brush: Small wires on a wooden handle (usually) that help remove loose particles such as corrosion, rust, and paint.

Wire strippers: A cutting tool used to remove the insulation or plastic coating off electrical wires. The groove in the blades stops short of cutting through the wire and enables you to cut through just the insulation.

Wood chisel: *See* chisel.

Power Tools

Whether you get a battery-operated or a corded tool is up to you and your wallet. Battery-operated tools have their pros and cons. Pros: there's no tripping over cords, and the tool can be used anywhere and is not restricted to being a cord's distance from an outlet. Cons: the batteries do run down, and if you don't have a second charged battery, you will need to wait. Also, some battery-operated tools will not have enough *oomph* to cut or drill through tough materials. The following are power tools referred to in this book:

Circular saw: A saw that rotates a round, flat steel disc with cutting teeth on a spindle. A guard surrounds and protects the blade and the user. The baseplate can be adjusted to cut material at a 45° angle or a 90° angle.

Drill: A gun-shaped tool used to rotate drill bits and other attachments rapidly into or out of various materials when the trigger is squeezed.

Hammer drill: Similar to a drill, with an added feature of delivering repeated blows or "hammering" a drill bit. This tool is used for drilling through concrete, stone, or brick and uses a strong carbide-tipped drill bit.

Jigsaw (also known as a saber saw): A saw with a thin reciprocating blade that moves up and down to cut through wood, metal, or plastic depending on the blade attached. The thin blade enables you to cut curves and shapes easily, and the base-plate of the saw can be turned to make angled cuts.

Magnetic bit attachment: A long, magnetic attachment that holds various hex bits on one end and a hex shank that fits into a drill or screw gun on the other end.

Miter saw (chop saw): A combination of a circular saw and miter table that pivots and locks into position to cut any angle from 0° to 45°. Some models are combination miter saws that enable the user to slide the saw while cutting to make compound cuts.

Rotary saw (tool): Similar to a router, this saw will spin the various attachments at high speeds. Use these to grind, polish, sand, cut, and carve wood, metal, tile, and plastic.

Router: A tool used to make grooves and edging shapes with a motor that spins a housing that holds various cutting bits or blades. The base can be moved up or down to change the depth of the blade.

Router with laminate trim blade: A trim blade is a long, round cutting blade for laminate. The wheel stops the blades from cutting into the material.

Screw gun: A tool used for fastening drywall with drywall screws. It looks similar to a drill except that it only accepts a magnetic bit attachment in its hex-shaped housing for attaching to the screw head.

Spray gun: A gun-shaped attachment with a container to hold paint used often with an air compressor to spray paint evenly. Some models do not require an air compressor.

Table saw: Made of a circular saw protruding up through the top of a table. The material is pushed up against the rip fence for ripping any material quickly and perfectly even. The rip fence is removed for crosscuts, and the miter gauge is inserted in the groove to push material across the blade. This blade can be angled from 0° to 45°, and the miter gauge can be moved from a straight 0° to a 45° angle.

Wet saw: A saw used for cutting through tile. The tile sits on a table that slides underneath the blade. Water flows over the carbide circular blade while the tile is slowly pushed through. The tray is filled with water to enable a hose to suck the water up to the blade.

Chapter Two

Hiring a Contractor

The repairs and renovations in this book will be a mixed bag of what you "can do" and what you "can't do." Of course, as you tackle projects you will not only build confidence, but also build know-how—which will fuel your confidence.

For the projects that you are not comfortable tackling (yet), you will be hiring a professional. For this reason, I provide a reference here of questions and suggestions for hiring a contractor for many of the repairs and renovations in this book.

Finding a Contractor

The best place to start looking for a contractor is in your own neighborhood. Ask your neighbors and friends if they have had to do the same repair or renovation you are planning on doing, and find out who they hired and if they liked the crew. Be wary of those contractors who solicit door to door.

Educate Yourself

Before you pick up the phone and call a contractor, be sure you've done your homework. What do you know about the job? Read the chapters in this book to under-

Tip: It's rare for a job to be completed on time and on budget for various reasons. Because remodeling a home can be an expression of self, many times the homeowner wants changes to the original plan of remodeling as they see their design come to fruition. This will add on to the time of completion and the cost.

stand the scope of the work, the details, and how things should be done properly. You will be taken more seriously if you know what you are talking about, and your lines of communication will be much better if you are familiar with the construction terms associated with your particular job. Remember, the more you do your homework, the more you will save yourself costly work changes down the line.

The Interview

Interview three contractors to get a price range of cost and to give you some choice as to whom you would feel comfortable working with.

Now it's time to schedule a meeting with the contractors:

- Be sure you don't overlap their meetings. This is rude to the contractor and can put them in a compromising position with their competition. It can also be uncomfortable for you.
- Look at your watch and make a note as to what time they show up for the initial meeting. Are they on time, or are they late? How late? Did they call to tell you they were going to be late? Believe it or not, this matters, because the way they treat you upon trying to obtain the job is a good indication of how they will treat you once they have the job.
- Pay special attention to see if the contractor is listening to you. Do you feel that they are understanding you and you are understanding them? This is one of the most important aspects of all relationships: communication! In my opinion, this is the area that matters most, even more than the price, because if you work with someone who doesn't communicate well or has a hard time understanding what you want, it can cost you more in the long run in work changes.

Questions to Ask

- How long have you been in business?
- Are you licensed?

- Have you done a similar job before?
- How many jobs do you have going on right now?
- Are you going to subcontract the work, or will it be your crew doing the work?
- What will be the work schedule? Hours a day? Weekends?
- How do you clean up at the end of the day?
- Do you seal off the work area? How do you handle the energy and health environment of the job? Dust?
- Does your work come with a warranty?
- Do you have workers' compensation and liability insurance?
- What permits do you need?
- Will I get a written contract?
- May I have references? People who had similar work done? Do you mind if I call them or see the completed job?

Checking Out the Company

- Be sure you contact the Better Business Bureau (BBB) to be sure there are no complaints against this company.
- Call the references, and see the completed job. Ask the homeowners if they were satisfied with the work, the company, and the time it was finished. They will be all too eager to tell you if something did not go right.

Written Contract

These are items you should check for within the contract:

- Be sure the contractor's name, address, and phone number are on the contract.
- Must have a payment schedule.
- Contractor is to obtain work permits.
- Estimated start and completion timeline—be sure to allow some reasonable flexibility to the completion time because so many jobs do go over.
- How they handle change orders.
- Details of materials to be used, such as color, size, product brand name, etc.

Word to the Wise:

Not in therapy? Well, if you and your significant other are living in the home together, you might want to consider going to couple's counseling before you tackle a big home repair project. Few things test a relationship more than remodeling your home. Keep those lines of communication open, and be patient. Home improvement can test your very last nerve, especially if you are hiring others to do the job!

■ Warranties covering work and materials.

■ Right to cancel within three days upon signing contract.

The Money

All contractors will require money up front to buy the materials needed for your project. Never pay more than half up front, and never pay the final payment until the work is completed according to the contract. The last payment of money is your leverage in getting the job done correctly and in a timely manner.

_____

Difficulty Key:

1 Beginner

2 Confident
   beginner

3 Intermediate

4 Advanced

5 Professional

Chapter Three

The Interior

Carpentry

This chapter will cover most repairs concentrating on carpentry to the walls, ceiling, floors; painting and wall covering; electrical upgrades; and telephone problem-solving. Aside from the kitchen and the bathroom, these are the areas that will most likely require fixes. If you need a repair to a wall in the bathroom, please see the bathroom chapter, because it pays special attention to the needs of walls that will be exposed to moisture. If you live in a region where moisture is a problem in all areas of your house, you may want to use the painting and repair tips found in the bath-room chapter.

Walls

Before I started construction, I really never gave much thought to walls and never thought about what was behind the wall I was looking at or what it was made of. It wasn't until someone started using terms like *studs, track,* and *drywall* that I realized I was clueless. When I went to the Union School, I had a lot to catch up on!

Framing

Outside walls, interior load-bearing walls, or partition walls all have studs that are usually made of wood 2×4s spaced 16" apart on center (o.c). If you have a farmhouse

Fig 3.1 - Wall Framing

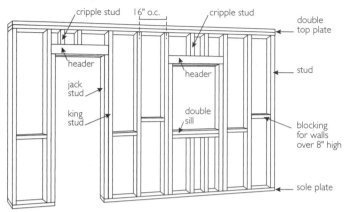

or an older home, you may have noticed that your framing is 20" or 24" apart on center. This is because years ago, 2×4s *really* were 2 inches by 4 inches and usually hand hewn. Because the lumber was a true 2 × 4 inches, it was able to carry more weight and be spread farther apart. Also, there were fewer restrictions on building. But nowadays, a 2×4 is not what it says it is. A 2×4 really measures 1½" × 3½" and by code, they should be 16" apart o.c.

What Are Your Walls Made Of?

The walls in your home may be covered by drywall, plaster, or paneling—most of which are susceptible to damage, be it cracking, holes from doorknobs, or nail pops. On top of the drywall or plaster, you may have wallpaper, paint, or a textured surface. This section will be one of the most used sections of the book because everyone has to deal with a wall repair or paint job at one time or other.

Paneled walls are the most obvious wall to detect. We all know this looks like wood with vertical grooves, giving it that look of faux joints. Drywall and plaster need closer inspection. Usually you can tell drywall by giving the wall a tap with your knuckles. If the wall has a hollow sound to it, then it's drywall. You may need to tap along a horizontal 16" section because it could happen that your first knock was right over a stud, giving it a feeling of a plaster wall. A plaster wall will feel solid no matter where you knock on it, and it will feel cool to the touch. Once you determine what kind of wall you have, you can then determine what kind of fix you'll need to repair it.

Repairing Drywall and Plaster Walls

Everything moves and changes with time. This goes for your house, too. A house will naturally settle over time. This shifting, no matter how minute, can cause cracks in the walls as well as nail pops. But the good news is, patching holes or fixing cracks

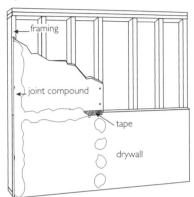

Fig 3.2- A Drywall Wall

framing
joint compound
tape
drywall

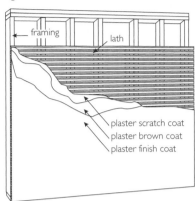

Fig 3.3- A Plaster Wall

framing
lath
plaster scratch coat
plaster brown coat
plaster finish coat

and nail pops are easy fixes. But it can get a little messy, so be sure to use a drop cloth to protect walls and furniture before you start a wall repair.

Drywall

Drywall is also known as wallboard or Sheetrock®. Sheetrock® is a name brand of drywall, just as Kleenex® is to tissues. Drywall is made of gypsum that is sand-wiched between two pieces of thick paper and along the edges to make a very durable and heat-resistant material. It has become incredibly popular because it is affordable and durable yet easy to handle and cut, which makes for a speedy installation. It also takes almost any decoration: paint, wallpaper, or a textured surface. The long edges are tapered to accept the drywall tape and keep the surface looking perfectly flat when finished. Usually you can find drywall in 4 × 8-foot sheets, but it can be special-ordered to your specifications. The thicknesses range between ¼", ⅜", ½", and ⅝". To bend drywall, wet the back and front paper. For a tight radius curved wall, you may have to use ¼-inch-thick drywall secured to the frame and double layered. Most residential walls are made of either ½-inch- or ⅝-inch-thick drywall, depending on the building codes in your area. I have noticed that the average thickness is ½" across the country. (It's important to figure out the thickness of your walls before you repair a patch.)

If It Were My House:

I always use drywall screws when working with drywall to prevent "nail pops." A nail pop is caused when a home has settled, or when the closing of doors creates a constant vibration that, over time, will back the drywall nail away from the stud, causing a little bump or "pop" at the location of the nail head. I have traveled across the country doing seminars, and I haven't been to a city yet that doesn't seem to be plagued by nail pops.

Fig 3.4- Make a "V" Groove

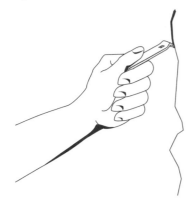

The sheets of drywall are nailed or screwed into studs, which, in residential homes, are usually made of wood. Metal studs are most commonly used in commercial property. I am, however, a big believer in metal studs for residential construction as well. More on that later.

CRACKS

DIFFICULTY: 1

TOOLS YOU MAY NEED: Can opener (a.k.a. church key) or utility knife, 2" or 3" putty knife

MATERIALS YOU MAY NEED: Mesh or paper tape, joint compound, 100-grit sandpaper or sponge, shellac-based primer/sealer

Small cracks: Make a "V" groove: To repair a crack, use the pointed end of a can opener. Starting at the beginning of the crack, run the can opener down with enough pressure to open up the crack. At first, it may feel strange to be making the crack worse intentionally, but you will get used to it. The V of the can opener is the exact size you need to create a V in the crack, widening it just enough to accept joint compound or vinyl spackling. You can make the same V with a utility knife if you extend the blade a little bit so the blade won't break. And be careful not to cut through the

---

Trick of the Trade:

After years of remodels and repairs, I have found that there is a real trick when applying joint compound. You want to apply a thin, smooth, and even amount of compound. To have control and to keep steady pressure on the blade, hold the handle in the palm of your hand and put your index and middle fingers on the back of the blade. This will enable you to put pressure evenly on both sides of the center point of the handle, and you will notice the difference in taping your joints! Put the joint compound on the blade, and starting at the top, pull the taping knife down the joint with the angle of the blade away from the point of contact.

Fig 3.5- Apply Joint Compound

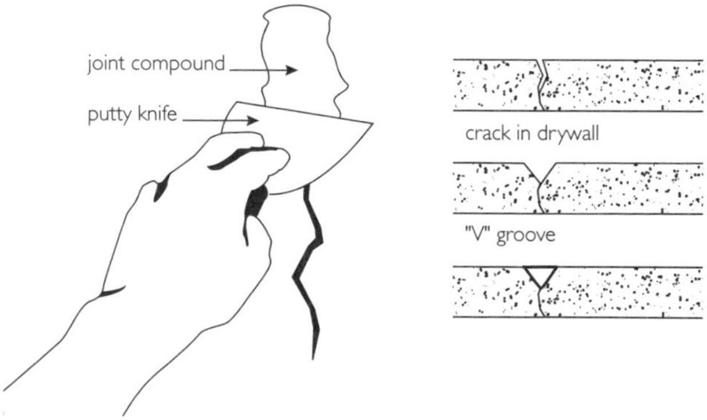

joint compound

putty knife

crack in drywall

"V" groove

drywall. I have noticed that if you use a can opener, you may still need to use a utility knife to cut any drywall paper that may have crumpled up while making the V with the can opener.

Lightly sand a 3" area on each side of the crack with 100-grit sandpaper so the compound will stick to the existing painted wall.

Use a putty knife to fill the crack with joint compound or vinyl spackling.

LARGE CRACKS OR CRACKS AROUND DOORWAYS AND WINDOWS
DIFFICULTY: 2
TOOLS YOU MAY NEED: Same as above, 6" taping knife, 10" taping knife
MATERIALS YOU MAY NEED: Same as above, vinyl spackle

Follow the previous steps for a small crack and then use drywall tape over the crack. There are two different kinds of tape: mesh tape and paper tape. I prefer the mesh tape, which has a resin on the back that sticks to the drywall and doesn't require the thin layer of compound underneath it that paper tape requires. If you are using the paper tape, you will need to lay a thin layer of joint compound over the crack, wide enough for the tape to lay on top of it, because this is the only way that this paper tape sticks to the drywall.

Whether you're using mesh or paper tape, use a 3" or 4" putty/taping knife to smooth on a thin layer of compound to cover the tape. This is your first coat. Let this dry overnight.

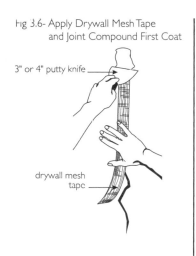

Fig 3.6- Apply Drywall Mesh Tape and Joint Compound First Coat

3" or 4" putty knife

drywall mesh tape

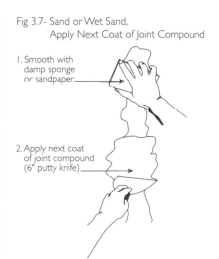

Fig 3.7- Sand or Wet Sand, Apply Next Coat of Joint Compound

1. Smooth with damp sponge or sandpaper

2. Apply next coat of joint compound (6" putty knife)

Fig 3.8- Prime and Seal the Surface

Then either sand the taped crack using 100-grit paper, or wet sand it with a sponge. (See the following details on wet sanding.) Be careful when sanding, because you don't want to sand off the tape. Next, you will use a 6" taping knife. Again, go over the crack with more joint compound or vinyl spackle. Let dry, then sand and repeat once more with a larger 10" knife.

Squeeze out most of the water from a wet sponge, and lightly go over the area until it is smooth. Wet sanding is useful for small projects in a finished home where you don't want much dust. It's also a good idea to wet sand if you are allergic to dust.

Use a shellac-based primer/sealer. Let dry, then finish the wall any way you choose (paint, wallpaper, texture).

PATCHING A HOLE
DIFFICULTY: 2

TOOL YOU MAY NEED: A drill with a Phillips bit attachment or a screw gun; utility knife; 4", 6", 10" taping knives; drywall keyhole saw

MATERIALS YOU MAY NEED: Piece of drywall, joint compound, furring strips or plywood for backing, mesh or paper drywall tape, 100- to 120- grit sandpaper or sponge, drywall screws (1¼" or 1⅝"), shellac-based primer/sealer

Although it is very durable, drywall is still susceptible to damage. Maybe you don't have a doorstop and the door handle went right through the wall, or maybe someone in the household needs to go to anger management therapy . . . right after they fix that hole they put in the wall! Fixing the hole in your drywall is almost as easy as hanging a picture to cover it!

Trick of the Trade:
For a small patch, go to your neighborhood hardware store and ask if there is a broken piece of drywall you can use for a patch. They will often have broken pieces in the back and will cut you a patch for no charge!

If the hole is as small as a doorknob, you can buy a peel-and-stick repair patch. Oftentimes, these are about 7 × 7-inch squares of sticky fiberglass mesh tape. In that case, go directly to the "Tape the Joints" section.

For bigger holes, get a piece of drywall that is the same thickness of your wall. It will either be ½" or ⅝", depending on your area's building code. To determine the thickness of your wall, take the lip on the end of the measuring tape, catch the back of the drywall, and read the measurement.

Cut the drywall patch and the wall: Now, here's what I do. Cut the drywall patch first. Take your measurement of the hole and then cut a square piece of drywall that will fit over the hole. It doesn't have to be perfect, because you will be using this piece as a template first to be sure it will fit. To cut the drywall patch, you will need a utility knife to score one side of the paper on the drywall. That side of the drywall will then snap over, and you just need to score the other side of the paper to snap it free.

Now that you have your patch, place it over the hole and trace a pencil line on the wall around it. I always put a little arrow at the top of my piece so I know which end is up when it's time to put in the patch. Using a drywall keyhole saw, cut through the drywall following your pencil line. When you have a hole that will accept the patch, you have two options. Option one: if your home center or hardware store has drywall repair clips, slide them on the edges of your drywall patch, at least two on each side, and slide it into place. This will keep the drywall flush to the surface of your wall and securely in place. It also removes the need for backing. If you use these repair clips then go to the "Tape the Joints" Section (page 33). Option two: because these repair clips are fairly new, I have always used backing to secure a patch.

Backing: Using scrap wood (this can be 1 × 2-inch furring strips, plywood, etc.), cut pieces, known as backing, to fit inside the hole you've made for the patch. You will need to have two pieces that are 3" longer than the length of the hole, so that when you get it behind the drywall, you can screw it to the existing wall. To hold the wood in place, you may have to put a screw in the middle of it so you can hold on and pull it toward you as you screw it in place.

Using drywall screws, secure the backing strips to the existing drywall, dividing the space evenly with the two strips. Use 1¼" screws if you have ½" drywall or 1⅝" if you are using ⅝" drywall.

Secure the patch: When you have something to screw the patch into, you can secure the patch onto your backing. Drive in the drywall screws so the heads only dimple the drywall and you will be able to put a coat of joint compound over them to hide them. If you drive the screw heads past the paper, it will not hold properly. You may only need to put in four screws, depending on the size of your patch.

Sand around the patch: Using 100-grit sandpaper, lightly sand the existing wall area around the patch, giving the wall some "tooth." This will help the joint compound adhere to the existing wall. Brush away the dust when you've finished.

Fig 3.9- Cut Drywall

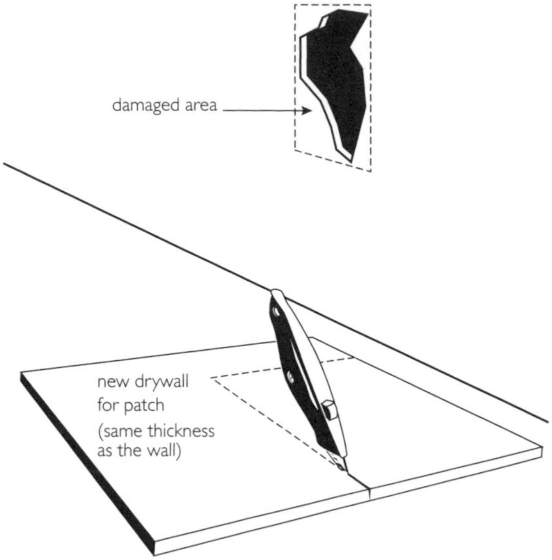

damaged area

new drywall
for patch
(same thickness
as the wall)

Fig 3.10- Trace the Patch

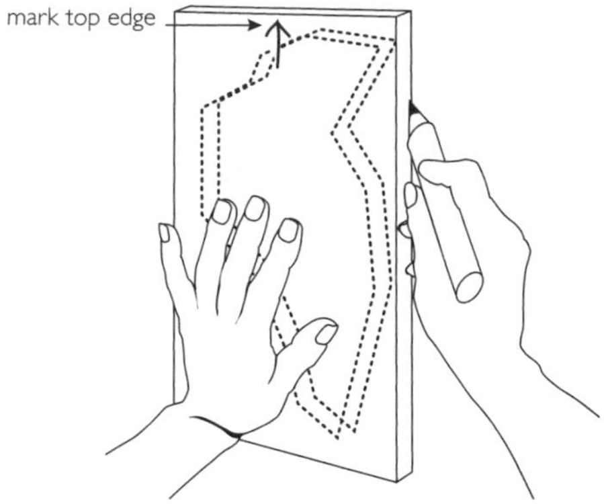

mark top edge

Fig 3.11- Cut Out the Damaged Area

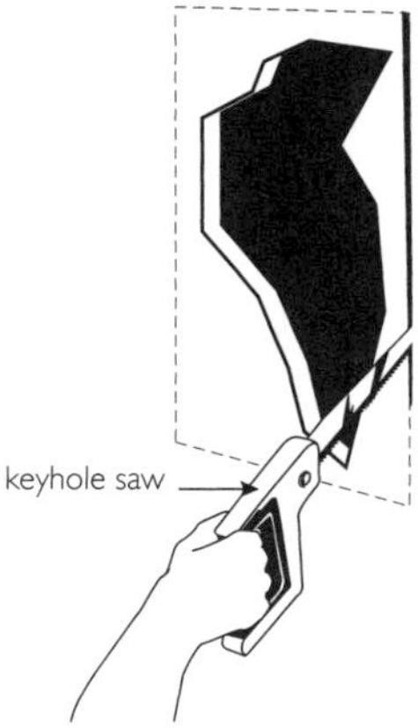

keyhole saw

Fig 3.12- Secure the Patch

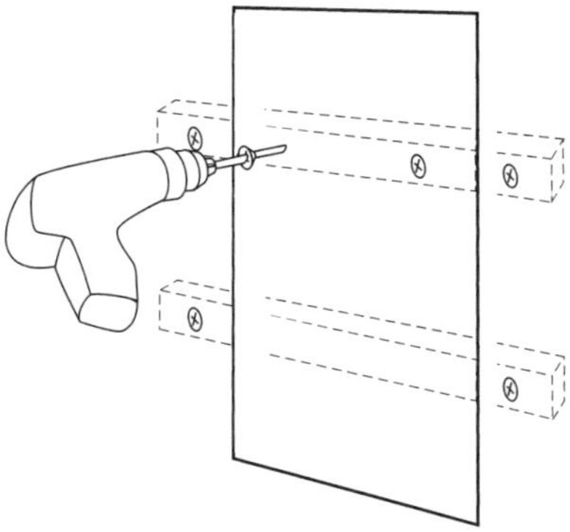

Fig 3.13- Tape the Joints

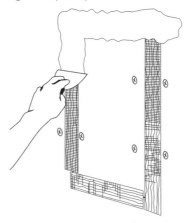

Tape the joints: Next you will need to tape the edges of the patch, or the joint. If you don't do this, the patch will crack later and you will just have to go back and do this step. I like to use fiberglass mesh tape because it has a sticky resin that adheres directly to the wall. Put the mesh tape over the seams or joint of the patch. You can cut the mesh tape with a utility knife or by planting your drywall knife where you want to cut the mesh tape and pull the tape at an angle. Run your 4" taping knife over the mesh tape to be sure it has stuck to the wall. If you use paper tape, you must first lay a thin layer of joint compound over the joint the same width as the paper tape, with the same size putty knife. Once you lay the paper tape over the joint compound, smooth it down with the putty knife to take out any bubbles or high spots.

Tape coat: The taping steps are the same with a patch as they are with new installation of drywall. You want to start out with a smaller blade and graduate to a larger blade by the third coat. This will hide the joint and give the wall a flat, smooth surface over the joints.

Now, whether you've used mesh tape or paper tape, you will need to put a thin layer or coat of joint compound over the tape. Using the same 4" taping knife, lightly spread a layer of compound over the tape. Check out the illustration on how to hold a taping knife (page 28). This will help you balance the knife and put on an even coat. Let this dry overnight. The next day, lightly sand the compound with 100- or 120-grit sandpaper. You just want to smooth the compound, so go lightly. Otherwise you will start to break up the mesh or the paper tape.

Apply the second coat of compound using a wider knife. I like to use a 6" or 8" knife for this. Smooth on a thin coat of compound. (Again, check out the illustration on how to hold a taping knife.) Let dry overnight.

Sand until smooth with 120-grit sandpaper.

Apply the third and final thin coat of compound using a 10" knife. This is the final coat, so make it stretch out so the edges lie smoothly on the wall. Let dry overnight.

Sand lightly.

Before I knew better, I thought I'd save time and get away with putting two coats of paint over a patch. The problem with this is that the patch needs to be sealed and primed

Tip: If you are a perfectionist, as I am, then this is a bit of advice for you: don't try to make the first couple coats perfect. There will be sanding and a couple more coats before this is completely finished. I have tried to do the "perfect" coat, and it was that last swipe that made the tape "accordion," and I had to do it all over again.

Trick of the Trade:

You can use a damp, flat sponge and "wet sand" this area if you want to cut down on dust. Wet sanding is the process of using a damp sponge instead of sandpaper to take down the high points and smooth the joint compound.

first, so the paint on top of it won't keep soaking into the patched area, giving you a different sheen than the existing paint on your wall. A few different companies make shellac-based primer/sealers. If you don't prime, then you will notice that the area where you applied the joint compound sticks out like a sore thumb in certain lighting! So always seal the deal with a primer/sealer, then paint, wallpaper, or texture.

NAIL POPS

DIFFICULTY: 2
TOOLS YOU MAY NEED: Hammer, nail set, drill with Phillips head bit, putty knife
MATERIALS YOU MAY NEED: Drywall screws, 100- or 120-grit sandpaper, spackle or joint compound, sealer/primer

My training as a union carpenter was in commercial buildings in New York City in the mid- '80s. Drywall was only hung with drywall screws, and we used metal framing as well. I never could understand why anyone would hang drywall with nails. I had many a debate with people from other parts of the country about the ease and flexibility of drywall screws. A drywall nail can't just come out of the wall and stud without hurting the drywall, whereas a drywall screw can. Move the clock ten years ahead, when I tour the country for different repair demonstrations and everywhere I go, almost everyone in the audience was suffering from "nail pops."

A nail pop is the term used when the drywall nail moves away from the stud it has been nailed to and the head pops the old compound out of the drywall and sometimes comes out so much that you can see the nail head. Nail pops occur from the natural shifting of a home and the shrinking of the studs behind the drywall. The lumber (2×4s) used to build the walls in your home are kiln-dried but still hold some moisture. Over time, these 2×4s will dry out, and as they do, they can squeeze that nail out and away from the wood, causing the nail to "pop" out of the wall.

Many theories exist on how to deal with nail pops. I've heard some people instruct the homeowner to just hit the nail back into place, cover with joint compound, seal, and paint. Do you see the problem with this? You are leaving yourself open to fixing it over and over again because it is already loose. If you hit the nail too hard, it will go past the paper of the drywall and won't hold the wall to the stud. Other people say to pull the nail head out of the wall and replace with a drywall screw, but then you run the risk of damaging your drywall with your hammer as you try to pry out the nail. Then you're left with a bigger problem and maybe a hole from the hammer.

This is what I do and what I would recommend for you to do: use a nail set, and pound that nail into the stud. Yes, drive that nail through the paper of the drywall and into the stud. Now, about 1" away from the nail, either above or below it, drive a drywall screw into the stud, being careful not to drive it past the paper of the drywall. You just want to dimple the paper. Do this to all the nail pops. It may take you a while, but believe me, if you do it right the first time, you can be assured that you won't have to do it again!

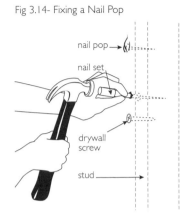

Fig 3.14- Fixing a Nail Pop

Once you have driven all the nails into the studs and put a screw in next to it, now you can sand the area around the nails and screw heads with 100- or 120-grit sandpaper. This will give the wall some "tooth" so it will hold the spackle or joint compound.

Spackle or joint compound is good for this repair, and you can buy small containers of either item. Use your putty knife and go over all the nail holes and screw heads. If the putty knife hits the metal of the screw head, then you have not driven it in far enough. Let this dry overnight and lightly sand with 120-grit sandpaper. Because the spackle or joint compound will shrink as it dries, you will probably have to go over the nail holes and screw heads with one more light coating of joint compound until it is perfectly flush with the existing face of the wall. Lightly sand until it is smooth and flush.

If It Were My House:

If you are ever going to remodel your home, please use drywall screws to secure the drywall to the studs.

Be sure you use a sealer/primer over the compound and then finish your wall with paint or texture.

Plaster Walls

Before drywall became popular, plaster was a widely used material to finish interior walls. In older homes or apartments, the walls are made of plaster. They are more noise-resistant and provide a very solid wall. Plastering is a dying craft, and no wonder, considering the work that goes into it. First, wood lath strips, which are rough pieces of wood approximately ¼" to ⅜" thick and 1⅛" wide, are nailed horizontally or at right angles to the studs. The plaster is applied directly to the top of the strips. The plaster is pushed into the spaces between the laths and slumps down behind the lath and forms what are called "keys." The keys are what hold the plaster in place.

Fig 3.15- Types of Lath

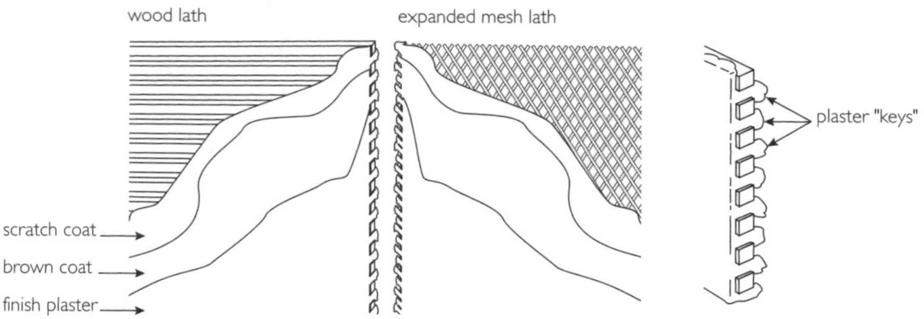

wood lath

expanded mesh lath

plaster "keys"

scratch coat

brown coat

finish plaster

Plaster is applied in three coats. The first two coats build up the thickness ⅜" to ½" and the last coat is the thin ⅛" finishing coat. The first is a "scratch coat" that helps stiffen up the wood lath and is combed over when wet (hence, scratch coat), which helps hold the next coat. The next coat is called the "brown coat." Lastly, a thin layer of plaster called the "white coat." (approximately ⅛") is applied.

Little-Known Fact:

Back in the good ol' days, carpenters would add horse, cow, or hog hair to bind the plaster for the scratch and brown coats. I've seen this to be true in most farmhouses and older apartment buildings I've worked in. There's nothing like cutting a hole in the wall, only to have a big fur-ball come out of it! In the twentieth century, wood fibers replaced the animal hair for binding.

Nowadays, for large patch jobs, contractors use metal lath that comes in rolls of 24". This is nailed to the studs to provide the structural foundation of the plaster. The metal lath has more holes and, therefore, more keys for the plaster. The application over the metal lath is the same as the wood lath. It's no wonder that so many people prefer the ease of drywall!

CRACKS
DIFFICULTY: 2

As your house settles, you may see a crack in your wall. Sometimes this can reoccur, especially if you live in an earthquake area. If it's very serious, you may want to seek an engineer's advice as to what is causing the reoccurrence, because it could be a structural problem. But in most cases, the fix is easy: the same for a plaster wall as for drywall. See "Cracks" under "Drywall." (page 29)

HOLES

With most plaster wall holes, the wood lath is still intact. If you have a small hole, I would recommend buying the peel-and-stick patch repair tape I suggested earlier in the drywall section. You just stick it over the hole and apply a couple coats of joint compound over it, allowing each layer of compound to dry before sanding. Use a shellac-based primer/sealer and then paint.

If you're patching a bigger hole, the process is different from the drywall repair. If the wood lath strips are intact, the repair requires just a few tools and materials. (If the lath is not intact, secure some lath strips or a piece of metal lath into the hole.)

PATCHING A HOLE

DIFFICULTY: 2

TOOLS YOU MAY NEED: A 3" putty knife, a paint brush

MATERIALS YOU MAY NEED: Bonding liquid, plaster, and shellac-
    based primer/sealer

Remove loose plaster: Remove any loose plaster with a putty or taping knife, and clean away the dust. I keep a thick, unused paint brush in my toolbox to remove the fine dust.

Apply the bonding liquid with an inexpensive paint brush. Drying time is usually in 15 to 30 minutes.

Mix only the amount of plaster you will need for the first layer, because the plaster sets up fast. The plaster shrinks when dry, so you will need to apply another layer of plaster. If the hole is deep, add some sand to the scratch and brown coats. The finish coat needs to be a thin layer of plaster and lime putty (35 percent plaster and 65 percent lime putty for a smooth finish).

Sand lightly if needed. (You will not be able to "wet sand" plaster.)

Finally, brush on a shellac-based primer/sealer. Let dry, then paint.

Plaster Walls of Today: My favorite client to date is fashion designer Betsey Johnson, who wanted sunflower-yellow plaster walls in her home. Instead of putting up lath on the studs, we installed "blue board," which looks like drywall but the paper on the finished side is blue in color. This dry-

If It Were My House:

I would go to the home store and get a bonding agent just for plaster walls. Plasterweld™ is the kind I use; it comes in a quart or gallon container. This stuff is great because it seals the area where you will be applying the plaster, immediately cutting down on the dust. It also bonds the plaster or joint compound like nobody's business!

Trick of the Trade:

"Hot mix" is what we use in the trade to prevent the plaster from setting up so quickly. The old-timers used lime to slow down the process, which is fine, but not too many contractors nowadays have lime on a jobsite. Hot mix consists of adding some plaster to joint compound (1 part plaster to 4 parts compound; add a little water till it's a creamy, peanut butter consistency) to slow down the plaster's setting process so you can work with it longer. Hot mix takes longer to dry.

wall is specifically designed for plaster and removes the scratch coat layer and requires only a final finish $\frac{1}{16}$" layer. To tint the plaster, you must use a dry oxide pigment in a slaked lime base with marble dust and apply with a flat, stainless-steel trowel. Many people use the term *Venetian plaster* to describe this kind of plaster finish. The finishing touch is a wax. Different name-brand waxes are used for this final finish. My plasterer used a butcher's wax on the finish plaster and burnished it (rubbed it) to a beautiful sheen.

In recent years, more and more companies are selling premixed Venetian plaster that is very easy to apply.

If It Were My House:

I've just instructed you on the proper way to repair a plaster hole, but there's another way I've used when I'm in a time crunch. I clear the hole down to the wood lath strips, removing all the debris. Then I cut a drywall patch that would fit into the hole, and secure the drywall patch to the plaster lath with a couple drywall screws (black screws with a Phillips flathead specifically used for drywall). I still use the bonding agent I mentioned in "Patching a Hole," and after that dries, I place mesh tape around the drywall patch. Lastly, I use joint compound instead of plaster. If plaster is not properly applied and then dries, it's quite a job to sand it down. Sometimes I find joint compound more forgiving and easier to work with than plaster. (See "Tape the Joints.") After you apply a couple coats of compound, then sand, seal, and paint!

PANELING

DIFFICULTY: 3

TOOLS YOU MAY NEED: Claw hammer, putty knife, nail set

MATERIALS YOU MAY NEED: Panel nails, panel adhesive, wood putty

Wall paneling is susceptible to stains, holes, or gouges. The best repair for wall panel is to replace the entire panel. First, you need to take the measurement of the panel and see if you can buy a replacement panel that will fit in stain color, as well as the width between the seams. Paneling comes in 4×8-foot sheets and is nailed to the studs with paneling nails with finished heads.

Remove a panel: You'll need to remove the baseboard and crown molding to remove the paneling. Oftentimes, if you pull the paneling off the studs, the nail pulls through the panel and stays on the studs, so just remove them or tap them into the stud. You may also notice that the paneling had adhesive on the studs. Remove the old adhesive with a putty knife.

Replace a panel: Use panel adhesive on the studs, and install the new panel with paneling nails in the seams if they land over the stud. Slightly set the nails with a nail set in the panel, and cover with wood putty that matches the stain.

Alternatives: If you have a hard time finding matching paneling, you might be able to pull some paneling out of a closet area and replace the damaged panel. Then re-

Fig 3.16 a- Removing a Wall Panel

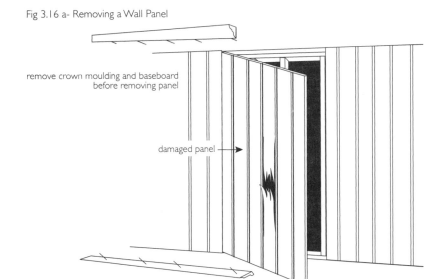

remove crown moulding and baseboard
before removing panel

damaged panel

Fig 3.16 b- Replacing a Wall Panel

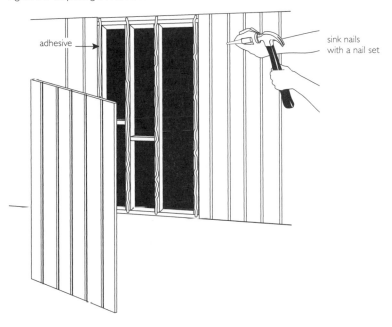

adhesive

sink nails
with a nail set

place that panel in the closet with some paneling that doesn't match, since it won't be seen much except by you. Or you can make one wall of the room a drywall side.

Another option: if you don't want to replace the paneling, you can hang a picture over that area if it's high enough, or if the damage is low, then you can install some wainscoting over the lower panels. I would level a line around the room at the height of your wainscoting and cut the panel with a circular saw set at a ⅜" depth. Remove the paneling and install the wainscoting. You can also patch the hole and paint the room or wallpaper it.

A friend of mine, sick of her paneling altogether but not up to removing it, simply painted over the whole thing, creating a very nice effect.

PAINTING PANELING

DIFFICULTY: 2

TOOLS YOU MAY NEED: Putty knife

MATERIALS YOU MAY NEED: Trisodium phosphate, rubber gloves, sponge, joint compound or auto body filler, 100-grit sandpaper

Fig 3.16c- Filling the Grooves

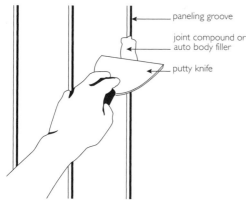

paneling groove

joint compound or auto body filler

putty knife

The first thing you need to do, if you choose, is to hide the seams. That will be the hardest part of the job. With your gloves on, wipe down the paneling with TSP (trisodium phosphate) while wearing safety glasses. This will degloss the paneling and remove any dirt or grease.

Now you have to fill the seams. You can fill them with either joint compound or auto body filler. Auto body filler can be found in your home center and definitely in automotive stores. When applied with a hardener, this putty sets up rock hard. It is a little harder to sand than joint compound, so I would go with the joint compound. Once you fill the seams with compound, then lightly sand with 100-grit sandpaper. You may have to go over the seams again lightly for a flush finish. Then use a primer/sealer before you paint.

Wallpaper paneling: You will need to prep the panel just like you would if you were going to paint it. After you use the primer/sealer, roll on wall sizing. *See* "Wallpaper (page 43)."

Paint

The fastest and least expensive way to uplift a room is by painting it. With so many beautiful colors to choose from, it's no wonder why a painting project is the top of the list for women to tackle.

Oil or Latex?

This used to be such a big debate about twenty years ago. But now, I can confidently say that with so many wonderful latex products out there, there's no reason to paint with oil. Latex dries faster and can be easily cleaned by water.

Picking the Finish

There are so many finishes to choose from: matte, satin, eggshell, semi-gloss, or glossy. Each have their benefits.

Matte: This is also known as a flat finish or flat paint and has no shine, which makes it easy to hide any imperfections on your wall. This is used throughout the house but not in the kitchen or bath, because you cannot wash stains off it.

Eggshell: Look in your refrigerator and take out an egg. The sheen of the egg is similar to the finish you will have, hence the name. It has a low sheen, yet you can clean it, which makes it a favorite for interior walls.

Satin: This has more sheen than eggshell and is used often in kitchens and baths because it can endure light scrubbing.

Semi-gloss: Years ago, this was the paint most of us used in the kitchen and bathroom because it can be washed over and over. It's shiny but not too glitzy. This paint is used on doors, cabinets, and trim.

Glossy: This is also known as "high-gloss" paint because it is very shiny with the look of enamel. This paint is usually used on doors, trim, cabinets, and furniture in a more formal or contemporary décor. Because it is so shiny, imperfections

Tip: Let's talk about picking out a color. What an ordeal that can be! If you're not sure of the color, my suggestion is to get a quart of paint of the color you like and paint a section of your wall. This will enable you to see the paint in different light and not break your piggy bank.

are easily seen, so be sure the surface has been prepped properly.

Ceiling paint: The rule of thumb with ceiling paint is that you want it to be a light color. If you put a darker color on the ceiling, it will make the ceiling feel lower than it is. If you put white on your ceiling, it will lift the feeling of the room. Most decorators and contractors will put a flat white on the ceiling.

HOW TO PAINT A ROOM

DIFFICULTY: 1

TOOLS YOU MAY NEED: Paint brushes, rollers, roller stick, five-in-one putty knife

MATERIALS YOU MAY NEED: Paint, paint tray, painter's blue tape, drop cloths

After you've picked out your color and finish, you can get ready to prep the room. You will find that prepping a room will take you more time than the painting itself, but don't cut corners. It will take you longer in cleanup if you don't protect your existing trim, floors, and furniture. Follow these steps:

Tip: With a hammer and nail, put holes in the indented lip of the paint can. This will allow the paint to drip back into the can and not puddle up around your lid.

- Remove all shelves, artwork, and photographs from the walls.
- Remove the furniture from the room, or put it in the middle of the room and cover well with drop cloths.
- Cover the floor with a drop cloth.
- Protect baseboards, moldings, all trim, and door frames with painter's blue tape. Mask the edges of trim to the wall.
- Mask around the ceiling edges.
- Cut-in (using a brush around any right angles) around all edges where you have masked off with painter's blue tape, applying about 3" of paint. I prefer an angled paint brush to give a nice bead.
- Pour your paint into a paint tray, and saturate a roller, being careful not to load up the roller so much that the paint drips off.
- Paint an N pattern in the wall, starting at one corner and working around the room. Once you make a 4-foot N with the roller, then go over it and fill in the

area. Use steady pressure, but not so hard as to create what is known as "ropes." Ropes are thicker lines of paint caused by the paint at the ends of the roller gushing out. Dip the roller in the paint tray, and repeat until the room is finished.

Fig 3.17- Paint an N

"Cutting-in": You will need to "cut-in" around the door casings, windows, and ceilings. Cutting-in means to apply the paint in a straight seam between the wall and ceiling or the wall and moldings. The best way to do this is to dip the tip of the brush in the paint and hold the brush at a 60° angle to the wall with a firm and steady stroke either going horizontally or vertically, depending on what you are cutting in to. Go horizontally near the ceiling and above door frames and vertically along the sides of the frames. Then turn the brush flat and smooth the paint away from the edge you are cutting in. I like an angled brush for cutting in because I can see the line better, and it gives me more control.

Tip: Don't take your lunch break in the middle of the wall. Be sure you paint to a corner before you take a break.

When painting around a window, cut newspaper to fit in the panes of glass. Dip the paper in a bucket of water, and stick the pieces to the window. Wipe away any dripping water. After you finish painting, peel off the paper. Use a window scraper with a razor edge to remove any paint on glass.

Fig 3.18- Cutting In

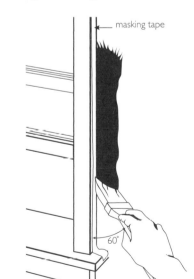

masking tape

60°

Your paint brush: Use the right brush for your paint and job. A soft nylon or synthetic brush works for latex and water-based paint. Look for split ends known as "flags." These will help retain more paint on the brush and spread it more uniformly. Use a natural hair brush for oil and alkyd-based paints. Work all brushes back and forth in the palm of your hand and remove any loose bristles. You don't want any coming out in your paint.

Trick of the Trade:

Sometimes we will put the roller sleeves in the freezer if we will be working with the same latex paint and color the next day. This will save you time and mess with cleaning at the end of the day. Just be sure the rollers are well covered. I like to put them in sealable plastic bags before putting them in the freezer. If you will be taking a short break, say an hour or so, you can simply slip the original roller wrapper over the wet roller.

For ceilings, floors, and chimneys, use a thick 3- to 6-inch-wide brush. My favorite is a 4" brush. For cupboards, large pipes, furniture, and wide base molding, use a 2- to 3-inch-wide brush. For smaller base molding, crown molding, and door trim, use a 1" to 2" brush.

When working with your paint brush, keep the bristles facing down as much as possible so you don't get paint caught in the metal collar around the paint brush. This will stiffen up the bristles at the root. Never dip your brush in the paint more than an inch.

A friend of mine who works on a classic wooden yacht has to do a lot of painting and varnishing and will use painter's blue tape to wrap the metal collar of the brush to keep it from caking with old paint and varnish. She also hangs on to old coffee cans with the plastic lids for brush cleanup.

Clean your brushes: On *Talk2DIY*, we had Brian Santos, "The Wall Wizard," on our show. He showed us the best recipe for cleaning brushes. In his book, *Painting Secrets from Brian Santos, The Wall Wizard*, he suggests the following: use a five-in-one tool to scrape off the excess paint from the brush. For *latex paint or water-based paints*, make up a solution of 1 gallon warm water to ½ cup fabric softener. Dip your brush into the solution, and swish the brush quickly through the mixture. The paint will settle to the bottom of the bucket. This works like magic!

For *oil-based paints*, Brian suggests getting three clean mayonnaise jars and filling the first jar two-thirds full of mineral spirits and the second jar with a 50/50 mixture of mineral spirits and denatured alcohol. Fill the third jar with just denatured alcohol. Once you scrape the paint off the brush, swish the brush in the first jar of mineral spirits for about ten seconds, then spin off the excess in an empty bucket. Next, swish the brush in the second jar of the 50/50 mixture for about ten seconds. Now swish the brush in the third jar of denatured alcohol for another ten seconds, and spin the brush in an empty bucket. Condition the brush in a solution of 1 gallon warm water and ½ cup fabric softener. This will neutralize the alcohol and restore the oils to the bristles.

After Brian appeared on our show and I saw a brush that he's used for twenty years that looked as good as new, I highly suggest using Brian's recipe for cleaning brushes!

Rollers: Rollers enable you to apply much more paint quicker than with a brush and without leaving brush strokes. Roller cages come in metal and plastic, and the roller sleeves or covers slide onto the roller arm. Remember, when choosing a roller cage, you get what you pay for. While you're at the paint store, pick up a roller stick. This will screw into the roller handle and save your back when you're painting the ceiling and tops of your walls. In a pinch, I have unscrewed my broom handle to use as a roller extension. Most broom handles will fit.

> **Safely Store Oily Rags:**
> Because oily rags can spontaneously combust, never pile rags. When working with oil paints and other oil-based materials, always store them in a metal container with a metal lid.

The thickness of the roller is called the "nap." You will see different-size naps at the paint store. The rougher or more textured the surface you are painting, the more paint you will need on the nap; therefore, choose a thicker nap. Think of a sponge. Choose the nap to fit your walls:

- Drywall, smooth plaster, metal, or smooth wood: use a short nap—⅛" or ¼"—although I usually like ⅜".
- Light textured stucco, smooth concrete, or rough wood: use a medium nap—⅜" or ½".
- Heavy textured stucco, brick, or concrete block: use a long nap—¾" or 1".

Cleaning your rollers: Open the can of paint and, using the arched side of the five-in-one putty knife, scrape the nap of the roller sleeve back into the paint can. (Oh! That's what that arch is for on that tool!) You may want to slide a plastic bag over the roller sleeve to pull it off the roller. Wear rubber gloves, and take the sleeve to your bathroom sink or slop sink, and rinse the sleeve a few times while you scrape the roller with the five-in-one tool until most of the paint has been removed. For water-based paints, dip the roller in The Wall Wizard's solution of 1 gallon warm water to ¼ cup fabric softener and run the five-in-one along the nap to remove the rest of the paint. Dry it with a paper towel, and you will be able to reuse it. For oil paints, follow the same directions as for cleaning brushes.

Paint pads: Paint pads are made of foam or a synthetic material and are great to use when applying paint in corners, nooks, and crannies. They're not very expensive, so when you are done working in a room, throw away the pad. They don't hold up as long as a regular brushes.

DECORATIVE PAINTING
DIFFICULTY: 2

I could devote an entire book to faux finishes. But until I can write one, suffice to say that there are many techniques for the same finish. Whether you use a plastic bag, a rag, a brush, or a feather, you can be assured you will have quite the arts and crafts weekend when faux finishing your walls. I have briefly described different types of decorative painting in the following paragraphs. For further information, techniques, and products, pick up a decorative painting book at your local paint store or bookstore.

Most faux paint jobs or decorative painting requires a base coat. Find out what your particular technique requires. I usually stick with a satin finish for a base coat.

Glazing or color washing: There are all sorts of glazing techniques and products. Some glazes are made of 5 parts paint to 1 part glaze, while others require tints or acrylic paints mixed with the glaze coat. Glazing can give you a soft effect or an antique-looking effect. A soft, blended effect is made by big, sweeping strokes that are random yet balanced, working in a 3-foot-square section at a time and then blending with more pressure on the dry brush at the end. Keep your body open and relaxed.

Crackle: Depending on the product, this is either a two- or three-step process. Some products require a base coat first. The crackle coat is applied next and then the top coat. It's the crackle coat that makes the top coat look cracked. Other products have the crackle additive in the basecoat, so you will just need to apply the top coat. In either case, this will give an antique look to your furniture or walls. Rub with antique wax or a watered-down brown paint. Many manufacturers specialize in the crackle look.

Ragging: Apply a base coat. Let dry and then apply the base coat color mixed with ⅓ white paint, keeping the same finish for both paints, that is, the base color and white would be the same satin finish. Submerge a rag in the paint, and squeeze off any excess paint, then start ragging the wall. I like to put on some music and put a rag in each hand and beat the walls to the music. Hey, whatever gets the job done!

Sponging: You can use as many colors as you would like. Generally, most people tend to use two colors. Roll on your base coat, then dip one sponge in paint #1 and pounce on your wall. I like to dab it on a piece of paper first to remove excess paint. After you have sponged the whole room, repeat with the second color and a clean sponge.

Marbleizing: This is a wonderful look and if done properly, it really does look like marble. This technique usually requires a base coat with 3 different colors of glaze. One coat may be wiped on and then some of it removed with a thin plastic drop cloth or plastic bag, the next stippled, and the next dabbed with a sea sponge. You can also use a feather to make the veins.

Wood graining: In my opinion, this is the hardest technique. It also requires a good many brushes and a couple glazes. This technique is usually done on bookshelves and cabinets. It can warm up a room if done properly. For complete instructions, buy a decorative painting book that features wood graining.

Stenciling: This can be a relatively easy technique. You can make your own patterns, buy them, or download them from the Internet. Usually, you tape the stencil on the wall, dip a stiff brush in the paint, being careful not to overload it, and lightly remove some paint off the ends on a piece of paper. Then pounce, lightly pound, and rub the brush on the stencil to make a flat pattern. Don't wipe over the stencil, because the paint will get behind the paper and smudge.

Stippling: Ask your parents or grandparents about stippling. This technique has been around for a long time. Stippling is also known as pouncing. The effect is a fine and sandy appearance. The brush used is a fat brush called a stippling brush and has dense bristles. You can use many colors of paint or just one color.

Wallpaper

Wallpaper can be a lovely finish for your walls. The downside is that if you get a hole in the drywall, you will need to repair the drywall and then fix the wallpaper—more work than painting over a patch. On *Talk2DIY*, I have more questions on how to remove wallpaper rather than applying it. But believe it or not, hanging or removing wallpaper can be quite easy.

WALLPAPER REMOVAL

DIFFICULTY: 2

TOOLS YOU MAY NEED: Putty knife, garden sprayer, scoring tool, sponges, rubber gloves, safety glasses, a 5-gallon bucket

MATERIALS YOU MAY NEED: Spackle, bucket of warm water, and The Wall Wizard's Magic Solution of 3 gallons hot water, 22 ounces wallpaper remover concentrate, ¼ cup liquid fabric softener, 1 cup white vinegar, 2 tablespoons baking soda

You have a few options when removing wallpaper. Hopefully the wall was prepared properly before the wallpaper was installed so it will come off easily. First, move the furniture to the middle of the room, and cover the floors with drop cloths. Plastic drop cloths are good because the pieces of wallpaper get stuck to it and you can just throw the whole lot away after you remove the wallpaper.

Scoring the wall: To remove wallpaper, you must first perforate the paper using a scoring tool. This tool fits neatly in the palm of your hand and has little teeth on a wheel, which punctures the paper. Work the scoring tool around the room, applying enough pressure to go through the paper but not too much pressure as to ruin the drywall underneath it.

Spraying the wall: *Turn off the power to the room.*

The best recipe for wallpaper removal comes from The Wall Wizard himself, Brian Santos, who showed Brad Staggs and me on *Talk2DIY* how well his solution works. In his book, *Painting Secrets from Brian Santos, The Wall Wizard,* he suggests his Secret Stripping Solution, which consists of the following:

3 gallons hot water
22 ounces wallpaper remover concentrate
¼ cup liquid fabric softener
1 cup white vinegar
2 tablespoons baking soda

Fig 3.19- Removing Wallpaper

Pour all the ingredients into a 5-gallon bucket, and mix it together. Fill a garden sprayer with this mixture, and spray the walls, working from the bottom up. Brian's solution remains active for fifteen minutes after its been sprayed, so work quickly. Go around the room and spray the walls three times, being sure the walls are thoroughly saturated. Using a thin plastic sheeting (.7 mil works fine), smooth the sheeting of plastic on the walls from top to bottom. The plastic will stick to the solution, make a tight vacuum seal, and not allow air to dry it out. Cut the plastic around the moldings, and let it set for at least three hours, although overnight is preferred. This solution will dissolve more than one layer of wallpaper adhesive and will come down like magic!

Steam machine: If you use the preceding solution, I don't think you'll ever have to use a steam machine, but just in case you run into the most stubborn wallpaper, you can rent one. Sometimes when a wall wasn't prepared properly or sealed and "sized," the paper has a hard time releasing from the wall. Sometimes there is more than one layer of wallpaper, which makes removal extremely difficult. If this is the case, rent a wallpaper steam machine. Hold this over the wallpaper for a couple minutes, and the hot steam will saturate the paper, allowing it to come off with your putty knife.

Remove any glue: With a scouring pad and a bucket of hot water, wash off any glue that may be left on the wall. I use a scouring pad and my putty knife to remove any leftover glue. Once your wall is dry, run your hand over the wall. If you feel any rough areas, lightly go over the wall with a 100- or 120-grit sandpaper until smooth.

Spackle holes: While removing wallpaper, you might have gouged the wall or maybe the scoring tool put some holes in your wall. Using spackle or joint compound, fill in any holes or tears in the drywall paper. Once the spackle has dried, then sand with 120-grit sandpaper. Remove any dust. Then, be sure you use a primer/sealer after you've finished. See "Painting" for more information.

Hanging Wallpaper

DIFFICULTY: 3

TOOLS YOU MAY NEED: Tape measure, screwdriver, putty knife, drywall knife, level, razor blades, straight edge, seam roller, smoothing brush, pencil

MATERIALS YOU MAY NEED: Drop cloth, sandpaper, spackle, wall sizing, wallpaper paste, plastic bucket, paint roller and ⅜" nap sleeve, water tray, sponge, stepladder

The most important aspect to hanging wallpaper is the prep work. If you have a folding table, please use it, because you will need a work area. You might want to cover the table in plastic because wallpapering can be a little messy. Cover your floors with drop cloths, and cover all the furniture and move it away from the walls. Remember to keep your leftover wallpaper in case you ever need some for a wall repair in that room.

Prep the walls: Remove all outlet covers and light switch plates with a screwdriver. Keep them in a sealable plastic bag so you don't loose the screws. Fill holes and cracks with spackle or a joint compound. Sand the walls smooth, and if you have gloss walls, then sand them to give the wall some "tooth" to hold the wallpaper. Wallpaper cannot go over a textured wall. With a damp sponge, wipe away the dust or dirt.

Seal/prime the wall: The wall needs to be sealed and primed properly with a wallpaper sealer/primer. This product is made just for wallpapering. I have seen some products that both seal/prime and size the wall.

Sizing the wall: Be sure you "size" the wall. Sizing is an adhesive solution that is applied directly to the wall and allowed to dry. It's basically a diluted paste to help adhere the wallpaper to the wall. This is an important step, because the last thing you want is peeling wallpaper! The sizing paste also makes wallpaper removal easier when you decide down the road to redecorate. You just put it on with a roller and brush as you would paint.

Mark a plumb line: Measuring from a corner in the room, mark the wall the width of your wallpaper minus ½" and plumb a line from the bottom to the top of the wall at that mark with your level. Your line should be perfectly straight up and down. This line is most important, because once you hang the first piece of wallpaper, you will be holding the wallpaper parallel to this line around the room.

Fig 3.20- Marking a Plumb Line

corner of room

width of paper minus 1/2"

Figure out the design: Unroll the wallpaper roll and look at the pattern to decide where you want it to go against the ceiling. I think beginning a full design at the ceiling looks best. Mark the spot on the back of the wallpaper with a pencil. Cut the wallpaper with a straight edge for length, giving yourself about 2" for trimming on the top and bottom. This piece will be your template to cut the rest of the pieces. Line up the patterns, and keep cutting your strips so they will line up properly to each other. I like to cut all my pieces at once.

Unpasted wallpaper: Placing the wallpaper pattern-side down on a large table, coat the back of it with the wallpaper paste using a paint roller. Always use the wallpaper paste recommended by the wallpaper's manufacturer.

Prepasted wallpaper: With the table covered with a drop cloth, fill a wallpaper water tray with water and submerge a strip in the water with the decorative side facing down. This will be rolled up, so press out all air bubbles, and soak for the manufacturer's recommended time. Then grab the

Tip: Go around the room and measure where each strip will end and be sure you don't end the wallpaper with a little strip at the corner where you started. This will also enable you to figure out how many strips of wallpaper you will need to cut.

Fig 3.21 - Booking Wallpaper

top of the sheet and pull it out of the water, being sure the whole back is wet. The paper will unroll as you pull up one end.

"Booking" means to fold one end of the paper over to the middle, paste to paste, and the other end of the paper, paste to paste. Be sure *not* to crease the folds. Allow the paper to book for about three to five minutes, according to the manufacturer's recommendations. Booking allows the paper to relax and the adhesive to activate. You can usually book about four or five sheets at a time.

Hanging the wallpaper: Take off your gloves, if you are wearing them, because you need to feel with your hands when hanging wallpaper. Remember when you marked the back of the wallpaper? Look for that mark, unbook that top part, and place the mark up against the corner of the ceiling. The paper will be slippery against the wall and easy to handle. Slide the paper so that the edge aligns with the plumb line mark on the wall. Using a smoothing brush, smooth the strip against the wall. Unbook the bottom half of the wallpaper, and smooth it into place. Keep close attention on the plumb line. The excess will overlap the ceiling, the corner of adjoining wall, and your base molding. Snip the corner of the paper at a diagonal to the corner of the wall. This will enable you to smooth the ½" strip side on the adjoining wall.

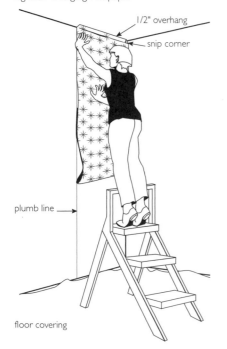

Fig 3.22- Hanging Wallpaper

1/2" overhang

snip corner

plumb line

floor covering

Smooth the paper: Always work from the top down at a diagonal and then from the center to the edges, forcing out any air bubbles with the smoothing brush. If you get an air bubble, immediately pick up the paper to the bubble and resmooth it. For stubborn air bubbles that just won't come out, poke the bubble with a pin and then smooth.

Trim the paper: Hold a taping knife so the blade meets the crevice of the baseboard and wall with the handle pointing up and laying up against the wallpaper. Cut the wallpaper with a straight razor. If you don't feel comfortable holding a flat straight razor in your hand, then use a utility knife. Always use a new blade, and keep moving the taping knife until you have trimmed the wallpaper. Do the same at the ceiling, holding the taping knife with the handle pointing down. With a damp sponge, remove any excess paste on top of the wallpaper, baseboards, and ceiling.

The second strip: Do the exact same thing with the next strip, but match the pattern to the first strip. Butt the edges together so you don't see any wall space between them, but not so tight as to overlap the edges. Do this over and over until you come to the corner where you started. I like to make a new plumb line as a guide on each new wall.

Seam roller: After about fifteen minutes, or until you have put up the wallpaper you've booked, go over the seams with a seam roller. Don't press so hard that you squeeze out the adhesive.

Cutting in around door and windows: Hang the strip and smooth it in place to the edge of the door or window. Just like you made a diagonal cut in the corner, you will need to cut in the corners around the door and window frame. This will allow you to smooth the paper against the wall using your smoothing brush. With the taping knife, trim the paper around the frame of the doors and windows using the same technique you used for the ceiling and baseboards.

D'oh! My friend Don used to own a late-1800s farmhouse in upstate New York that had beautiful wallpaper throughout the house. One hot summer evening, we were all gathered around, eating dinner, and noticed that the gold rose wallpaper was actually hung upside down! The roses were growing down the wall instead of up! It took us quite a few years before we noticed it. I bet the installer must have had a heart attack (or a good laugh) the day he/she noticed the mistake. Always double-check your pattern to be sure the paper is laying in the right direction!

The light switches and outlets: Before cutting the paper over the light switches and outlets, shut off the power to the room. With the razor blade, cut an X over the hole, and remove some of the paper, leaving a smaller hole than the actual electrical box.

Check out the pattern where your cover will go, and cut a big enough piece of wallpaper to go over the cover with room for adjustments. I usually make mine about 6 × 6 inches. Put your cover back in place, notice where the pattern lands around it, and try to match it up. Dry fit the paper around the cover, making slits through the hole for the switch. Apply wallpaper paste to wallpaper, book the piece for about three minutes, then apply on the wall or outlet cover and fold behind the cover. Let dry and then reattach the covers over the receptacles and switches.

Wallpaper Repair

DIFFICULTY: 2

As with drywall, the wallpaper can get damaged from moving furniture or children's horseplay. Hopefully, you have some wallpaper that you saved when you first installed it.

Paper lifting off the wall: If the installer put up the wallpaper and squeezed out too much of the paste behind it, then, in time, the wallpaper can come away from the wall. Fix this by lifting up the loose wallpaper and spreading a thin layer of wallpaper paste underneath it. Smooth it down lightly with a smoothing brush or a wide putty knife. Clean the wallpaper with a damp cloth.

Blisters: If you have an air bubble or a piece of dirt under the paper, it will cause a blister. Just cut the blister with a sharp razor blade along a pattern line if possible, take out any debris, and spread a thin layer of wallpaper paste up underneath with the edge of a putty knife. Smooth down with a damp cloth, and clean off any excess paste.

Tears or holes: You know that wallpaper you saved in the attic? You'll need it now. Find the pattern where the hole is on the wallpaper, and find where that pattern is on the saved roll of wallpaper. Now, cut out a square patch larger than you'll need. Place the patch over the tear or hole until the pattern matches up, and tape into place with painter's blue tape. (Test the tape in a corner area to be sure the tape doesn't pull off the wallpaper.)

Now with a sharp razor blade or utility knife, cut on the line of the pattern to make an irregular patch big enough to cover the damage. You will need to apply pressure, because you will be cutting through the existing wallpaper, too. Remove the cut patch, and peel away the existing wallpaper over the damaged area. You can patch the area with a little spackle, let it dry, and seal it. If the area is flat or the hole is small and you don't think anyone will knock an elbow into that area, then put the wallpaper paste on the back of the patch and match it over the cut

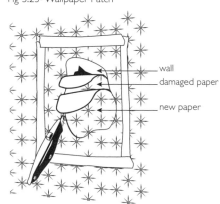

Fig 3.23- Wallpaper Patch

wall

damaged paper

new paper

out. Smooth and remove any excess paste on the wall. If you have done this properly, you should not be able to see the patch.

Wall Fasteners

What is Murphy's Law? Wherever you want to hang something you can be sure you won't hit a stud! Whether you have drywall or plaster walls, if you hang something with some weight to it and don't hit a stud, you'll need a wall fastener to hold the piece on the wall. Even if you want to screw into brick or concrete, you will need an expansion anchor. There are different kinds for different walls, such as expansion anchors, screw-in anchors, molly screws, toggle bolts, and others that expand behind the wall. When hanging something big or heavy, go with a larger fastener. The fastener package will tell you how much weight it will bear. Most anchors will come in different sizes for different wall thicknesses. Drywall anchors come in ½" and ⅝" sizes. Use a #6 screw for less than 10 pounds of weight, which should penetrate at least 1" into the wall, and an #8 screw for more than 10 pounds, which should penetrate the wall at least 1½".

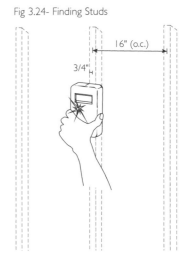

Fig 3.24- Finding Studs

16" (o.c.)

3/4"

DIFFICULTY: 2

Expansion anchors: These are for use with solid material walls: brick, concrete, or metals. When the screw or bolt is threaded into the anchor, it expands. Lead anchors are also used in solid materials. The least effective anchor is the plastic expansion anchor. I stopped using them altogether because too often they would spin as I was driving in the screw.

You can also buy amazing concrete screws. First, you need to drill the proper pilot hole in the concrete with a hammer drill, and then they screw right in.

Drywall anchors: These anchors are only for drywall—not plaster—walls.

Threaded drywall anchors: These came out a few years ago and have made hanging anything in drywall a breeze. With the tip of your screwdriver or a magnetic Phillips tip on your screw gun, you can screw these anchors right into the drywall. This takes away the step of drilling first. The other nice thing about these anchors is

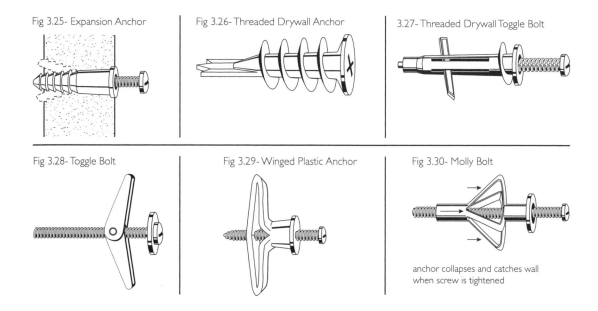

Fig 3.25- Expansion Anchor

Fig 3.26- Threaded Drywall Anchor

3.27- Threaded Drywall Toggle Bolt

Fig 3.28- Toggle Bolt

Fig 3.29- Winged Plastic Anchor

Fig 3.30- Molly Bolt

anchor collapses and catches wall
when screw is tightened

that when it's time to renovate or move, you can just unscrew them from the wall and spackle over the hole. Can you tell that these are my favorite? No muss, no fuss!

Threaded drywall toggle bolt: This is basically the same principle as a threaded drywall anchor. You screw them into the wall, and when the screw is inserted, the toggle flips over and holds the back of the wall. If you're going to hang something heavy, use these!

Winged plastic anchors: I like these, too, but they do require a pilot hole first. Drill a hole no bigger than the thickness of the shank of the anchor. Pinch the wings together, and insert the pinched wings into the hole, then hammer into place. These come with a little plastic push-tool (usually red) that you need to insert into the anchor. This will drive the wings open in the back.

Molly bolts: I like using these bolts for hanging something in a hollow door. Use a very small molly bolt for this application. Drill a pilot hole, insert the molly bolt, and let the teeth underneath the collar catch into the wall. As you tighten the threaded bolt, it will expand the anchor on the back of the wall or the inside of your hollow door.

There are more heavy-duty molly bolts for drywall. Some have a point that you can nail in, and some require a pilot hole, but they all expand, catching the back of the drywall.

Plaster walls: The problem with plaster walls is that you have the plaster and the lath, and sometimes that thickness can be anywhere between ¾" and 1" thick. So what wall anchor should you use? Well, you can never go wrong with a toggle bolt.

Toggle bolts: These are the "Mac Daddy" of wall anchors. There are two parts to this bolt: the toggle, which looks like a spring-loaded wing, and the machine screw that the wing screws on to. They come in many different lengths and thicknesses of the screw and toggle. This is the fastener to use in a ceiling for sure! They can hold an incredible amount of weight. They'll take away a huge chunk of wall before the anchor will come out.

Toggle bolts need to have a pilot hole big enough for the diameter of the toggle (wing) when pressed together. Once you drill the pilot hole, be sure you put the toggle on the bolt properly, with the flat part of the toggle facing you as you put it in. The flat part, when opened, up goes against the back wall. (Don't do what I have done and put them in backward. They won't hold a thing that way and can be pulled right back through the hole.)

The trick to this anchor is that as you screw in the bolt, you need to pull the bolt toward you; otherwise, the toggle will just spin. Pulling the bolt toward you allows the toggle to catch the back of the plaster or drywall.

Wainscoting

Wainscoting is a wall treatment applied to the lower part of the wall that not only protects the walls, but can transform a room, giving it a country feel or an upscale, formal look. Traditional wainscoting is made of solid wood with vertical and horizontal members surrounding flat wood panels and is often found in older homes. This type of wainscoting was installed by a talented finish carpenter. Today, however, because of paneled wainscoting and bead board, you can get a wonderful look by doing it yourself!

Installing Wainscoting

DIFFICULTY: 4

TOOLS YOU MAY NEED: Level, measuring tape, stud finder, hammer, drill with drill bits and a Phillips driver bit, nail set, putty knife, miter saw, clamps, safety glasses

MATERIALS YOU MAY NEED: Panel adhesive, putty, 120-grit sandpaper, 4d finish nails. 4d nails are "4 penny" nails that are 1½" in length. This is an old term when 100 nails would cost 4 cents for this length in a pound. The "d" stands for "penny."

There are three components of modern-day wainscoting: the paneling or bead board, the chair rail, and the baseboard. First, you must install the panels or bead board planks. You can also buy bead board panels that will give you the look of bead board at a lesser price.

Remove the old baseboard: I do not recommend placing wainscoting panels on top of existing baseboards, although I have seen it done. I guess if the top of the base-board is thick enough, you could possibly get away with it. Everyone else, remove your baseboard. You will also need to remove all outlet covers.

Layout: Wainscoting can be applied at a height of 32" to 36". My feeling is it's a combo of personal taste and the measurement of the chair backs that will live in the room, because the chair railing goes on top of the wainscoting. Chair rail was designed to protect your walls from the top backs of your chairs. After you've established your height, draw a continuous level line around the room with a 4-foot level if you have one. If you have a laser level, this will come in handy to lay out the room.

Trick of the Trade:

When using your level to lay out an entire room, be sure you keep flipping your level after each mark. Don't flip it upside down; flip it left to right. In case your level is a hair off, flipping the level will compensate the discrepancy.

Locating studs: With the stud finder, go around the room and find the center point of your studs. Set the stud finder on the wall and press the button to let the stud finder calibrate. When it's ready, while still pressing the button, drag the stud finder across the wall. The moment it beeps or lights up, that is the *edge* of the stud. You will need to measure ¾" over from that mark for the center point of the stud. (Studs are made of 2×4s, but are really 1½" × 3½". Therefore, the center of 1½" is ¾".) Make your marks on the level line for reference when installing.

Cutting the bead board/panels: I like to go around the room and take the measurement from the floor to the level line. Because of settling, shifting, or the original installation, your floor is not going to be the same height all around the room. The smallest measurement is the high spot in the floor. Cut all boards or panels ¼" shorter than the smallest measurement so you can fit it in quickly. Wainscoting panels come in 48" × 32" or 48" × 96" panels. Bead board is sold in a range of widths and are usually tongue and grooved, meaning there is a routed or channeled groove down the center of one edge of the plank and a "tongue" that is contoured to fit in the groove on the other edge of the plank. These planks are usually sold in 8-foot lengths.

Start installation: If you have an outside corner, start there. First, you will need to install corner molding from the level mark to the floor. Add panel adhesive to the back of the molding, and secure it with nails. The first panel will butt up against this corner molding. If your room doesn't have an outside corner, start in the inside corner. In either case, you may have to trim the edge so it lays into the corner nicely. To trim the paneling or bead board, use a jigsaw or a block plane. Paneling is thinner and easier to plane than bead board, but neither should give you much difficulty. If you're going to paint over the bead board, don't stress making everything perfect, because you can go back and caulk the gaps later.

Depending on if you're using a long, 48" panel or installing tongue-and-groove planks, apply some panel adhesive on the wall in horizontal or zigzag lines for planks. Set the panels in place, and nail 4d finish nails every 8" to 10" down the studs and along the bottom of the panels.

For the planks, remove the tongue on your first plank with a jigsaw or table saw. Place the now flat edge in the corner, and toenail (at an angle) a 4d nail into the groove and into the wall along the other edge. Be sure you use a nail set to sink the heads in. This way the nail head won't interfere with the tongue fitting into the groove.

Remember, the first panel or plank needs to be perfectly plumb—straight up and down— and up to the level layout line. As you continue around the room, you will have to cut the panels or planks to fit in the corners.

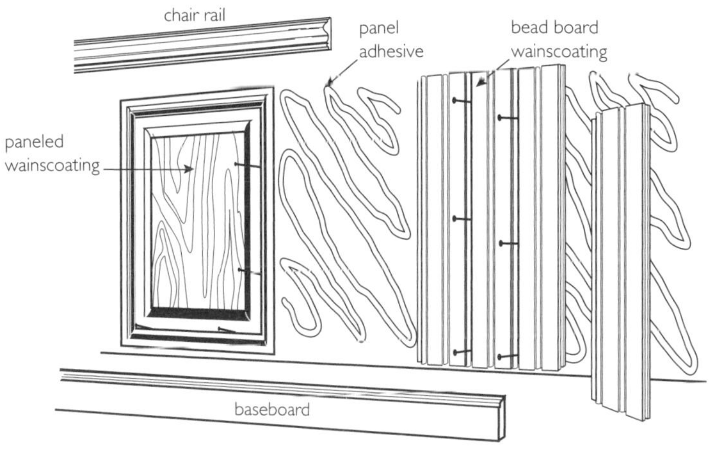

Cutting around outlets and windows: Take the measurements of the outlet holes, and use a jigsaw to cut the panels or planks. You

Fig 3.31 - Installing Wainscoting

chair rail

panel adhesive

bead board wainscoting

paneled wainscoting

baseboard

Trick of the Trade:

When using panel adhesive with panels in the trade, we push the panels up against the panel adhesive on the wall and then pull them away from the wall. Lean the face of the panel up against you for a couple minutes to allow the adhesive to form a slight skin. Then push the panel back on the wall and into place. This will actually help to suck the panels to the wall.

will need to measure from the level layout line to the top of the outlet and from the side of your last panel or plank to the side of the outlet. Measure twice, and cut once! Because you will be adding to the wall, you may need to buy longer machine screws to bring the outlets or switches out flush to the face of the wainscoting and extend the receptacle boxes.

Now you will need to apply the base molding and chair rail. See "Moldings."

Every year the building industry designs new products and materials to help us combine steps. For instance, in some areas of the country, you can buy base molding with a groove on the top for the wainscoting to fit in. In this case, you would install the base molding first and then the paneling.

Moldings

Moldings add the finishing touch to a room, and you can bring up the value of your home by simply installing molding! You can use various types of moldings to beautify your walls: baseboards, chair rail, picture, and crown. All these come in various sizes and profiles. Moldings can come in different wood grains and are sold as a solid piece or finger-jointed to make the long lengths. If you are going to paint the molding, buy finger-jointed molding. It will save you money in the end, and no one will see it once it's painted.

Whether you are going to paint or stain your moldings, you will need to use a nail set to push the head of the nail below the surface of the face of the molding and putty over it with wood putty. If you're going to paint, you can use caulk to hide any gaps. Putty will have to be used if you're staining.

Because all molding but crown molding is cut the same, I will share how to make proper miter cuts in the "Baseboard" section.

Installing Molding

DIFFICULTY: 3 to 4

TOOLS YOU MAY NEED: Drill with drill bits, hammer, level, compass, miter box/saw, nail set, measuring tape, pencil, putty knife, backsaw, clamps, safety glasses

MATERIALS YOU MAY NEED: Molding, wood putty, 6d finish nails, masking tape, wood glue, caulk, damp rag

BASEBOARD:

Baseboard is a way of finishing off a wall. Even the most basic room will have baseboard; whether it's made out of vinyl or wood will depend on the budget. Whether you're applying baseboard on top of wainscoting or just need to replace it, the application is the same. First, you want to be sure the baseboard is level and that it doesn't slope down if your floor isn't level. This will stick out, especially if you have wainscoting installed level. Start at the low end of the room (if you have wainscoting, it will be the longest measurement from the floor to the level line or chair rail) and at a corner.

Baseboard comes in many different profiles and sizes. You can install it flush to the floor, which will require you to scribe the baseboard to the bottom of the floor. Scribing is the process of leveling your baseboard and using a compass. You remember compasses from math class, right? One end is a point and the other end holds a pencil. If you use quarter-round molding on the bottom of your baseboards, you can omit scribing the profile of the floor.

Scribing: Place a length of baseboard on the floor (usually 8 feet long), and put a level on top of it in the middle. Add shims or a wedge underneath the bottom of the baseboard

> **Hint:** If you need to scribe the baseboard, level it, mark it, make your miter cut, then cut the scribe line.

to the left or right end to make it perfectly level. With the compass point touching the floor, bring the pencil point to the edge of the board on the end with the shims/wedge. Holding the baseboard in place against the wall, drag the compass along the bottom of the baseboard. This is the mark you need to cut with your jigsaw. After you cut along this line, when you put the baseboard back on the floor, it will follow the contour of your floor and the top will be level.

Fig 3.32- Scribing Baseboard

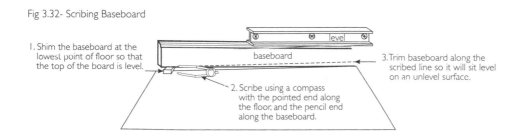

1. Shim the baseboard at the lowest point of floor so that the top of the board is level.

level

baseboard

3. Trim baseboard along the scribed line so it will sit level on an unlevel surface.

2. Scribe using a compass with the pointed end along the floor, and the pencil end along the baseboard.

Nailing into place: With your stud finder, locate the studs with a light pencil mark that you can remove later just above the height of the baseboard. (Remember: most stud finders light up on the **edge** of the stud first.) I recommend drilling a pilot hole—a small hole that's slightly smaller than the nail you use so the wood won't split. I recommend a 6d finish nail, which is 2" in length. Go the hardware store and ask for a "6 d" finish nail. The "d" stands for "penny," which is a trade term that originally meant how many you could buy for a penny. I also like to use panel adhesive or construction adhesive behind the baseboard. Just apply a squiggly line on the back before nailing into place.

Tip: If you're using an power miter saw, be sure to locate the clamp so it doesn't get in the way of the arm of the miter saw when cutting.

Miter cuts: This is what separates the women from the girls and the men from the boys . . . miter cuts! You can use a miter box or a chop saw, also known as a miter saw, to make your miter cuts. The key to making a proper miter is precision and patience.

Inside corner: The inside corner is made by two baseboards coming together with each having an inside 45° angle that will make a 90° or right angle. Let's say that we start in a left corner and work around the room left to right. Make the left inside 45° angle by placing the baseboard up against the back of the fence of the miter box or the electric chop just as it would sit on the wall. I suggest screwing the miter box to your work table and clamping the baseboard to the back of the miter box so it doesn't move. You will be making the miter cut on the left side of the baseboard.

With the backsaw, insert it in the farthest groove to the right, and push it in until it goes through the back groove. Lightly pull the saw toward you to enable the saw to bite into the baseboard to start the cutting. Cut through the baseboard with back-and-forth strokes. When cutting the baseboard to fit into a right inside corner, place the baseboard flat up against the back fence, clamp it, and put the saw in the farthest left grooved angle, pushing it through to the back groove, and cut the angle.

Outside corner: All outside corners need to be mitered. Two outside 45° angles make up a 90° angle, also known as a right angle. If you are working from left to right and come to the outside corner on your right, put the baseboard in place against the wall and mark the top of the baseboard right at the corner. Use a fine pencil point for this. Place the baseboard up against the back fence of the miter box or chop saw with the baseboard extending to the left. Slide it over until the mark you

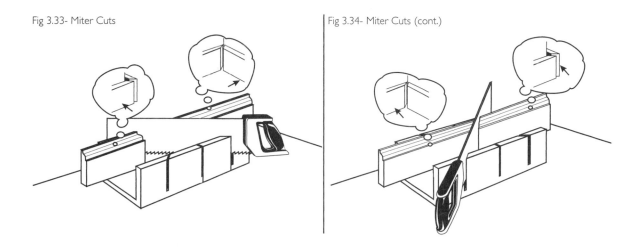

Fig 3.33- Miter Cuts

Fig 3.34- Miter Cuts (cont.)

made comes up to the left groove on the back of the miter box. Clamp this down, push the backsaw through the grooves, and lightly pull back on the saw, starting the cut of the baseboard. Continue to cut back and forth. For the other piece, you will need to hold the baseboard off to the right of the miter box or chop saw. Because this will be the first cut, you won't need a line to cut on. The saw now goes through the far left groove and into the back groove. Cut through the baseboard.

Jointing at the middle: You have two options: a butt joint or a splice joint. I prefer the latter because a butt joint stands out too much. Remember to always use wood glue between your joints before nailing into place.

Butt joint: Obviously, a butt joint is easier because you just need to make two straight cuts and push them together. To make a straight cut, place the baseboard in the miter box and put the saw in the middle of the miter box in the straight grooves. Clamp your work to the back fence of the miter box or chop saw and cut your 90° angle, which is a straight cut.

Fig 3.35- Butt and Splice Joint

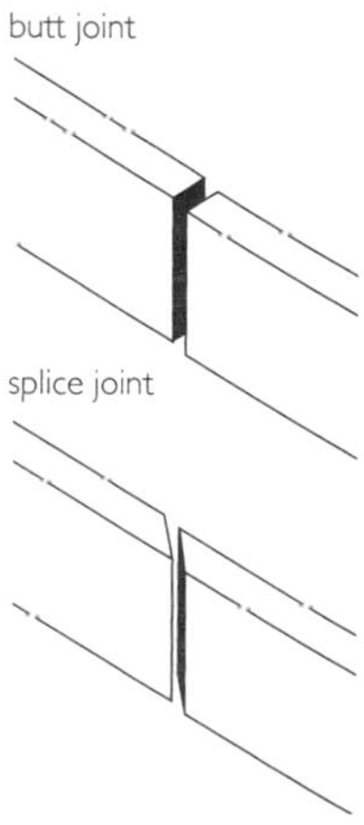

butt joint

splice joint

Splice joint: This is also known as a kerf joint. It is basically cutting the baseboard on an angle and fitting the next piece in at an angle. If you're working from left to right, and have a long wall, and need to marry two baseboards together, cut the first board at an outside corner angle. So cut the right side of the board by placing it into the miter box, clamp it down, put the backsaw into the farthest groove on the right, push it through catching the back groove, and cut. The next piece of baseboard will need to have an inside miter on the left end. Place it into the miter box with the backsaw going through the far left groove in front and through the back groove. When placing this on the wall, the second baseboard will tuck neatly into the angle of the first baseboard.

Cope joint: This joint is only for inside corners and is a favorite among woodworkers because walls in most homes do not meet at perfect 90° corners. If you are going to stain the baseboard, you may want to learn this joint. A cope joint looks perfect no matter what the angle of your corner is . . . and let's face it, it's hard to find a perfectly square corner in a room. This is a more complicated joint, but it's my favorite, because once you get the hang of it, you will only use cope joints for inside corners.

In a cope joint, one piece of molding is cut straight and butted into one side of the corner. The other piece is coped along the profile of the molding, making it push right into the butted piece.

First, you will need to make an inside angle (see "Inside Corner", page 62). Take your pencil and run the side edge of the lead along the edge of the profile. That's the edge where the angle cut starts. This will help you see the line of the profile you will be cutting.

You will need to put the blade in the cope saw with the teeth facing up in the direction of the handle. Unlike most American saws, the coping saw cuts on the pull stroke, not the push stroke. The blade is very thin so it can turn easily. Lay the base-

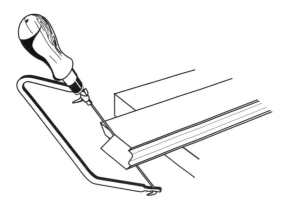

Fig 3.36- Cutting a Cope Joint

board flat on your work space and clamp it down. You will notice that the top of the baseboard will go into a point. The very top point will need to be cut straight up from the first small profile curve. Starting at the top of the baseboard, lightly push the cope saw down, starting a groove. You may need to do this a few times so the blade doesn't jump out at you. Now pulling the blade back and forth, keep the blade angled into the baseboard so you are cutting the profile at a 45° angle with the coping saw blade. Keep moving it back and forth, staying mindful of cutting the edge of the profile and the angle of the blade. Once you get to the straight part of the baseboard, turn it around and cut it straight up. You do not need to hold an angle when cutting on the straight part of the profile, although I do just a little so I will have less to rasp if it needs to be altered a bit.

Trick of the Trade:

Take it from me—you will need to get a wood rasp if you want to get good results on your molding joints. I have never cut a coped joint that I didn't need to tweak a little bit with my wood rasp.

CHAIR RAIL:

This is a wonderful accent for your home. It can be installed plain or as a cap to wainscoting. A chair rail is a molding for a specific purpose: to protect your walls from the backs of your chairs. That's the intention. So if you want to install chair rail, you can determine that measurement with your chairs. Most chair rail is installed between 32" to 36". Install the chair rail the same way you would baseboard, except you do not need to scribe the chair rail—just be sure you keep it level around the room. Start in one corner and work around the room left to right. Make the miter cuts just as you would baseboard.

PICTURE MOLDING:

Once upon a time, people would hang their pictures from picture molding so as to not puncture their walls with nails. Picture molding is in my apartment in Manhattan and can be found in older homes. It is installed near the ceiling, depending on what the builder wanted. Sometimes it can be installed directly under the crown molding, and other times it can be installed about 8" below it. It really depends how high the ceilings are. In my apartment, it's installed about 8" below the ceiling all through the house except the kitchen and bath. The top of the molding is rounded. The picture molding hardware looks like an S from the side. One side hooks over the molding, and the other side is a hook to catch the wire from the picture frame. Obviously, the pictures weren't hung way up at the ceiling, so the wires were long, hanging the pictures at eye level.

The installation is the same as installing chair rail except the location is near the ceiling.

CROWN MOLDING:

In my opinion, crown molding makes a room look elegant and sophisticated. It requires a good bit of know-how and a *lot* of patience. Are you up for it? Because it goes on the wall at an angle touching the ceiling and the wall, you need to keep it at an angle when cutting it. That sounds simple, right? Well, here's where it gets tricky. You have to cut it upside down in the miter box or miter saw.

This is what I do: I write "ceiling" on the bottom of my miter box or power miter saw and then I write "wall" on the back fence of the miter box/miter saw. I do this because I get confused. Yes, after years of doing this, my mind can wander and I forget. Plus, because you're working on a ladder, you have to go up and down a good many times, and I don't like to have to go back and forth more times than necessary. With that said, let's start at an inside corner.

Inside corner: Similar to baseboard, you can cut two crown moldings at an inside 45° angle to make up the inside corner, or you can cope it. First, the 45° angle: hold the crown molding up to the ceiling at an angle with the bottom flat part of the crown touching the wall and the top flat part, touching the ceiling. Write "ceiling" on the back of it where it touches the ceiling. Starting in a corner and working left to right, with a pencil, draw the angle line across the face of the molding. The bottom left side of the crown will have a point, and the angle will go to the right once cut. These marks help me when I'm down off the ladder and cutting the miter.

D'oh! I installed crown molding for someone who I just adore. The joints were perfect. The job was beautiful . . . well, almost. I applied the crown molding upside down. I didn't notice until I had finished the entire room. My friend, who I call Pop, let it slide! Phew. Don't do what I did. Be sure you know how the crown molding goes.

First, cut a small piece of crown molding about 2" or 3" wide. Place it on the inside of a framing square, being sure the edges contact the framing square flat. Write down the measurement where the molding ends on each side of the square. Make the reference marks on the bottom of the miter box and the back fence, measuring from that back corner. You will want to keep the crown molding positioned at these marks when cutting it.

Look on the molding where you have written "ceiling," and place the molding upside down in the miter box. With the ceiling side on the bottom of the miter box and the other side up against the back wall of the miter box, place the backsaw in the direction of the line you drew on the face of the molding. Or you can remember it this way: "Upside down and reverse." This means to keep the molding "upside down" (to the way it sits on the ceiling and wall) with the profile facing you, and "reverse" means that if you are cutting for a left inside cut, then you will need to cut the miter toward the right. Place the backsaw blade in the miter box in the far left front groove and the far right back groove. This will position the saw to be cutting toward the right.

Remember:

    Left inside corner: Upside down and reverse
                                (cutting toward the right, with
                                the handle of the saw over to the left)
    Right inside corner: Upside down and reverse
                                (cutting toward the left, with
                                the handle of the saw over to the right)

Outside corner: The recipe for cutting inside corners does not apply for outside corners. If you are working left to right and you get to an outside corner on the right, then place the crown molding upside down and against the back of the miter box, and cut it toward the right. Go in the same direction.

Remember:

    Right outside corner: Upside down and cut toward
                                   the right
    Left outside corner: Upside down and cut toward
                                   the left

Jointing in the middle: Always use a splice joint in the middle. It is made of two miter joints, an outside and an inside, that marry together. Always use wood glue in the joints. See "Baseboards."

Coping a joint: Of all the joints, this is the hardest yet the most rewarding when you get it right. Cut an inside miter first (see "Inside Corner" page 62), put the molding flat down on your work table, and clamp. Lightly rub the edge of your pencil on the profile of the crown molding. This will help you see the profile better. Cut the profile using the coping saw, working it back and forth and holding it at a 45° angle to cut into the crown molding along the profile. Remember to have the blade with the teeth point up toward the handle. You will need to stop and remove the coping saw from time to time when it gets stuck and start sawing at a different angle to free up the blade. Use a wood rasp to remove any excess to make the joint tight. See "Baseboard," "A Cope Joint." (page 64)

Trick of the Trade:

My first carpentry foreman, Dennis Currier, taught me a great trick for crown molding for a room that doesn't need to be jointed in the middle. Make your measurements from corner to corner, and cut your molding 1/16" less than the measurement. Screw all four pieces of molding together from the back at the corners. Now lift the entire crown molding up to the corners. You will need four people to help you hold the crown molding up in place. Do a dry run first, take it down, glue, and then nail into place.

Fig 3.37- Door Casing Reveal

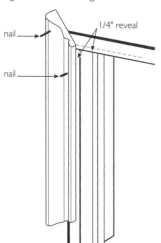

Nail in place: Using 6d or 8d nails, depending on the size of your crown molding, nail the molding into the studs in the wall and into a joist in the ceiling. Use latex paintable caulk or wood filler to fill any gaps.

CASING:

The molding around the doors and windows is called door casing, or just casing. You have different widths and profiles to choose from, like all moldings. Unlike the previous moldings, the key to cutting casing is to lay it flat on the bottom of the miter box and up against the back fence.

When installing casing, leave ¼" all around the jamb. This is called a reveal. It finishes out the door and window jamb (frame). Be sure to lightly mark this reveal with your pencil so you can follow the line when nailing it. Nail the casing in place using 6d finish nails through the outer, thicker edge to hit the stud and 4d finish nails through the thinner side into the jamb.

DOOR STOP:

The door stop is the thin molding that the door shuts to. It literally stops the door. To cut the miters of door stop, place it flat on the back fence of the miter box and make your angled cuts as you would with inside corner moldings.

Doors and Windows

Doors

Interior doors are needed for privacy and not security. All doors that lead outside your home need to be solid wood or metal to give you proper security. In older homes, you will have interior doors that are solid as well, but those of you who have priced solid doors know why interior doors are usually hollow! They cost a lot less money!

The problem, of course, is that because they're hollow, they're susceptible to damage. I remember when I was about eight years old. I was dancing to the Jackson 5, and I decided to give it a twirl. I threw myself off-balance, and my heel went right through my bedroom door. Ouch! There are two repairs you can make: 1) apply a veneer over the door, or 2) get a new door.

APPLY NEW VENEER OVER THE DOOR

DIFFICULTY: 3

TOOLS YOU MAY NEED: Screwdriver, hammer, paint roller, utility knife, paint brush

MATERIALS YOU MAY NEED: Contact cement, dowels or sticks, block of wood, 100-grit sandpaper, stain or primer/paint

Fig 3.38- Trimming Veneer

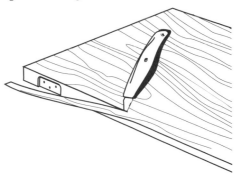

Depending on the cost of a new door, you might just want to buy a new door, or you can add a ⅛" veneer over the damaged side of the door. Veneer is a thin sheet of wood. Buy the sheet larger than the door. You will need to remove the handle and take the door off the hinges by removing the pins.

Lay the door on your workbench or sawhorses, sand the damaged side of the door, and remove all dust. Then, in an open area, use a paint roller to distribute contact cement on the side of the door. Then roll contact cement on the veneer. Let both dry. Contact cement works when the glue is dry and then sandwiched together. Lay a couple pieces of sticks or broom handles over the door, and lay the veneer over them. These sticks or broom handles will keep the veneer from touching the door until you have it in place. Then, by working top to bottom, remove a stick at a time and press the veneer down on the door, working from the middle out. Keep removing the sticks until the veneer is firmly in place. With a block of wood, tap around the veneer to be sure it has good contact to the door.

Trim the excess veneer around the door with a sharp utility knife and sand.

Stain or prime and paint the door, then replace the door handle. You may need to make adjustments to the strike plate on the jamb by moving it out if the veneer was applied to the inside of a door.

REPLACE A DOOR

DIFFICULTY: 3 to 4

TOOLS YOU MAY NEED: 1" wood chisel, hammer, screwdriver, combination square, tape measure

MATERIALS YOU MAY NEED: Dummy stick (1"×2"), door, new hinges

When replacing a door, you will need to mortise out the hinges and drill a hole for the door knob. *Mortise* means to cut a groove. You do this so the hinges will have a groove to fit in flush to the edge of the door. Hold a piece of lumber (1"×2") or a

Fig 3.39- Mark Hinge Location Using a Dummy Stick

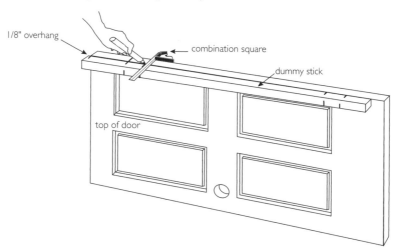

dummy stick up to the top of the jamb (door frame). Mark on the stick with a pencil exactly where the hinges are. Draw a ⅛" line on the top of the stick. Now transfer these marks to your door. Hold the stick on the edge of the door with the top of the door on the ⅛" line. This will give your door ⅛" between the door and the top of the jamb.

Have a friend hold the door on its side with the edge up. Using a combination square, square off these marks on the edge of your door. Take the measurement of the depth of your hinge on the jamb, and mark that depth on the edge of your door. Once you have transferred these measurements to the door, then you can mortise the hinges.

To mortise the hinges, use a 1" chisel at a 90° angle to the edge of the door, cut around the outline of the hinge. Hold your hammer on the side when hammering at a chisel. Holding the chisel at a 45° angle, make a series of relief cuts in the marked areas where the hinges will be. These will be chips that will come right off and will make it easy to flatten the area. Keep working the chisel to remove enough of the wood so the hinge sits in flush.

Use a drill bit slightly smaller than the shank of the screw to make pilot holes for the screws. Then screw the hinge into place.

The hinges on the door need to align with the hinges on the door frame. Lightly tap them up or

Fig 3.40- Mortise the Hinges

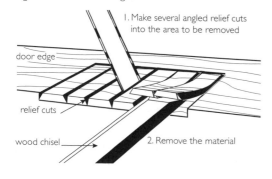

down if they are a hair off. Then push the pins down into the hinges.

REMOVING A DOORKNOB
DIFFICULTY: 2
TOOLS YOU MAY NEED: Screwdriver

Taking off a doorknob will help you understand how easy it is to install one. On one side of the door where the privacy lock is, you may have a round cover or escutcheon around the knob with two screws in it. Remove these screws with a Phillips screwdriver. This will release the knobs.

Another type of doorknob has a little tab that needs to be pushed with a flat screwdriver to release the knob, which will allow the escutcheon to come off. This will expose the screws underneath that hold the knob to the other side.

To remove the latch cylinder, use a Phillips screwdriver to unscrew the two screws holding it into place. Slide the cylinder out of the door.

INSTALLING A DOORKNOB
DIFFICULTY: 3
TOOLS YOU MAY NEED: Drill with a 2⅛" hole boring attachment, ⅞" spade bit, screwdriver, 1" wood chisel, hammer, combination square, tape measure
MATERIALS YOU MAY NEED: Pencil, doorknob assembly

If you're replacing a door, you will need to take off the old knob and install it on the new door. Use the old door as a template for location of the doorknob. If you buy a new doorknob, instructions and a template will come with the new hardware.

To get the exact location of the hole for the knob, find the center of the strike plate on the doorjamb. Close the door, and transfer the middle point to the door. Transfer this line lightly using a pencil with the combination square around both faces of the door. Take the door off the hinges and have someone hold it steady with the edge up, or you can clamp it.

Now for the latch. At the transferred pencil line and the

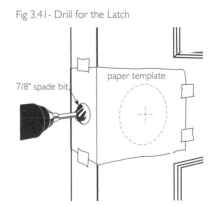

Fig 3.41 - Drill for the Latch

⅞" spade bit

paper template

center of the edge of the door, tap a nail in and then remove it. This will help start your drill bit. Using a ⅞" spade bit, drill into the door, holding the bit perpendicular to the edge.

Then drill the hole for the knob. Lie the door flat and use a 2⅛" diameter hole saw on your drill at the transferred mark of the old door or where the template tells you. When drilling through the door, apply pressure and release, then repeat. Once the inner drill bit pokes out the other side, flip the door and begin to drill from the other side.

Now you will mortise the latch. I like to set the latch in the edge of the door and screw into place. Then I use a utility knife to score around the latch. Remove the latch and tap around the perimeter line of the latch with a 1-inch-wide chisel. Hit the chisel with the side of the hammer. Now make relief cuts with the chisel, holding it at a 45° angle. Remove all the wood so the latch sits flush with the door edge. If you have a plate that goes over this, you will need to mortise deep enough to allow for the plate. Make a pilot hole with a drill bit slightly smaller than your screw in the holes of the latch. Don't screw the latch plate down until the doorknob has been assembled.

Finally, install the doorknob assembly. Insert the doorknobs in each side, aligning the stems to fit horizontally into the holes of the latch. After you have lined up the doorknobs, insert the machine screws and tighten down by hand. Then use a Phillips screwdriver and tighten down the screw closest to the latch but not too tight. Then tighten the other screw. If you put too much tension on the screws, they will not allow the doorknob to work properly.

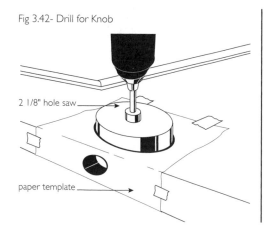

Fig 3.42- Drill for Knob

2 1/8" hole saw

paper template

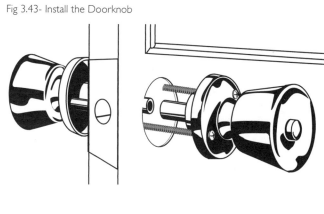

Fig 3.43- Install the Doorknob

A SQUEAKY DOOR
DIFFICULTY: 1

There's nothing like having a home alarm system built into your hinges! *EEEer-rrrrkkkkkk!* There are a few products that I have used on a squeaky door.

Graphite powder: Graphite is what we write with in our pencils. At the hardware store, you can buy graphite powder, which comes in a little tube. Pull up on the pins of your door hinges, and blow graphite into the hinges by squeezing the tube. This is a favorite among the pros. Caution: if you have a light-colored rug or carpet, you may want to stick with ball bearing grease or lubricating spray, because the powder could stain the carpet if you blow out too much of it.

Ball bearing grease: This is my next favorite choice, because it really gets in there and lubricates the knuckles of the hinge. Take one hinge pin out at a time, and lather the pin and between the knuckles with ball bearing grease.

Lubricating spray: A few lubricating sprays out there work well. Just spray it on the hinge and work the door back and forth, getting it into the joints. Protect your floors, carpets, and rugs when doing this.

Windows

STUCK WINDOWS
DIFFICULTY: 2

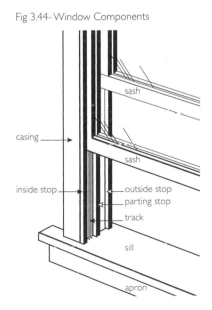
Fig 3.44- Window Components

Before there was the plethora of home security, my dad drilled through the sashes of the windows and used a nail to keep them shut tight. If you move into a home and you can't get a window open, check first to see if there is a nail holding it closed. If so, use needle-nose pliers to pull out the nail.

The biggest problem with windows is that they get stuck from dirt, humidity, or paint, or maybe the house, along with the windows, has settled. Usually, when people paint their homes they'll pay close attention to the windows . . . except they forget to open the window about an hour after they have painted and the paint seals the window shut.

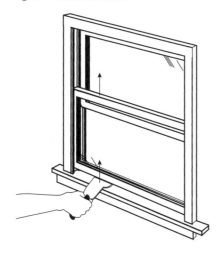

Fig 3.45- Release the Sash

With a sharp utility knife, score the paint around the seams of the sashes of your window and the stop. Now try it. Still stuck?

Wedge a putty knife into the frame against the sash, releasing it from the stop or the track. Do this all around the window, getting the putty knife up underneath the window and releasing the sill from the window frame.

Still stuck? With a block of wood against the stubborn area of your window, give it a few gentle hits with your hammer. You have to give enough of a tap to do something, but not so hard as to break the glass. This should release the window.

First you must be sure you don't have any paint in the channel or track. This will cause the window to continue to stick. Remove any paint or dirt using paint thinner on a rag. Wipe off all paint, and lightly sand with 100-grit sandpaper. If you just have dirt, you can remove that with a household degreaser. Then use some paraffin wax in the channels. Paraffin wax (sold at your hardware store) is a staple for your toolbox!

For metal windows, use a lubricating spray in the tracks.

The Ceiling

The ceiling is usually covered with plaster, drywall, and in some cases, bead board. A ceiling is different from the wall in the respect that there are joists or trusses to nail or screw into rather than studs. If you have a floor or attic above, you will have joists. If you have neither above, then you will have trusses. Unless, of course, you have a cathedral ceiling, and in that case, you'd have none of the above. Repairs are made the same as walls, but because you are dealing with overhead work, be mindful to wear safety glasses, dust masks when necessary, and a bandana or hat to cover your head.

Water-damaged plaster ceilings can get very messy. Sometimes it can come down in pieces, while other times it comes down in big chunks. Be sure you cover your floors well with a drop cloth, and always remove loose pieces with your arms extended away from your body, rather than right over your head!

When installing drywall on the ceiling, make yourself a couple drywall jacks. They look like Ts made out of 2×4s. Make these 1" or 2" taller than the height from the floor to the joists. In the trade we call them "dead men," because all they do is hold the load of the drywall once you get it into place so you can secure them with screws. Believe me, if you have to repair an entire room and you're holding up ½" or ⅝" drywall, you get really tired, so you do need to have something hold the weight! When installing a lot of drywall on the ceiling, rent a drywall lift for the day. Put a sheet of drywall on the lift, crank it to the ceiling, and screw it into place.

Because the repair to a ceiling is the same as walls, see "Drywall and Plaster" in the "Walls" section of this chapter.

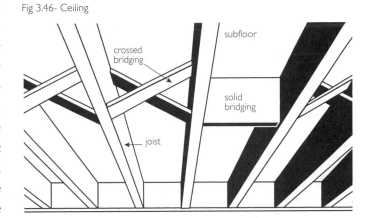

Fig 3.46- Ceiling

crossed bridging

subfloor

solid bridging

joist

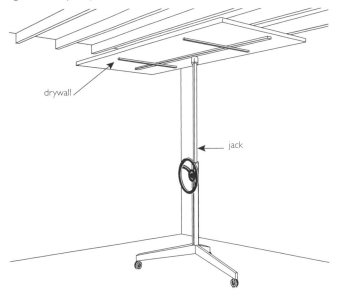

Fig 3.47- A Drywall Jack

drywall

jack

Floors

There are all sorts of floor coverings: hardwood, cork, carpet or rugs, vinyl 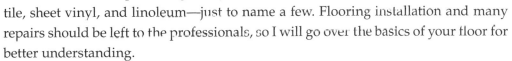 tile, sheet vinyl, and linoleum—just to name a few. Flooring installation and many repairs should be left to the professionals, so I will go over the basics of your floor for better understanding.

First, you have floor joists that support the floor and are usually 16" apart o.c. (on center). On top of the joist lies the subfloor, which is nailed or screwed into the joists. Building paper or asphalt felt is laid on top of the subfloor and overlaps 2½". Building paper is a red rosin paper that acts as a barrier to protect against dust infiltration

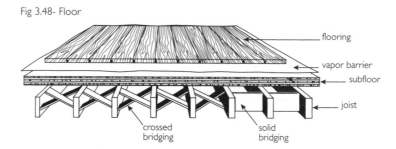

Fig 3.48- Floor

flooring

vapor barrier

subfloor

joist

crossed bridging

solid bridging

and minimize squeaks. A layer of 15-pound asphalt felt does the same thing and provides a moisture protection.

The Subfloor

DIFFICULTY: 3

When your floor is damaged, oftentimes the subfloor will be, too. For hardwood floors, you need to have ¾" plywood underneath. If you make a repair to the subfloor, be sure you or the contractor uses screws to secure the floor to the joists. This will help to prevent future squeaking, because a screw is harder to back out of the joists than a nail.

Hardwood Floors

DIFFICULTY: 5

Many solid hardwood floors are made of ¾" oak strips that are anywhere between 1½" to 3¼" wide. These hardwood floors are held together by a tongue-and-groove system, and each piece is nailed in through the groove and into the subfloor. A flooring nailer slips into the tongue of the board. When the plunger on the nailer is struck by a heavy rubber mallet, it drives the nail through the board and into the subfloor—all with one whack! I suggest hiring this job out, because a professional can install hardwood floors probably at least four times faster than you can. Using that flooring nailer will wear you out! I would

If It Were My House:

Not only would I use 2" wood screws securing the subfloor, but I would also use construction adhesive on the joists underneath the subfloor to prevent floor squeaks.

recommend that even the strongest individual rent a floor nailer that hooks up to a compressor. It will save your back.

When I was on the Discovery Channel's *Gimme Shelter,* I showed how to install a solid hardwood oak floor. I thought after thirteen years of being a union carpenter, I would have the kind of arm that could strike that plunger hard enough to send that nail deep into the wood. It was an old nailer (more up-to-date nailers are easier to use), and every strike landed it about ⅛" shy of setting in the board. I finally had to use the flooring nailer that is attached to a compressor, and I couldn't believe how easy it was!

> **Tip:** If you are having a new floor installed in your home, be sure the flooring is delivered to your home about one or two weeks before it is installed so it can acclimate to your home's humidity level. If you do not do this, the flooring might expand or contract, and can either buckle the floor or cause it to have many gaps.

Refinishing a Wood Floor

DIFFICULTY: 5

Many of you may have bought a home and noticed that when you lifted up the carpet, hardwood floors were underneath. Then you wanted to sand them and refinish them, thinking that if you did the work yourself, you'd save yourself some money. Great in theory, but *hire out this job!* Everyone I know who has sanded their own floors has botched up the job to the point that they either lived with it or they had to hire a flooring company to fix it. Do not let this be you. Working those drum sanders is a real talent and worth the money.

Always be sure your floors have at least two coats of finish on them—or better, three coats. Finish comes in a high-gloss, semi-gloss, or a matte finish.

Other popular floor coverings are bamboo and cork, which are thinner and incredibly durable. Both can be sanded and refinished.

Floating Floors

DIFFICULTY: 4

Floating floors have become very popular in the past ten years. These engineered floors lock together and are more resistant to moisture than solid wood. Some of the big name brands are Pergo®, Harris Tarkett®, and Dura-Wood®, to name a few. Many systems are 9/16" thick, and widths vary up to 7½" wide. This is a popular flooring system because the boards are edge-glued to each other but not glued or nailed to the subfloor, hence the name "floating floor," making it an ideal product to go atop a concrete floor. The only requirements for a floating floor is that the subfloor must be clean, level, and dry.

Installation over a concrete slab requires a 6-millimeter (mil) plastic sheeting over the slab. In the case of a wood subfloor, use building felt paper for a vapor barrier. Foam pad is cut to fit in the room and the butted edges are taped together. This gives the floor some insulation and a comfortable feel under your feet. The joints are staggered just like a solid floor. There must be a gap all around the perimeter of the room—usually the thickness of the board for expansion. The baseboard trim or quarter round will cover this gap.

This is a durable and easy-to-maintain flooring system. I have installed quite a few of these floors, and they look great.

A Squeaky Floor

DIFFICULTY: 3
TOOLS YOU MAY NEED: Drill with magnetic Phillips bit extension, drill bits
MATERIALS YOU MAY NEED: Wood glue, wood screws, L brackets, wood wedges

When I was growing up and I wanted to raid the refrigerator at night, I would know just where to walk in our home so I wouldn't wake up the family. One wrong move and I'd be busted by my mom, who has those mothering bionic ears!

From below: Fixing a squeaky floor is really easy if you have a basement or crawl space below and can get to the joists from underneath.

To locate the squeak from below, have someone at the squeaky floorboard while you are underneath the joist. When you've located the squeak, see if there is a gap between the floor board and the joist. From here, you have two options:

- Spread some wood glue on wood wedges, and tap them in the gap. Then use a wood screw and toe screw through the joist, the wedges, and into the floorboard, being careful not go through the floorboard. You may need to make a pilot hole for your screw.

▪ Screw an L bracket into the joist and then screw it into the floorboard with the drill. Be sure your screw doesn't go through the flooring. I would try a #8 ¾" flat head wood screw.

From above: For this fix, you will need a trim screw, which is a smaller thread screw with a very small head you can cover with putty. Drill a pilot hole with a drill bit that is smaller than the shank of the screw. (You do this so the screw doesn't strip or break in half because the floor is made of such hard wood.) Find the area of the squeak, and use a trim screw through the face of the floorboard. Use putty to cover the hole. Let dry, and lightly dab some polyurethane over the putty to seal it.

If you have a squeak under a carpeted floor, you can buy a kit with break-away screws that can be screwed through the carpet and then broken off at the floorboard. Be sure to follow the manufacturer's instructions.

Carpet

DIFFICULTY: 5

Lately, hardwood floors seem to be all the rage, but if you ask me, there is nothing better than a soft thick-pile of wall-to-wall carpet under my feet. Wall-to-wall carpet can turn your home into one big piece of furniture if you like to sit and lie on a carpeted floor.

If you are thinking about installing carpet in your home, *hire out this job!* This is a heavy job and hard on the knees. I've installed wall-to-wall carpet in my apartment, and I can't believe I can still walk. I would never do that again. Plus, years later, I had to hire someone to "re-kick" the carpet in place because it had stretched out and I was too light in weight to give it enough *oommmph!*

Before carpet is installed, two rows of tack strips are nailed around the perimeter of the room with the tacks facing the wall. When the carpet is laid in, the carpet is "kicked" into place with a carpet kicker. You "kick it" with your knee. Trust me, these installers are worth their money! After the tack strips are nailed in, then the padding underneath the carpet is installed. You have a few choices: fiber, rubber, or foam padding. Ask the carpet manufacturer what it suggests. I've always heard that fiber will hold up longer but give a firmer feel under the feet.

Before you or the carpet installers get to work, you might want to consider the following:

- Who is going to remove the existing carpet and padding, and how much will it cost?
- If furniture needs to be moved, who will move it? If the installers move it, find out if there is an extra fee.
- If appliances need to be disconnected, set that up before the day of installation.
- If there are remnant or leftover pieces of carpet, who will remove them? (Always keep a remnant in case you ever need to make a repair!)
- Find out the best cleaning method for your type of carpet.

Fixing a Stain in Your Carpet

DIFFICULTY: 3

TOOLS YOU MAY NEED: Carpet knife or a carpet cookie cutter

MATERIALS YOU MAY NEED: Remnant of matching carpet, double-stick tape, carpet glue

Many books out there help you with the removal of gum, wine, pine sap, and a plethora of other stains, so I will only show you how to repair those stubborn stains or cigarette burns that only can be fixed by a patch. Hopefully, you have kept a remnant of carpet for a repair. If not, you can cut a patch out of a corner of your closet or someplace that won't show.

Find the direction of the nap of the carpet, and place a piece of masking tape pointing in that direction. Find the direction of the nap on the remnant, too. You will need to install the patch in the same direction.

Trick of the Trade:

To find the direction of the nap of your carpet, lay a piece of paper on the carpet and roll a pencil back and forth over the paper. The direction the paper moves in is the direction of the nap. It doesn't matter which way you lay the paper or the pencil. The paper will always move in the direction of the nap.

Fig 3.49- Finding the Direction of Carpet Nap

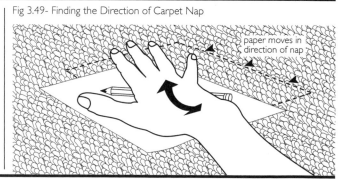

paper moves in direction of nap

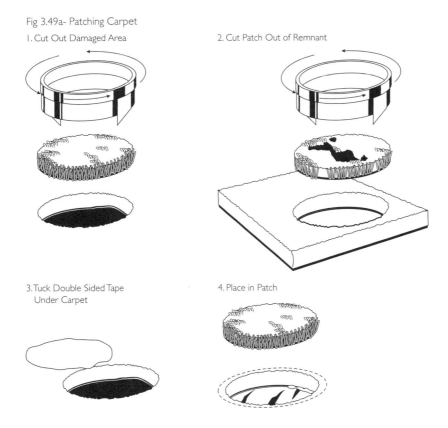

Fig 3.49a- Patching Carpet

1. Cut Out Damaged Area

2. Cut Patch Out of Remnant

3. Tuck Double Sided Tape Under Carpet

4. Place in Patch

Using a carpet cutting tool that looks like a cookie cutter with a little blade on it, turn it until you cut free a round hole in the carpet. Only cut through the carpet—do not cut through the padding underneath. Then turn the cutting tool around the remnant and remove the round patch. Cut some double-stick tape a little bigger than the hole. Lift the carpet and install the double-stick tape so it holds underneath the back of the carpet and sticks to the padding underneath. Apply some carpet glue (seam sealer) to the edge of the hole, and place the round patch into the hole with the nap facing in the direction of the nap in the carpet. Let this dry overnight and then vacuum.

For a bigger patch over padding, you will need to cut a bigger patch with a carpet knife. This cutting tool has a square-end razor blade that slides into the L-shaped casing just like a utility knife. The bonding needs to done with a heat-bonding tape and a carpet heating iron. For this bigger repair, I would suggest hiring a carpet expert.

Rugs

Do you know the most common problem with rugs? No matter how you wear them, they still look like a rug! No, I mean rugs that you walk on! They have a tendency to wrinkle, buckle, or slip, and that can mean a dangerous fall. Always use the proper padding for your rug. It's well worth it!

Electrical

You may be like me—a little wary of working with electricity. For good reason, too! I think it's healthy to have a bit of worry. If we replace worry with respect, it helps put us back in an empowered state of mind. I think of electricity like the ocean—a mighty force that you can enjoy, but if you don't play by the rules of the force, it can take you down. I think I'm starting to write a philosophy book, so let me change gears and go back to electricity. First things first. Where is the breaker box or fuse box located?

If Your Power Goes Off in a Room

First things first, *shut off some of the appliances or lights* you were using. When the electricity comes back on, you don't want to keep tripping the breaker or blowing the fuse.

Tip: Find out what room each circuit breaker feeds by having someone in the house when you flip it off. Write the room(s) or appliances that match the circuit breaker next to the switch for future reference.

Next, locate the breaker box or fuse box. Hopefully, you know where it is. If you don't, now is the time to find out. If you have a fuse box, the fuse that services that particular room has blown and needs to be replaced with a same-amperage (amps) fuse. If you have a breaker box, trip the circuit breaker that feeds the room. You will notice the tripped breaker because it is in between the ON and OFF setting. Flip it OFF first and then flip it ON.

If Your Power Goes Off in the Whole House

Check to see if the power in the rest of your house works. If it's not on, then you might need to flip the main breaker. If the electricity in your home is off, there's a good chance that a power line has gone down in your area or there is a power failure with your local electric company. Call a neighbor and see if they are experiencing a problem. Or go out and look around the neighborhood at the other houses. If they also have no power, call your electric company and report a problem.

> **Tip:** It's always good to have a telephone in your house that is not wireless and is plugged directly into the phone jack. If your power goes out, your phone will still work.

If your neighbors have power and you have tripped the main breaker, then go outside and look at the wires that feed your home. If you notice a line is down, *do not touch it* and keep all pets inside and others away from it. Immediately call the emergency number for your electrical company.

The Breaker Box or Fuse Box

DIFFICULTY: 1

Every once in a while your circuit breaker or fuse that feeds the outlets and lights to your kitchen may get overtaxed. You may be pulling so much power in your kitchen that it may "trip" the circuit breaker or "blow" a fuse. Maybe you were using your mixer, toasting some raisin bread, microwaving some popcorn with your lights and your fan on while watching the TV you've set up in the kitchen. For some reason, this usually happens at the most inopportune time—when you have company. Well, it can rattle your cage a bit, but don't panic! The solution is usually very easy and can be dealt with immediately. Always know where your breaker box or fuse box is located. If you have an older home, you might have a fuse box; newer homes will have a circuit breaker. Here's the difference:

A fuse: When a fuse "blows," it needs to be replaced. The term *blow* is just a term and not a cause for alarm. There are two types of fuses: cartridge and plug, which screw in.

Cartridges look a lot like a shotgun shell and are mounted in a little rack. You just need to pull them out of the bracket and push a new one in with a plastic cartridge puller. The *ferrule contact* is round on each end, can be pulled straight out, and is used for large appliances. The *knife-blade contact* has a hook on one end and is the main electrical fuse for the entire house.

Fig 3.50- Cartridge Fuse

Plug or screw-in fuses literally screw in and out like a

lightbulb. There are three types of fuses: standard, time delay, and S-type. The S-type are the most common. Some have a tiny glass window on top and metal threads on the bottom. When too much current flows through the fuse, the metal wire inside melts and the fuse "blows." You can usually tell when a fuse blows because the window gets a little black. The most common size fuses are 15- and 20-amp ratings. You must always replace the same-amp fuse with the one that has blown.

Safety First: Never change a fuse or reset a circuit breaker if you are standing in water. Clean up the wet floor first, then reset the breaker or fuse.

Tip: It is a good idea to keep a few spare fuses around. Keep them in the drawer where you keep your flashlights.

A circuit breaker: When a circuit breaker "trips," it needs to be reset. When you look inside your breaker box, you will see the breaker that has been tripped because it will be between the ON and OFF positions. To reset a breaker, you just flip it OFF first, then flip it to the ON position. It's that easy! Now you know why newer homes and older homes that have been rewired have circuit breakers.

But first, be sure you correct the problem before replacing the fuse or resetting the circuit breaker. Turn off some of the appliances you were using, and use one at a time when your electricity comes back on.

If you notice that your circuit breakers have been tripping more than usual, it may be that you've recently added an appliance or two, such as a new monster microwave, perhaps? The existing circuit breaker may not be able to handle the increased load. You may want to call an electrician to come out to swap the circuit for one with a higher-load amp.

Fig 3.51- Circuit Breaker

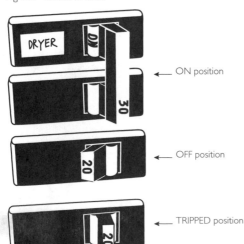

← ON position

← OFF position

← TRIPPED position

Replacing Your Outlets

DIFFICULTY: 3

TOOLS YOU MAY NEED: Screwdriver, circuit tester, wire stripper

MATERIALS YOU MAY NEED: Wire nuts, electrical tape, three-prong outlet

If you have an outlet and the plastic around the receptacle has broken, you need to replace it. Also, older homes usually have two-prong outlets that are not grounded and need to be upgraded with a three-prong grounded outlet. To do this, you have two options: rewire your entire home with a ground wire, which requires a professional, or you can install a GFCI outlet (ground fault circuit-interrupter), which has a circuit breaker built right into the outlet. The outlet won't be grounded, but it will trip the circuit breaker inside the GFCI outlet and protect you from electrical shocks caused by faulty extension cords or plugs. For detailed instructions see "Installing a GFCI Receptacle" in the "Electrical" section of Chapter 4 (page 181).

If you have a three-prong outlet that needs to be replaced, you already have a ground screw in the receptacle box and will need to replace it with a new, three-prong outlet.

Turn off the power to the outlet at the breaker box or fuse box. Remove the faceplate: With a flat screwdriver, remove the outlet's faceplate. Unscrew the mounting screws that hold the outlet to the receptacle box, and pull out the outlet. Remove any tape around the outlet, and notice how the wires attach to the outlet.

Notice the wiring: You will see that the white (neutral) wires are connected to the silver-looking screws and the black (hot) wires are connected to the brass screws. These screws are also referred to as "terminals." A green screw is the terminal for the ground wire. The ground wire is usually an exposed copper wire.

End of the run or middle of the run: A room is usually wired on the same circuit, so you will have the electricity feeding the light switch and some, if not all, of the outlets in a room. To figure out how to wire the outlet, you must first determine if your outlet is at the end of the run or in the middle of a run. If the outlet has a single cable with just one white wire, one black wire, and a copper wire (if it's grounded) coming out of it, then that outlet is at the end of the run.

Wiring an "end-of-the-run" outlet:
   ▪ Look at your new outlet with the holes facing you and find the silvery screw, which is usually at the top left of the outlet. Screw the white (neutral) wire to this silver screw.
   ▪ If there are two brass screws on the right-hand side of the outlet. Screw the black (hot) wire to the bottom brass screw.

Fig 3.52- "End-of-the-Run" Outlet

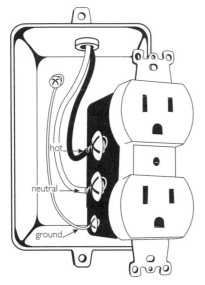

Fig 3.53- Strip the Wire

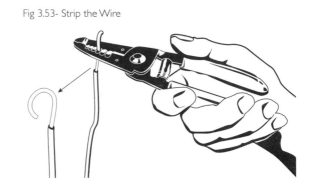

- The ground wire (copper) needs to be secured to the green terminal screw in the outlet and then attached to the green ground screw at the back of the receptacle box. You can also do this by pigtailing the copper wire to the copper wire coming out of the cable and the copper wire that is attached to the ground screw on the receptacle box. See the "Definition of a Pigtail" section. (page 88)
- Wrap electrical tape around the side of the outlet three times to insulate the wiring on the outlet.
- Mount the outlet into the receptacle box with the mounting screws, and replace the faceplate with your screwdriver.

When attaching the wires to the screws (or terminals) of the outlets, remove about ¾" of the insulation from the end of the wire with your wire strippers. If you don't have wire strippers, then lightly cut through just the plastic insulation with a utility knife and pull off the end with pliers. Use needle-nose pliers to make a small hook at the end of the wire. Attach this hooked wire around the screw with the hook ending on the right of the screw and then tighten the screw.

If you have two cables entering the receptacle box (usually one from the top and one from the bottom), you have a middle-of-the-run outlet. The wiring is just a little different.

Fig 3.54- "Middle-of-the-Run" Outlet

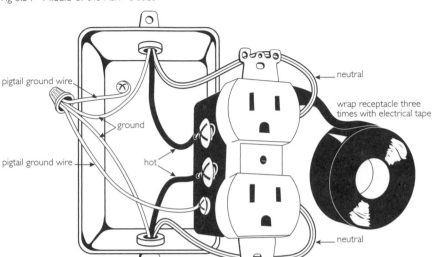

pigtail ground wire

ground

pigtail ground wire

hot

neutral

wrap receptacle three
times with electrical tape

neutral

Wiring a "middle-of-the-run" outlet (shut off power to the outlet):

- ▪ With the holes of the outlet facing you, locate the silver screw on the outlet. It may be on the top left-hand side of the outlet. You can "pigtail" a neutral wire from this neutral terminal on the side of the new outlet and attach it to the two white (neutral) wires coming out of the receptacle box with a wire nut.

- ▪ Attach the black (hot) wire coming out of the top of the receptacle to the top brass screw.

- ▪ Attach the black (hot) wire coming out of the bottom of the receptacle to the lower bottom brass screw on the right side.

- ▪ Pigtail the ground copper wire to the other copper ground wires. Then attach these to the green ground screw on the receptacle box.

- ▪ Now wrap electrical tape around the outlet over the screws three times. This insulates the wiring and ensures that you do not get an electric shock if you take the outlet out when it is hot. (Which you're not supposed to do without shutting off the breaker.)

- ▪ Mount the outlet to the receptacle box with the mounting screws and screwdriver and replace the faceplate.

Fig 3.55- Pigtail

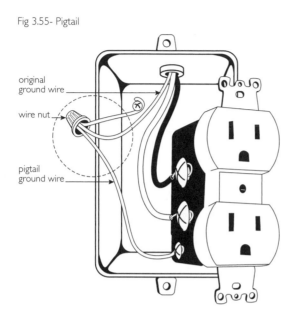

original
ground wire

wire nut

pigtail
ground wire

Definition of a Pigtail

A pigtail is a short wire used to join two or more wires to the same screw terminal on an outlet or switch. The pigtail wire bridges the connection, because having all the wires under the one terminal screw would be too cumbersome and possibly ineffective. The pigtail wire is the same color of the other wires it is connected to, and all wires are attached together under a wire nut.

Installing or Replacing a Standard Wall Switch

DIFFICULTY 3
TOOLS YOU MAY NEED: Screwdriver, circuit tester, wire stripper, needle-nose pliers
MATERIALS YOU MAY NEED: wire nuts, electrical tape, standard wall switch

Turn off the power to the switch: Most problems with switches are caused by a loose wire or the breakdown of internal components of the switch.

Check the wires: With the power off, take the faceplate off the switch and unscrew the switch from the receptacle box. Check to see if the wires are screwed in properly and that no bare wire is touching the receptacle box unless it's the ground copper wire. If a wire has become loose, tighten it to the terminal (screw). Turn the power on to see if this has fixed the problem. If it has, turn the power back off and wrap electrical tape around the switch's terminal three times before screwing the switch back into place. This will keep the wires in place and keep the hot wires insulated.

Test the switch for power: Go back to the circuit breaker or fuse box and turn on the power. With your circuit tester, touch one probe to the hot terminal screw, which should be the top screw that has a black wire wrapped around it, and the other end of the probe to the receptacle box. If the light goes on, power is going to the switch. This means that the switch has broken down and needs to be replaced.

Replace the switch: Turn off the power to the switch.
Take notice of how the other switch comes out. This is how you will wire the new switch. The hot (black) wire will go under the darker brass terminal screw, and the neutral (white) wire will go under the light-colored terminal screw. If your ground screw is connected to your old switch, mount it the same way on your new switch at the green terminal screw. Otherwise screw into the back of your receptacle box.

You may need to cut off broken-down ends of the wire. Use a wire stripper to expose about ½" of bare wire. Make a hook using needle-nose pliers, and attach the hooked wire with the hook going clockwise around the terminal screw. Wrap electrical tape around the switch a couple times. Gently push the wires back in the box, and screw the new switch to the receptacle. Install the faceplate, and restore power.

Installing or Replacing a Standard Dimmer

DIFFICULTY: 2
TOOLS YOU MAY NEED: Screwdriver, circuit tester, wire stripper, needle-nose pliers
MATERIALS YOU MAY NEED: Wire nuts, electrical tape

Whether you're replacing a dimmer or installing one, be sure you buy a dimmer with the proper wattage. For instance, a chandelier that uses seven 100-watt lightbulbs would *not* be able to use a 600-watt dimmer because you would need a dimmer that could handle 700 watts. Dimmers are either dial-type or slide-action. Only use dimmers if you have an incandescent bulb—the most common type of lightbulbs.

Don't use a standard dimmer for a fan. See "Installing a Ceiling Fan Wall Control."

Turn off the power to the switch.

Remove the knob and cover plate: If you have a knob or a toggle, it will pull right off. With your screwdriver, remove the mounting screws that hold the cover plate in place.

Fig 3.56- Test the Circuit

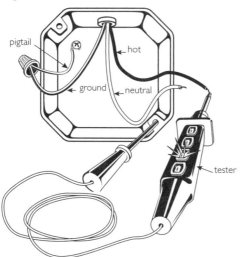

Test for power: It's always a smart move to be sure you've turned off the correct breaker or fuse and use a circuit tester. Remove the wire nuts, and touch one end of the tester probe to one set of wires, and touch the other probe to the metal junction box. If you have a plastic receptacle box, then touch the other end of the probe to the other wire. The power has been shut off if the light won't go on.

Connect the wires: Use your wire strippers and remove ½" of the plastic insulation from the ends of the wires on the dimmer. Connect the green (ground) wire first. Twist it around the bare copper wire coming out of the electrical box in your wall, and screw on a wire nut securely. Now do the same with the black (hot) wire to the black wire and the white (neutral) wire to the white wire. The good news is that the switch wires are interchangeable and you really can't make a mistake! Push the wires into the electrical box, and screw the fixture into the box. Screw the faceplate back on, push on the knob or toggle switch, and turn on the power.

Ceiling Fans

Ceiling fans create a wind chill effect that speeds up the evaporation of perspiration on the skin. They can make an 80-degree room feel like 72 degrees. They are so popular because most of them draw less electricity than a 110-watt lightbulb. When you use a ceiling fan with an air conditioner, you can save up to 40 percent on your energy bill by setting the air conditioner at a higher temperature.

Did you know that by changing the direction of the fan blades, you can help to heat a room? That's right! Because hot air rises to the top, if you flip the switch on the fan housing, you can change the direction of the blades. This will suck the air up to the ceiling and transfer the warm air out to the room and down the walls without causing a wind chill effect. This can lower your winter energy bill by 10 percent. Never flip the switch while the fan is on or the blades are moving.

INSTALLING A CEILING FAN

DIFFICULTY: 3 to 4
TOOLS YOU MAY NEED: Screwdriver, circuit tester, wire strippers, linesman's pliers
MATERIALS YOU MAY NEED: Metal junction box, lock washers, wire nuts, electrical tape, ceiling fan

Have I sold you on a ceiling fan? You can buy fans with lights and with remote control options. Most ceiling fans need to be installed 8 to 9 feet from the floor to the blades. Determine the height of your room. If you have a high ceiling, you may need to buy a fan with an extension downrod that will bring the fan closer to the floor.

If you have a light fixture in the middle of your ceiling, you're ready to install the fan. If you don't have a light fixture in the middle of your ceiling, you will have to run electricity to the center; therefore, I would suggest hiring an electrician.

Turn off the power to the fixture at the breaker box or fuse box.

Remove the existing light fixture: With a screwdriver, remove the fixture from the ceiling. This usually requires removing a couple screws and then the light fixture will hang by the wires. Using a circuit tester, touch the prongs on each wire to be sure the power is off. Be sure you hold the fixture while you disconnect the wires.

Reinforce the junction box: Because the ceiling fan is heavy and spinning blades around over your head, you want to be sure it's in your ceiling securely. You will need a metal junction box held by four legs or cross braces to the joists. If you don't have that, you will need to buy a heavy-duty brace bar that runs between the joists and is secured by screws to the joists. If you have an attic above, reinforcing the junction box will be a breeze. If you have a second floor above you, then you may need to remove some of the drywall to properly secure the junction box. See "Patching a Hole" in the "Drywall" section (page 30).

Assemble the fan: Take the fan out of the box and check out how the fan blades are assembled. You can either as-

Trick of the Trade:

Those of you who don't want to go up inside your ceiling have another choice. You can surface-mount a square piece of plywood big enough to cover the span of two joists. A 24" square should do the trick. Just be sure you fasten the plywood securely to the joists and cut out a hole in the middle for your wires to come through the box. Then you can secure the junction box to the plywood. To finish it off, you can install molding around the plywood.

semble the blades comfortably on the ground, or you can install them after the fan is secured to the ceiling. It depends if you can get your screwdriver between the fan blades and the ceiling. I'll let you make that call. Either way is fine.

Install the hanger pipe: If your fan has a hanger pipe, which is much shorter than an extension downrod, then often it needs to be placed in the hole on top of the motor and the wires pulled up through the center of the pipe. The hanger pipe will have a set screw to keep it in place after it is threaded down.

Mount the hanger bracket: Install the hanger bracket on the junction box with screws. Hopefully, the manufacturer has provided you with lock washers; if not, buy some because they help prevent the screws from loosening from the fan's vibration. Install these under the nut.

Attach the fan to the hanger bracket: Many hanger brackets hold the fan in place while you make the connections. Check out the instructions for your fan. You may want to have a friend on a ladder next to yours to keep the fan in place and help you with installation.

Fig 3.57- Attach the Fan to the Hanger Bracket

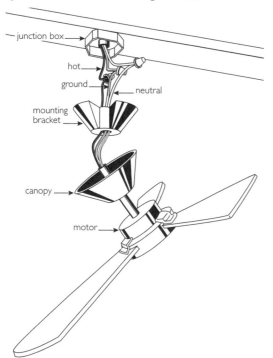

junction box

hot

ground

neutral

mounting bracket

canopy

motor

Connect the wires: You may need to remove ½" of the insulation from the end of the wires with wire strippers. Now twist the black wire from your ceiling to the black wire on the fan using your hands and then twist it tighter with linesman's pliers. Twist the white wire in your house with the white wire of the ceiling fan. Cap both sets of wires with wire nuts to keep them together. The bare copper wire is the ground wire, which should be attached to the green ground screw in the metal junction box. You may have to pigtail this to attach to the existing ground wire and the box. See "Definition of a Pigtail. (page 88)"

Attach the cover plate: After you've hung the fan in place, push the wires into the junction box and attach the fan's cover plate, which hides the hole in the ceiling. The cover plate usually slips over the screws provided on the fan's housing.

Attach the blades: If you haven't attached the blades to your fan, do it now.

Blade balance: You may notice that your ceiling fan wobbles. This is usually because the blades aren't balanced properly. Most ceiling fans will have weights to attach to the fan. You can also tape a coin or two to the top of the blade(s) in a pinch.

Light kit: If you're installing a light kit with your fan, follow the manufacturer's instructions. Usually the power to the light comes through the blue wire, which means the fan's blue wire and black wire need to attach to the black (hot) wire in the junction box. Always check the manufacturer's instructions.

INSTALLING A CEILING FAN WALL CONTROL
DIFFICULTY: 3+
TOOLS YOU MAY NEED: Screwdriver, circuit tester
MATERIALS YOU MAY NEED: Ceiling fan wall switch, wire nuts, electrical tape

The problem with some ceiling fans is that the cords that hang down can lop you in the head every time you walk underneath—especially if you're tall—and most fans usually only give you three fan speed options. Having this control at the wall switch makes life a whole lot easier. First, you must buy a ceiling fan wall switch. This looks like a regular dimmer, but it is not. A regular dimmer will burn out if you attach a ceiling fan to it.

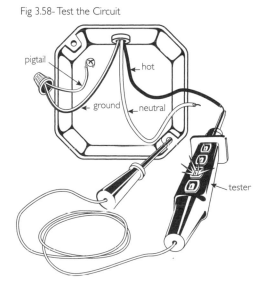

Fig 3.58- Test the Circuit

Prepare the fan: Turn on the ceiling fan and set it to its highest speed.

Shut off the power at the breaker box or circuit breaker.

Remove the old switch: Remove the faceplate, and unscrew the mounting screws with a screwdriver.

Circuit tester: It's always a good idea to use a circuit tester to be doubly sure the power is off to the switch.

Wiring: There are two wires coming out of a control switch. It usually doesn't matter which wire you hook up to the white (neutral) wire or the black (hot) wire, although I always suggest to match the color of the wire. Twist one wire of the switch with one of the wires coming out of the wall, and cap with a wire nut. Do the same with the other wire. I like to wrap the wire nut and wires with electrical tape just to be sure they stay together.

Test the control switch: Push the dimmer into the receptacle box, replace the mounting screws, and tighten. Replace the faceplate using your screwdriver. Turn on the power, and test the control.

CEILING FAN AND LIGHT ELECTRONIC CONTROL

Yon can buy electronic controls or switches that will enable you to control the light and the fan at your light switch. You can wire a receiver in the fan and a transmitter in the wall switch. There are also battery-operated, and remote control versions. Because there are many different models, I suggest buying the model that best fits your needs and follow the manufacturer's directions.

Telephone Repair

Static on the Line

DIFFICULTY: 1

Not too long ago, a phone was loaned to the user by the phone company for a monthly fee. Then, if something went wrong with the phone, you were covered. Nowadays, most people own their own telephones. Unless the phone is dropped, it will last a long time, but as we all know, electronic products are susceptible to problems from wear and tear. My father sold systems for the phone company, so I've always saved myself a bushelful of money by running my own phone lines in my house and making the proper repairs when I could. The most common phone problem is static on the line. This can be caused by too many phones on one line, problem with the jack, a faulty cord, or a weak cordless phone battery.

Check the phone: Unplug a phone from another room at the jack and plug it into the jack that's giving you static. If you don't have static on the new phone, then the problem is likely something with the cords of the original phone. Proceed to "Check the Cords."

Too many phones on one line: To check if you have too many phones on one line, disconnect all the phones from their jacks except the one with static. Pick up the receiver. If you have static, then go to the next step. If you don't have static, then plug in another phone and recheck the original phone for static. Keep doing this until you have checked all the phones. Oftentimes, you will hear static after the fourth or fifth phone is installed. If you can live without the phone that causes the static, you'll save yourself some money. Otherwise, you will need the phone company to install a second line.

Check the Cords

DIFFICULTY: 1

You'll need to check three cords: the coiled cord from your receiver to the phone base (this one does not apply to those of you who have a cordless phone), the cord that connects the base of the phone to the jack, and the cord that connects the jacks to each other in a multiple jack situation.

Coiled cord check: If your kitchen phone has static, try replacing the coiled cord with a coiled cord from another phone. If this stops the static, all you need to do is to replace the coiled cord. I replaced my kitchen wall phone with a 25-foot coiled cord. This allows me to walk all over the kitchen with the phone. If this doesn't fix the static, proceed.

Check the cord to the jack: Remove the cord from the base of the phone to the jack. These have a little plastic release arm that you have to pull back to get it out of the back of your phone and the jack. If you replace this cord and there is no more static, you have found the problem; otherwise, proceed.

Check the Jack(s)
DIFFICULTY: 2

First unplug all the phones in the house from their jacks (at the jack). There are two kinds of jacks: surface mounted, which mount on top of the baseboard, and flush mounted, which mount flush or even with the wall surface. The fix is the same for both.

Safety first: Phones operate on a very low voltage level, but if you get a call in and a phone rings, the ringing phone uses a higher voltage level. You could get a shock if the phones are connected and a call comes through. You know that Murphy's Law is always in effect, so just be on the safe side and unplug all phones.

Remove the jack faceplate. Some have a screw in the middle, while others just pull off and snap on. Inside you will notice four wires. These wires are color coded: green, red, yellow, and black. They are screwed down by a screw to their connections also known as posts or terminals marked (G) for green, (R) for red, (Y) for yellow, and (B) for black. Be sure all the screws are tight with the wires wrapped under and around them. Sometimes the plastic coating or insulation of the wire is preventing a good contact on the terminal. If you notice this is the case, unscrew the screw a couple turns and take off the wire. Using wire strippers or your utility knife, remove some of the insulation to expose more of the copper wire. Put the wire back on the terminal, and tighten the screw. If the static exists, try replacing the jack.

Remove the jack: Disconnect all the wires from the jack by releasing the screws a couple turns from each terminal. Remove the screws that hold the jack's base plate with your Phillips or flat screwdriver. Wiggle out the wires, and replace the jack.

Fig 3.59- Phone Jack

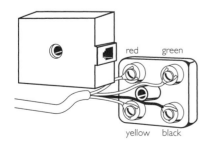

Replace the jack: Jacks are inexpensive, and the easiest jacks to install are the surface-mounted jacks. If you're replacing a flush-mounted jack, I suggest replacing it with a similar one. Attach the base plate in the same area and reconnect the wires—green to green, red to red, and so on. Put the faceplate on the jack by snapping it on or screwing it on and see if that has fixed the problem.

Cordless phones: A weak battery will cause static in your phone line. To fix this, recharge your battery. If you keep noticing your cordless phone has static, replace the battery. When your cordless phone's battery starts to lose the charge quickly, it's also time to replace the battery. There are so many different types of batteries out there it will boggle your mind, so bring the battery with you to the electronic store.

Call the phone company: If you still have static, then most likely your problem is coming from outside.

No dial tone on the phone

First check to see if it's just one phone with no dial tone. If so, then you might want to go through the checklist for "Static on the Line. (page 94)" But if none of your phones have a dial tone, it could be one of the following:

Unpaid bill? Hey, hasn't this happened to all of us one time or another? With struggling economic times, we may have had to juggle some bills, and we may have ended up with a dead phone line. No problem; call the phone company. Usually, they are very receptive to helping you out and making a plan. For those of you who went on vacation or just forgot to pay your bill, same goes for you: just call the phone company and see if your dead phone can be fixed with a payment.

Did your alarm go off in your house? Sometimes a short in your alarm system can cause a phone line to go dead. Call the alarm company, and follow their instructions. They'll probably tell you to call the phone company.

Did your neighborhood experience a storm or maybe a car crashed into a telephone pole? A downed telephone line will take out everyone's dial tone. Check with your neighbors to see if they're experiencing the same problem. If you have a cell phone, call the phone company and let them know you're experiencing trouble on your land line.

Difficulty Key:

1 Beginner

2 Confident
beginner

3 Intermediate

4 Advanced

5 Professional

Chapter Four

The Kitchen

The kitchen has more than its share of potential problems. It's one of the places in the home that contains all areas of the trades: plumbing, carpentry, electrical, and in many cases, gas. This would explain why most people devote an entire kitchen drawer to an assortment of tools.

Plumbing

Most plumbing problems are easily fixed, provided you understand the basics of plumbing, plumbing connections, and which tools do what job. I used to think plumbing was super complicated. It wasn't until I wanted a washing machine in my apartment in New York City that I rolled up my sleeves to plumbing. I was amazed at how easy it really was if I was willing to buy the right tools and ask a lot of questions. The hardest part was trying to tell the guys behind the counter at the hardware store what I wanted to do and then describing the existing conditions accompanied by my rudimentary drawings. With a lot of help and many trips to the hardware store, I was able to put in a wonderful stackable washer/dryer in my kitchen, and I saved a ton of money by doing it myself.

Okay, maybe you won't put in your own washing machine from scratch, but with the proper tools and a bit of patience, you can tackle most plumbing problems. When your home was built and what part of the country you reside in will determine what your pipes are made of. For instance, some areas of the country are restricted by building code not to use PVC. It's always good to know your building codes when making repairs on your home.

When I was new in construction, I got confused by many of the plumbing terms. For example, *vent*, *stack*, *line*, and *waste* may conjure up something more complicated than what they are—pipes. They are all pipes, but pipes with different purposes.

Your home's plumbing:

- The water comes into your home through a pipe known as the **main supply line.**
- First, it passes through the **water meter** so your town can determine how much water you're using and overcharge you for it.
- Usually near your water heater, your supply line/pipe is spliced in two so one pipe fills up your water heater. This is called a **branch line.** The other line/pipe distributes cold water throughout the house to sinks, dishwashers, toilets, and washing machines.
- The heated water in your water heater comes back out of the heater through a pipe and is distributed to the sinks, dishwashers, and washing machines throughout the house.
- All fixtures and most appliances have a **waste pipe** or **drain line** that leads to the **sewer line.**
- Waste water flows through these pipes by gravity, but to work properly, they must be vented—meaning they need air above them. To vent a waste pipe, another pipe is connected above the waste pipe and is called a **vent pipe.**

Fig 4.1 - Household Plumbing

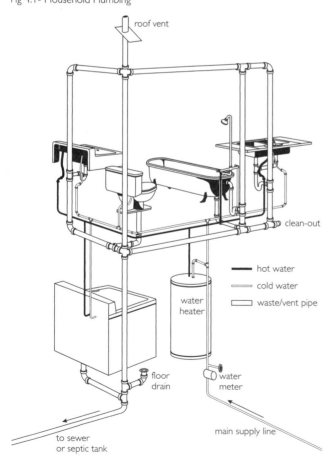

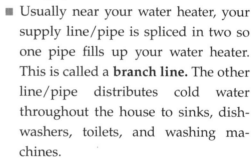

- All the vent pipes return and connect to one central and bigger pipe known as the **waste and vent stack.**
- The waste and vent stack lead out of the house through the roof known as the **roof vent.**
- The **floor drain** is usually found in the basement area.
- The **drain cleanout** is found at the end of the waste or drain line of your fixtures. Sometimes this can be found outside your home.
- The **main shutoff valve** is usually found near the entrance of your water supply line. You will notice that I use the terms *shutoff valve* and *supply valve* interchangeably throughout the book.

Copper Pipe: Cutting and Joining Pipes

DIFFICULTY: 3+
TOOLS YOU MAY NEED: Tubing cutter, hacksaw, emery cloth, propane torch, spark lighter
MATERIALS YOU MAY NEED: Soldering paste (flux); straight, elbow, or T-joint fitting

Always *turn off the supply valve* to the pipe you are working on. If you cannot find a shutoff valve in the area you are working, you may need to go to the main supply valve located near the water meter, and shut off the water there.

Cutting: The best way to cut copper pipe is by using a tubing cutter. You could also use a hacksaw, but I wouldn't because a tubing cutter is ridiculously easy to use and makes a perfect cut.

Place the tubing cutter blade over the pipe where you want to cut it. Tighten the knob on the handle until the cutting wheel and the rollers sit firmly on the pipe. Turn the cutter one rotation around the pipe and then retighten the knob. Repeat a couple times and then rotate the wheel in the opposite direction after tightening the knob. The pipe will come apart easily.

Remove metal burrs: On the other side of the tubing cutter is a triangular piece of metal. Just place the opening of the copper pipe in this metal triangle, and twist to ream or file any sharp metal pieces.

Sand and smooth: Using an emery cloth, the "plumber's sandpaper" that can be found in soldering kits, sand the outside and inside of each end of the pipe. Roughing up the metal will help in the adhesion of the ends that will be joined together.

Fig 4.2- Cutting Copper Pipe

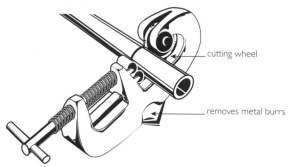

cutting wheel

removes metal burrs

Fig 4.3- Smooth the Pipe

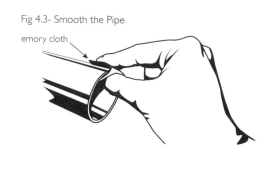

emory cloth

Fig 4.4- Apply Soldering Paste

FLUX

Fig 4.5- Solder the Pipe

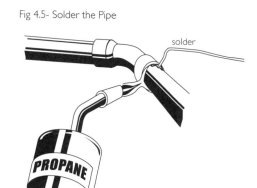

solder

PROPANE

Soldering paste: Apply a thin layer of (lead-free) soldering paste called "flux" with a flux brush that looks like a small paint brush. This, too, comes in the soldering kit. With the brush, coat 1" of the end of your pipe on the outside with flux. Flux helps draw the solder into the joint.

Prepare the fitting: A "fitting" is just a connection piece that pipes fit into, hence the name. Fittings come in different shapes and sizes depending on what you need them to do. A straight fitting joins two pipes together in a continuous line, an elbow fitting is needed when making a turn, and a T-joint fitting will split a supply line. The inside of the fitting will also need to be scoured with an emery cloth or wire brush and be coated inside with flux.

Fig 4.6- Pipe Fittings

continuous   elbow   T-joint

Insert the pipe inside the fitting on each end so it slides to the bottom of the socket, and twist slightly to spread the flux.

Unwind about 10" of the solder wire, and bend it to a 90° angle about 2" from the end.

Start the torch: With one hand holding the torch and the other hand holding the spark lighter, turn the knob on the torch counterclockwise until you hear the gas escaping. Flick the spark lighter until the torch has a flame. Set down the spark lighter, and adjust the flame so that the inside blue flame is between 1" and 2" in length. Always keep the torch in your hand, and be mindful of the flame.

Solder the pipe to the fitting: Hold the tip of the blue flame to the center of the fitting until the soldering paste (flux) begins to sizzle. Immediately, touch the solder to one end of the joint. You will notice that the solder melts quickly. You may not think it, but ½" or ¾" of solder is enough to seal that pipe to the fitting. Immediately solder the other side and remove the flame. If you keep the flame on it too long, the heat will burn off the soldering paste and not allow the solder to flow in properly. Careful! These pipes are *Hot!*

Check the seal: After the pipes and fittings have cooled, turn on the supply valve and check your fitting. If there is any kind of leak, you will have start all over. But first you must reheat the fitting to take it apart.

Safety Precautions:
Before lighting your propane torch, put on your leather work gloves and, if you're working overhead, definitely put on safety goggles. Use a heat-resistant pad behind the joint you're soldering. You should also have a fire extinguisher on hand, just in case. This isn't to scare you; it's just good to be mindful when working with fire.

Taking Apart a Soldered Joint

DIFFICULTY: 3

TOOLS YOU MAY NEED: Propane torch, spark lighter, groove-joint pliers, emery cloth

You must heat the fitting to free the pipes. Light your propane torch with the spark lighter, giving yourself a 1" to 2" flame, and hold the tip of the blue flame to the center of your fitting. When you see the solder start to melt, take your groove-joint pliers and twist the pipe out of the fitting.

Remove the old solder by heating the end of the pipes and letting the old solder drip away from it. Then use an emery cloth to polish the ends down to the copper.

Be sure you buy new a fitting, because cleaning the old one is too hard and time-consuming, plus a new fitting is very inexpensive.

Hint: Most people tend to refer to CPVC as PVC. It is important to know the difference when making a repair.

Rigid Plastic Pipe: Cutting and Joining

DIFFICULTY: 2

TOOLS YOU MAY NEED: Hacksaw or tubing cutter or miter saw, permanent marker, emery cloth

MATERIALS YOU MAY NEED: Cleaning primer, proper solvent cement for your type of pipe

Rigid pipe has become very popular. It's lighter in weight, easy to work with, and less expensive. You will need to check out the building code for your area. You can do this by doing a "building code" search on the Internet and type in your town/city/state, or you can call and ask a contractor in your area.

The following are rigid plastic pipes:

- **ABS** (acrylonitrile-butadiene-styrene) is black in color and used for DWV (drain-waste-vent lines).
- **PVC** (polyvinyl chloride) is usually white or cream colored and used for drain lines, vent lines, and cold water only. PVC is becoming more popular than ABS because it is more rigid.

    Both ABS and PVC come in these sizes: 1¼", 1½", 2", 3", and 4" inside measurements. The smaller 1¼" and 1½" are used for drain traps under sinks. The 1½" and 2" are used for showers and tubs. The 4" is always used for toilet drains, and the drain lines and vents can use either 2", 3", or 4".

- **CPVC** (chlorinated polyvinyl chloride) is also white and used for hot and cold water supply lines. The sizes vary from ½" up to 2".

Fig 4.7- Cutting Rigid Plastic Pipe

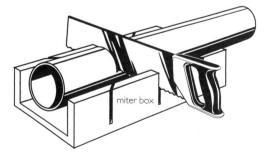

miter box

Cutting: You must make the cuts in a straight line for them to seal properly in their fittings. You can either cut them with a tubing cutter, a hacksaw, or a miter saw. I like the miter saw—fast and perfectly straight. Remove the burrs from the inside and outside of your cut piece with a utility knife or an emery cloth.

Fig 4.8- Smooth the Pipe

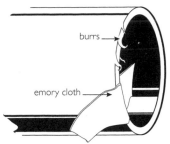

Fig 4.9- Connecting the Pipes

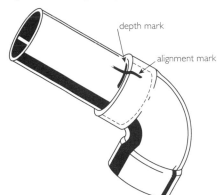

Alignment marks: Test fit all fittings and pipes first by assembling them without glue. Make a depth and an alignment mark with a permanent marker on both the pipe and the fitting. You will need to work fast when the glue is applied, so this will guide you to the right spot.

Smooth the pipe: Using an emery cloth, sand and smooth the pipe from the alignment mark to the end of the pipe and remove the dust.

Primer and Glue: ABS, PVC, and CPVC use a glue that melts the fittings together.

> **Tip:** PVC and ABS are *not* interchangeable and need a special fitting to connect them. Always use the glue that goes with the pipe.

- **ABS** pipe uses ABS glue and does not require a cleaning primer before gluing.
- **PVC** pipe *does* require a cleaning primer (purple) that cleans and prepares the pipe for the PVC glue.
- **CPVC** pipe uses a cleaning primer (either the purple PVC primer or CPVC primer) and requires CPVC glue.

For PVC and CPVC, apply the primer to the outside of the pipe and the inside of the fitting and allow it to dry.

Working one joint at a time, apply a liberal amount of solvent cement (glue) to the end of your pipe and a thin film on the inside of the fitting. Slide the pipe into the fitting with a twisting motion to spread the glue. Position the pipe so the alignment marks match up, and hold in place for about twenty to thirty seconds to allow the glue to set up. Gently wipe away any excess glue without disturbing the joint.

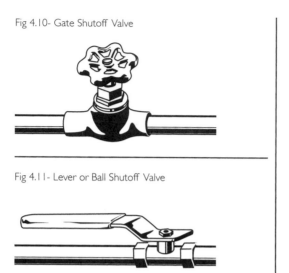

Fig 4.10- Gate Shutoff Valve

Fig 4.11- Lever or Ball Shutoff Valve

Fig 4.12- Fixture Shutoff Valve

Where's your shutoff valve? This is most important! Know where the shutoff valve is for the fixture you're working on. This will allow you to shut off the water just in the area you're working on. Also, know where the main shutoff is to your home or building. This will shut down all the water for your home.

Most main shutoff valves are located near the water meter and are usually in the basement. Sometimes they are near the water heater or near the wall closest to the street. They look like a metal wheel-shaped knob (gate valve) or a lever (ball valve). It's a good idea to know where this valve is and mark it with a hanging tag.

Gate Valve: Using a rag over the knob to help get a grip, turn the metal knob clockwise. You may need to use a lubricating spray if it is stuck. If you still can't turn it, you can use groove-joint pliers or an adjustable wrench, depending on the stem of your gate valve.

The Sink

Plenty of problems can occur in a sink:

- ▪ Clogged drain
- ▪ Leaky faucet
- ▪ Leaky handles

- Leaking below the sink
- The disposal problem

Why is it that most sinks work fine until we're throwing a dinner party? Usually this is because we don't properly maintain our plumbing. Because so much food waste seems to go down our sinks whether we have a garbage disposal or not, we tend to have a buildup of grease and food that can block the drain. To break down the grease buildup, occasionally run hot water down your drain. When you start to sense that water is not flowing well, use a plunger and then run hot water.

Your home has either a single sink or a double sink, or one with a garbage disposal.

Shutoff valve: To shut off the water to your sink and dishwasher, look in the cabinet underneath your sink. You should have two valves. One shuts off the cold water, and one shuts off the hot water.

THE CLOGGED DRAIN
DIFFICULTY: 1–2+
TOOLS YOU MAY NEED: Plunger, pliers/plumber wrench, bucket, plumber's hand snake

A clogged drain can be caused by the following:

- Buildup of food and grease that clog the trap or even further down the line.
- An obstruction in a vent. A venting problem is rare and most likely won't be your worry.

If your drain is draining slowly, try using a home remedy first. Heat up about a cup white vinegar, pour the vinegar down the drain, and add a few tablespoons baking soda. You will see it foam up. Let it sit until the foaming stops and then rinse with hot water. Hopefully, this will clear your drain.

Commercial drain cleaners might do the trick, but many are caustic and the acid will eventually eat through your pipes if allowed to sit long enough. Often the drain cleaners don't work and you'll have to go into the waste pipe anyway. Then you'll risk getting the acid on you, which is why I recommend a homemade drain cleaner. If you really have your heart set on buying a drain cleaner, buy a noncaustic drain cleaner (sodium hydroxide or copper sulfide based), and always wear eye protection when plunging.

START OFF BY USING A PLUNGER

DIFFICULTY: 1

TOOLS YOU MAY NEED: Plunger, clamp

THE SINGLE SINK:

This is your basic single sink without a garbage disposal or dishwasher attached. Put the plunger over the opening, and begin to rapidly plunge up and down about six to twelve times. Repeat a few times if necessary. If this allows the water to drain properly, then run hot water for a couple minutes to be sure the problem gets flushed to the bigger waste pipe.

THE DOUBLE SINK:

Determine which side is clogged. Insert the strainer/stopper in the drain of the side that is *not* clogged. You need to seal off the drain of the unclogged side so that when you use the plunger on the side of the clog, the air and debris don't pass through the drain to the sink that works. Put the plunger over the drain hole. Begin to pump the plunger up and down. You may need to run a little water to help the seal around the plunger. After six to twelve plunges, release the plunger by pulling straight up. You may have to repeat several times. Flush any debris down the drain line with hot water. If this doesn't do the trick, then you might need to remove the trap.

Tip: If you can't get a good seal around the plunger, use some petroleum jelly around the drain. This will give better suction.

Fig 4.13- A Single Sink

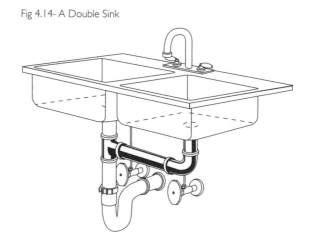

Fig 4.14- A Double Sink

Oftentimes, both sides are clogged. In this case, block the drain on one side. Plunge. Then block that drain and plunge the other side.

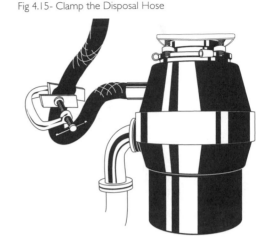
Fig 4.15- Clamp the Disposal Hose

THE SINK WITH A GARBAGE DISPOSAL

If you have a double sink, then stop up the drain on the side that does *not* have the clog.

Check underneath your sink to see if your disposal has a ribbed hose from the garbage disposal to an air gap located on top of your countertop, which is usually a chromed dome. You need to clamp this hose closed so when you start to plunge, the water won't spray all over the place.

Then begin to pump the plunger over the drain. You may need to run some water to be sure you get a good seal around the plunger. Do this several times. Run hot water to flush any debris. If this doesn't fix the problem, then proceed to removing the trap.

REMOVING THE TRAP

DIFFICULTY: 2+

TOOLS YOU MAY NEED: Groove-joint pliers or plumber's wrench, plumber's hand snake

MATERIALS YOU MAY NEED: Bucket

All sinks have either a P-trap that comes out of the wall or an S-trap that comes out of the floor. The traps are called P-trap and S-trap because of their shape. I think the P-trap looks more like a U-trap, but I never got to cast my vote on plumbing names. The trap is necessary for two reasons:

> **Hint:** When you need to remember which way to turn the nuts on a fixture, try the old plumber's saw: lefty loosey, righty tighty. Turn left to loosen; turn right to tighten.

■ This shape helps catch items such as rings and small objects. The weight of the object will sink to the bottom of the curve and won't go back up and out the waste. I'm sure this has saved many a relationship!

■ This U-shape also holds a portion of water in the curve after you shut off your faucet. This water is what stops the sewer gas from seeping up through the drain line and into your home. It also is what will hold soap, grease, and other debris.

Fig 4.16- Remove the Trap

If plunging doesn't unclog your sink, you'll need to remove the trap underneath the sink. First you'll need to get a bucket underneath the P-trap, and you may want to wear some rubber gloves. Use groove-joint pliers or a plumber's wrench to loosen the nut holding the top of the trap to the extension piece. The slip nuts are held in place by rubber or plastic washers. To remove it from the connection, you need to slide the nut and the washer down.

Repeat this on the other end until the trap is free. Empty the contents into your bucket. You should be able to clean the P-trap successfully. If there is nothing in the trap, you need to go to the next step.

Hopefully, if you are looking for a ring or piece of jewelry, you will find it there. If it's not there, get ready for the bad news . . . it has been lost down the main waste pipe.

SNAKING THE WASTE PIPE
DIFFICULTY: 2+

If there is nothing obstructing the P-trap, then there is a deeper problem. You will need a plumber's hand snake for this fix. I think it's a good idea for every home to have one of these on hand. I checked out a plumber's snake that can be used by hand or attached to a drill that retails for less than $35. Having a plumber come out to do the same thing could cost you up to $150.

The plumber's snake looks like a disc-shaped gun. It has a pistol grip and a flexible ribbed cable that extends out of the end. The disc holds the flexible cable and has a crank handle on it. The end of the cable is a spiral coil. This spiral coil is what will grab the hair, grease, or object that is clogging your drainpipes when the crank handle is turned. If you have the kind of snake that attaches to your drill, you activate the drill to turn the coil.

With the P-trap removed, you go directly into the drain line/pipe that returns into the wall. If you have an S-trap and can get to the fitting, you can remove it and

go directly into the drain on the
floor. Otherwise, keep the S-trap in
place and snake through the top of
the trap. Keep feeding or pushing
the snake into the pipe until you
meet resistance. This usually means
you've reached a bend in the pipe.
Give yourself some extra slack in
the snake, set the lock, and begin to

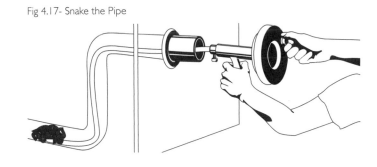

Fig 4.17- Snake the Pipe

turn the snake handle clockwise as you continue to push. This will get it past the
bend. Now release the lock and continue to push the snake farther into the drain
line.

When you hit solid resistance, you've reached your clog. Again, set the lock, give
yourself some extra slack, and continue to crank the handle to turn the cable while
pushing in. If it slowly starts to move, then the clog is probably a soap or grease clog.
If it's a bit harder, it might be food, hair, or a sponge. After you turn the crank a few
times, unlock the cable and continue to turn the handle while applying steady pressure. Repeat a few times and then retrieve the cable by pushing the cable into the
disc-shaped gun. Hopefully, you will find something icky on the end of the coil. You
will probably need to do this a few times to be sure you cleared everything. Then
run the hot water to flush the system of any debris.

If you come up with nothing at all, the problem is deeper and you may need to
clear a drain that is on the same branch line or go directly in the main waste or vent
stack.

This is when I call in the plumber.

THE LEAKY FAUCET

DIFFICULTY: 3

TOOLS YOU MAY NEED: Phillips/flat screwdriver, utility knife, prybar, groove-joint pliers,
adjustable wrench, seat wrench

MATERIALS YOU MAY NEED: Heatproof grease, washer, O-ring, stem assembly, valve seat

Turn off the supply valve.

In my opinion, a leaky faucet is tortuous. Once my ears fix on that sound, I'm
doomed. No amount of meditation can drown out that sound.

For those of you who experience a leaky faucet in the middle of night and can't get to sleep, tie a string around the faucet and let it hang down to the bottom of the sink. The drip will now slide down the string and down the drain without that awful dripping sound. This will allow you to get a good night's sleep so you can tackle the fix the next day.

A leaky kitchen sink faucet can be caused by a worn-out washer, O-ring, or seal.

Many faucet styles have repair kits that you can buy with all the replacement parts, including these faucets:

Helpful Hint: Cover your drain so you don't lose any parts down it.

- Compression type
- Ceramic disc–type cartridge
- Ball-type sleeve-type

COMPRESSION FAUCET OR TWO-HANDLE FAUCET:

A leaky faucet occurs when water passes between the washer, at the end of the stem assembly, and the valve seat. To determine which washer needs changing, put your hand under the dripping water. If it's cold, you need to change the washer in the cold handle. And you guessed it—if it's hot, you need to change the washer in the hot handle. Hardware stores sell replacement washers, O-rings, and valve seats.

Remove the handle:

TOOLS YOU MAY NEED: Phillips/flathead screwdriver, prybar

Remove the little metal or plastic cap on the top of the handle/knob. It will usually have an H (hot) or a C (cold) written on it. You should see a tiny notch in the rim of the cap where you can slip a small screwdriver to pry it up.

Using your Phillips (+) or flathead (−) screwdriver, depending on the screw head, remove the screw. Pull up on the knob seated on top of the stem assembly. You may need to rock it back and forth as you lift up on it. Sometimes I've had to use a small prybar to pry it off. If you use a prybar, protect the sink and the handle by wrapping a rag around the prybar. You want to avoid giving it a good shove in one place, as many knobs are made of plastic and too much muscle can crack the knob. Pry it gently but firmly at several points around the handle.

Removing the stem assembly:

TOOLS YOU MAY NEED: Groove-joint pliers or adjustable wrench

To replace the washer or O-ring or to inspect the valve seat, you must remove the stem assembly. This is what the knob/handle is screwed to; when turned to the "on"

Fig 4.18- Compression Faucet

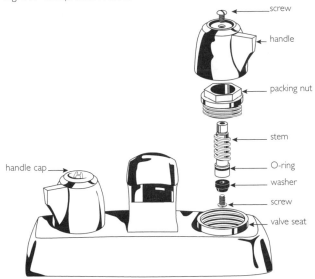

screw

handle

packing nut

stem

O-ring

washer

screw

valve seat

handle cap

Fig 4.19- Remove the Handle

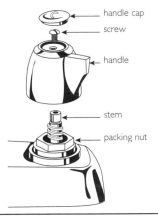

handle cap

screw

handle

stem

packing nut

Fig 4.20- Stem Assembly

retaining nut

stem

O-ring

washer

screw

Fig 4.21- Replacing the Washer

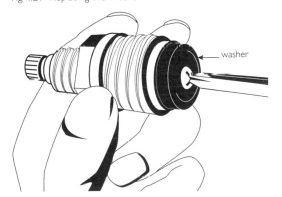

washer

Fig 4.22- Replace the O-ring

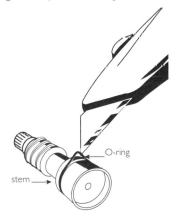

O-ring

stem

position, it allows the water to go through the faucet and it acts as a valve. If the retaining nut is round, use groove-joint pliers; otherwise, use an adjustable wrench to unscrew the stem assembly. Feel around in the hole with your finger. What you are touching is the valve seat. This is what the stem assembly sits on. If it feels rough in there, you need to replace the seat. A rough seat wears away a washer. See "Replacing the Valve Seat."

Replacing the washer:
TOOLS YOU MAY NEED: Screwdriver

MATERIALS YOU MAY NEED: Washer, penetrating oil, heatproof grease

Most likely, you'll need to replace the washer at the end of the stem assembly. The washer is a flat, black or red rubber ring that's attached to the bottom of the stem by a screw. Remove the screw with your screwdriver, and replace the washer that fits neatly into the round indentation. (Washers are sold in package of various sizes.) Be sure you feel around the valve seat before putting the stem assembly back in place.

Replacing the O-ring:
TOOLS YOU MAY NEED: Utility knife

MATERIALS YOU MAY NEED: O-ring

A broken-down O-ring will make the faucet leak at the base of the handle. Because you have the stem out, it's best to replace the O-ring, which is a thin, black rubber gasket within the stem assembly. The stem assembly is made up of a retaining nut and a spindle. Unscrew the threaded spindle from the retaining nut.

Use a utility knife to cut off the O-ring, and replace it with a duplicate size. Use heatproof grease and coat the O-ring and stem assembly before putting it back together. This will help ensure a good seal and will make it easier to take it apart in the future.

You can find a 2-ounce container of packing grease in the plumbing section of the hardware store. I always have a little tub of grease in my toolbox, and it seems to keep forever. If you don't have any grease around, you can use petroleum jelly or a drop of dishwashing liquid around the O-ring.

Tip: If you cannot get the nut from the spindle, try adding some penetrating oil such as 3-in-1 household oil in the joint and wait a few minutes before trying again. If you still cannot get it to budge, you will have to replace the stem assembly.

Replacing the stem assembly:
MATERIALS YOU MAY NEED: Steel wool or new stem assembly

If any part of the stem assembly looks corroded and badly worn, you're probably going to need to replace the entire

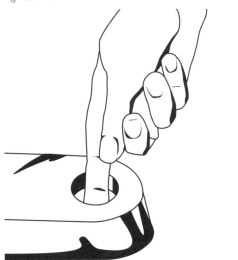

Fig 4.23- Feel to Check the Condition of the Valve Seat

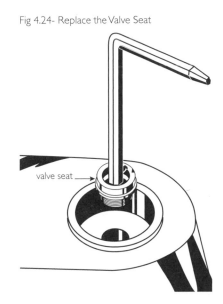

Fig 4.24- Replace the Valve Seat

valve seat

stem assembly. A new stem will come with a new washer and O-ring. Be sure you take the old stem assembly with you when you go to the hardware store. If the stem has only a small amount of corrosion, you can lightly buff with steel wool. Clean the stem of all particles and steel wool residue.

Replacing the valve seat:
TOOLS YOU MAY NEED: Seat wrench (L-shaped wrench)
MATERIALS YOU MAY NEED: Valve seat
If you stick your finger into the hole and feel that the valve seat has nicks or rough areas, you will need to replace the valve seat. This can occur from a stem assembly with a worn-out washer grinding on the valve seat, or it can be from mineral deposits within your water system grinding away at the valve seat. To remove the seat, place a seat wrench (L-shaped wrench) into the middle of the valve seat, and remove it by turning it counterclockwise. I suggest taking the valve seat to your hardware store so you are sure to buy exactly the same kind. Then secure the new seat using the L-shaped wrench.

Resurfacing the valve seat:
TOOLS YOU MAY NEED: Seat-dressing tool
If you cannot get the valve seat out, before you toss the entire fixture, there's one last fix. You can try to resurface the valve seat. Take the retaining nut to the hardware

Fig 4.25- Resurface the Valve Seat

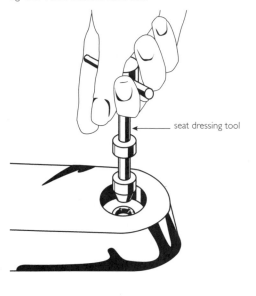

seat dressing tool

store and get a seat-dressing tool that fits the inside diameter of your retaining nut. The retaining nut is part of the stem assembly. See "Replacing the O-ring." Slide the retaining nut over the seat-dressing tool, and screw it in the faucet body—not tight. This will keep the tool directly in the middle and in place to resurface the valve seat. Pressing lightly, make two or three clockwise handle rotations. Take the nut and tool out of the faucet body, and reassemble the stem assembly. Good luck!

ONE-HANDLE FAUCETS:

Ceramic disc–type cartridge faucet: This faucet has a single handle that lifts "up" and rotates laterally left and right. This leaky faucet needs to have the ceramic disc or seals replaced.

Fig 4.26- Ceramic Disc Faucet

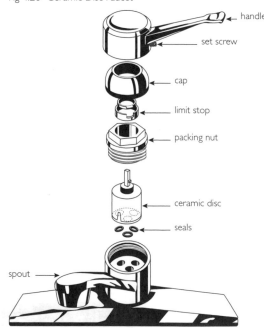

handle

set screw

cap

limit stop

packing nut

ceramic disc

seals

spout

Removing the handle:

TOOLS YOU MAY NEED: Flat screwdriver, hex wrench

Because you already have the supply valve to your faucet shut off (you have, haven't you? Go ahead, I'll wait), you should next cover your drain so you don't lose any pieces. Lift up on the faucet handle and locate the set screw. This will likely be covered by a small plastic cap. Use your fingernail or a small flat screwdriver to remove the cap. Most set screws are hex heads. Use your hex wrench (also known as an Allen key) to remove the screw. Remove the handle by lifting up.

Removing the Ceramic Disc:

TOOLS YOU MAY NEED: Groove-joint pliers, screwdriver, or adjustable wrench

MATERIALS YOU MAY NEED: Electrical tape, vinegar, scouring pad, possibly new seals or a new ceramic disc

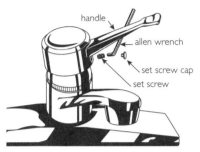

Fig 4.27- Remove the Handle

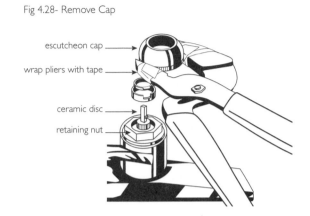

Fig 4.28- Remove Cap

Remove the round escutcheon cap with groove-joint pliers. The escutcheon cap is that domed cap directly underneath the handle. Apply some electrical or duct tape on the teeth or jaws of the pliers to prevent damage to the escutcheon cap. The ceramic disc will be held down by mounting screws or a retaining nut. Use a screwdriver to remove the screws, or use an adjustable wrench to remove the retaining nut.

Lift the ceramic disc out and flip it upside down. You will see three openings with rubber seals inside of them. Especially with hard water, mineral deposits will attach to the seals, preventing them from working properly. Oftentimes, if they're in good shape, you can clean these seals and openings with a scouring pad and a little vinegar. Rinse everything with clear water and reassemble. If you can see that the seals are beyond help, take the ceramic disc to the hardware store and buy new seals that will fit into the cylinder openings. If you have trouble finding the proper seals or if the openings look really bad, you can always replace the ceramic disc with new seals already part of the assembly. Replace the disc, and reassemble it and the handle.

Cartridge Faucet or One-Handle Faucet: This faucet has a single handle that lifts up and rotates left and right, similar to the ceramic disc faucet.

Removing the handle:
TOOLS YOU MAY NEED: Flat or Phillips screwdriver
Take the metal or plastic cap off the top of the handle. This will allow you to get to the screw. Close off the drain, and use your screwdriver to unscrew the screw. Remove the handle by tilting it backward and lifting it up.

Fig 4.29- Cartridge Faucet

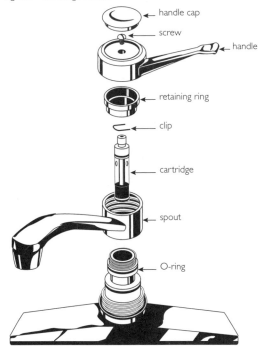

- handle cap
- screw
- handle
- retaining ring
- clip
- cartridge
- spout
- O-ring

Fig 4.30- Remove the Handle

Removing the retaining nut and replace cartridge:

TOOLS YOU MAY NEED: Groove-joint pliers

MATERIALS YOU MAY NEED: New cartridge

Using your groove-joint pliers, remove the retaining nut or ring by turning it counterclockwise. Look for a U-shaped retaining clip holding the cartridge in place, and remove it with your pliers. (Your faucet may not have this clip.) Using your pliers, pull the stem of the cartridge up and out. Take this cartridge to your hardware store so you're sure to buy the exact replacement. When putting the new cartridge back in place, be sure the tab faces forward.

While you're at it, you might as well replace the O-rings. These prevent leakage at the base of the faucet. You've gone this far; it would be a shame not to replace them as well. The O-rings lie underneath the spout.

In My Toolbox:

A 2-oz. container of packing grease can be found in the plumbing section of the hardware store. I always have a little tub of grease in my tool box, and it seems to keep forever. In a pinch, if you don't have any grease around, then you can use petroleum jelly or a drop of dishwashing liquid around the O-ring.

Replacing the O-rings:

TOOLS YOU MAY NEED: Utility knife

MATERIALS YOU MAY NEED: O-rings, heatproof grease or petroleum jelly

First, you need to take off the spout. Pull the shank of the spout up while twisting it. Cut off the old O-rings with your utility knife, and replace them in the grooved part of the faucet body. These are the two thin black pieces of rubber wrapped around the stem. Use heatproof grease and

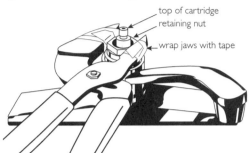

Fig 4.31- Remove the Retaining Nut

top of cartridge
retaining nut
wrap jaws with tape

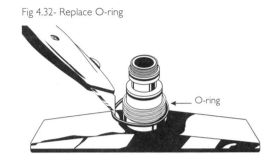

Fig 4.32- Replace O-ring

O-ring

coat the O-rings and stem assembly before putting it back together. This will ensure a good seal and will make it easier to take it apart in the future.

Putting it back together: After you have replaced the O-rings, place the spout on the faucet body, and put the new cartridge in place with the tab facing forward. Slip on the retaining clip, tighten the retaining nut/ring, screw the handle in place, and replace the cap on top.

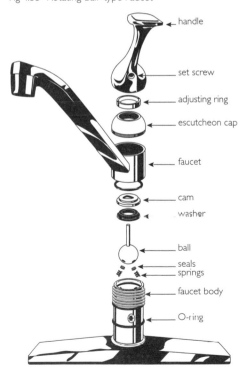

Fig 4.33- Rotating Ball–type Faucet

handle
set screw
adjusting ring
escutcheon cap
faucet
cam
washer
ball
seals
springs
faucet body
O-ring

Rotating ball–type faucet: This is a single-handle faucet that pivots over a dome-shaped cap. This faucet is a little more complicated because is has a few more parts to it. Be sure you cover the drain so you don't lose any parts, and *turn off the water supply.*

This faucet will leak for a few reasons: worn valve seats, springs, a damaged ball, or a loose adjusting ring—all of which can be replaced. First, see if the adjusting ring is loose. This is the easiest and quickest fix, because the adjusting ring is located underneath the handle.

Removing the handle:

TOOLS YOU MAY NEED: Hex wrench

The handle is usually held on by a setscrew. Place your hex wrench or Allen key into the hex head of the setscrew, and turn counterclockwise. Remove the screw, and lift off the handle.

Tip: Tracking your disassembly will help you when it's time to put it all back together. When there are a lot of parts to disassemble, I lay out a piece of paper and write the step number next to the part. This way, when I need to reassemble my faucet, I do the numbers in reverse. Those of you with a digital camera can take photos. Then I put my disassembled faucet parts that I need to replace into a locking plastic bag that I take to the hardware store. This keeps everything together, and the icky parts don't get on my clothing.

Tighten the adjusting ring:
TOOLS YOU MAY NEED: Cam tool

You'll need a cam tool, which looks like a stubby, flat, open-end wrench. Place the cam tool into the slots of the adjusting ring that lies on top of the cap. If you can tighten it by turning clockwise, put the handle back on and see if it still leaks. If it does, proceed to the next step. Of course, you'll have to remove the handle again—you knew that!

Removing the adjusting ring: Using your cam tool, loosen the adjusting ring by turning counterclockwise.

Removing the faucet cap:
TOOLS YOU MAY NEED: Groove-joint pliers

MATERIALS YOU MAY NEED: Electrical tape

Wrap the jaws of your groove-joint pliers with electrical or duct tape so you don't nick or mar the finished cap, and remove by turning the cap counterclockwise.

Removing the rotating ball:
MATERIALS YOU MAY NEED: Possibly a new rotating ball

To take out the ball, pull out the faucet cam that controls the direction of the ball and the rubber washer underneath it. Remove the ball, and check for damage. If it is

Fig 4.34- Remove the Handle

hex wrench

set screw

plastic bag

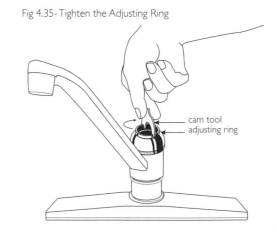

Fig 4.35- Tighten the Adjusting Ring

cam tool
adjusting ring

Fig 4.36- Remove the Adjusting Ring

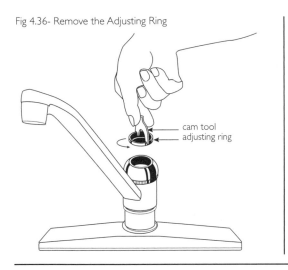

cam tool
adjusting ring

Fig 4.37- Remove the Faucet Cap

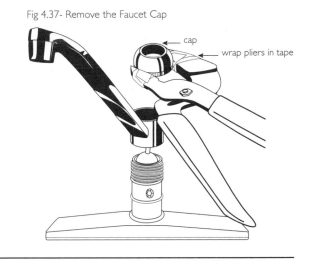

cap
wrap pliers in tape

Fig 4.38- Remove the Rotating Ball

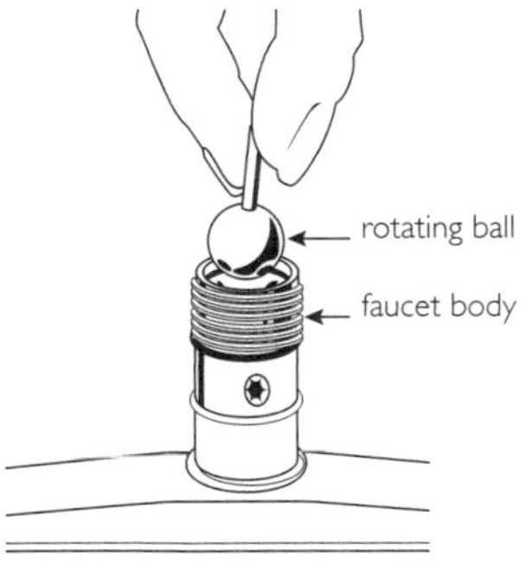

rotating ball
faucet body

Fig 4.39- Replace Seals and Springs

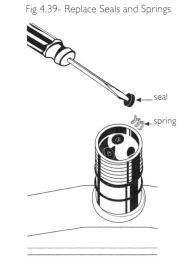

seal
spring

damaged, then take it with you to the hardware store and get a replacement. Also check the valve seats and springs.

Replacing the seals and springs:

TOOLS YOU MAY NEED: Flat screwdriver

MATERIALS YOU MAY NEED: Seals and springs, heatproof grease or petroleum jelly

If your rotating ball looks good, you'll need to replace your seals and springs. If your rotating ball is damaged, you might as well replace the seals and springs while you're at it!

Insert a flat screwdriver into each valve seal and pull up. This will remove both the valve seal and the spring. Using heatproof grease or dish soap, coat the new valves seal's edges and place back into their seats.

Fixing the leak under the faucet:
TOOLS YOU MAY NEED: Flat screwdriver, utility knife
MATERIALS YOU MAY NEED: O-rings, heatproof grease or petroleum jelly
If your faucet leaks at the stem of the faucet, you need to replace the O-rings. There are usually two located on the stem of the faucet assembly, and they are usually black in color. Using your flat screwdriver, pry the O-rings away from the shank of the faucet and cut them with your utility knife. Replace these with new ones, and coat the O-rings with some heatproof grease.

Reassembling the faucet: Were you keeping track of how this was disassembled? Now just do the reverse when putting it back together. Slide on the spout; insert the ball, the cam washer, the cam into the notch of the faucet body; and screw on the faucet cap with the groove-joint pliers with tape on them. Screw down the adjusting ring with your cam tool, place the handle on, and tighten your set/screw.

Congratulate yourself! You just saved yourself a lot of money by repairing this yourself!

REPLACING YOUR FAUCET
DIFFICULTY: 3

If you want a new faucet, you can easily replace it yourself. First, you need to *shut off the supply lines,* usually underneath your sink, and remove your old faucet.

Removing the old faucet: A faucet is connected to supply tubes that feed the water into the spout. Some faucets have the copper supply tubing pre-attached to the faucet shank. Other faucets will have the flexible supply tubes connected to the tail-pieces.

Removing the supply tubes:
TOOLS YOU MAY NEED: Adjustable wrenches or groove-joint pliers
For this project, adjustable wrenches are better, but most of us may only have one wrench. If this is you, you can use your groove-joint pliers. Supply lines or pipes

lead from the shutoff valve to the faucet. To disconnect the copper tubes that are pre-attached to your faucet, use one wrench on the end of the supply pipe nut and the other wrench or groove-joint pliers on the valve nut.

If your wrench handles are at a 45° angle, push them away from each other to loosen a connection. Push them together to tighten a connection.

If the supply tubes are connected to your tailpiece, you need to use your adjustable wrench or groove-joint pliers to loosen the coupling nut at the end of the supply tubes that attach to your tailpiece.

Removing the sink sprayer hose: If your sink has a spray attachment, it will be hooked up to the faucet underneath. You will need your groove-joint pliers to remove this coupling nut from the faucet shank.

Remove the mounting nuts:
TOOLS YOU MAY NEED: Groove-joint pliers
Most faucets are attached to either the sink itself or the countertop by bolts or tailpieces with mounting nuts. Many faucets come in separate pieces and are mounted individually by a nut. These nuts are referred to as mounting nuts, locknuts, or hand tighten nuts. To remove these nuts, you must go underneath the sink. Because

Fig 4.40- Disconnect the Supply Tubes

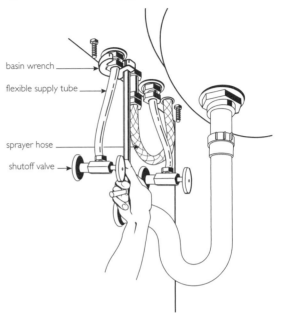

basin wrench

flexible supply tube

sprayer hose

shutoff valve

Fig 4.41- Loosen or Tighten a Connection

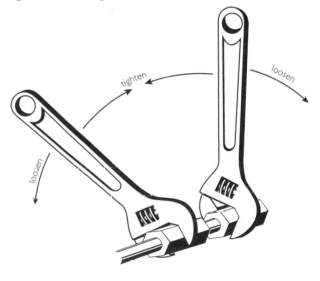

tighten

loosen

loosen

you're going to be working in a tight area, I like to double up a couple towels underneath the sink and get myself as comfortable as I can.

First, you can try loosening the mounting nuts by hand, but if they're too tight, use your groove-joint pliers to remove the mounting nuts along with any washer or gaskets.

Disconnecting your supply lines:

TOOLS YOU MAY NEED: Groove-joint pliers, adjustable wrench or basin wrench

In addition to the tailpieces with mounting nuts to keep the faucet from shifting, a two-handle faucet will have the supply lines attached. Other faucets will have the supply lines attached to the pre-attached copper tubing. Disconnect your supply lines by using your groove-joint pliers, adjustable wrench, or, if you're tight on space, your basin wrench.

If you have flexible supply lines, you will be able to reuse them with no problem. If the tailpieces are connected by copper tubing, which is not flexible, oftentimes it will need to be replaced. I would suggest replacing it with a flexible line.

Removing your faucet:

TOOLS YOU MAY NEED: Putty knife

Your faucet may be sealed underneath with plumber's putty or silicone. You might need to push a thin putty knife underneath the faucet to release the seal. Be careful to not damage the sink. When your faucet is out, scrap away any leftover seal or residue so your new faucet will have a good seal to it. Always install your faucet according to the manufacturer's direction. The good news is that they usually come with an easy-to-read diagram.

Fig 4.42- Cleaning the Faucet Aerator

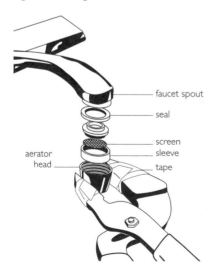

faucet spout

seal

screen
sleeve
tape

aerator
head

CLEANING YOUR FAUCET AERATOR

DIFFICULTY: 2

TOOLS YOU MAY NEED: Groove-joint pliers

MATERIALS YOU MAY NEED: Electrical tape, old toothbrush, toothpick or pin, penetrating oil

Dirt and minerals can interrupt the flow of water and air through your faucet's spout. To clean the aerator, you must remove it. Tape the jaws of your groove-joint pliers with electrical tape so you don't scratch the aerator when unscrewing it. After you've removed it, disassemble the parts. I set them in a line—exactly how they come apart. Clean both the screen and disc with soapy water and an old toothbrush, or soak it in a kitchen/bath product that dissolves lime. You may need to use a toothpick or a pin to remove small bits of dirt from the disc. Put the screen and disc back into place. If you have a lot of mineral deposits around the threads of the aerator, try adding some penetrating oil on the threads and screwing it back on the end of the spout. If it's in bad condition, then bring it to your hardware store and get a replacement.

Unclogging a Sink Sprayer

DIFFICULTY: 2

When the water coming out of your sink's sprayer starts to shoot out from one side, chances are good that the sprayer is clogged with the same dirt and minerals that can clog your faucet aerator. Or if the water is dribbling out, you may need to replace the hose. In either case, the fix is easy and you'll wonder why you waited so long to make the repair.

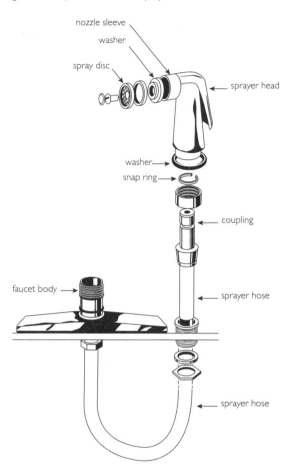

Fig 4.43- Components of a Sink Sprayer

nozzle sleeve
washer
spray disc
sprayer head
washer
snap ring
coupling
faucet body
sprayer hose
sprayer hose

Removing the head:
TOOLS YOU MAY NEED: Possibly a screwdriver, old toothbrush, toothpick or pin
MATERIALS YOU MAY NEED: Lime-dissolving product or vinegar

The problem is most likely in the sprayer head. Depending on your model of sprayer, you may have a sleeve at the end of the sprayer that unscrews, or you may have a little screw at the end of the nozzle you need to unscrew with a screwdriver. Sometimes this screw will have a little cover over it. Remove the cover to expose the head of the screw. When you have removed that screw, you can remove the washers, the sleeve, and the disc. If you have a newer model, the pistol-like head unscrews from the hose. (I like to run the water through to see if the water comes out easily from the hose. If not, then you'll need to replace the hose.) You'll probably notice that there are pieces of dirt caught in the disc or that there is a buildup of minerals from the water. Soak the pieces and the spray head in a lime-dissolving product or white vinegar for a couple hours. You can brush away these deposits with an old toothbrush. You may need to use a pin or a toothpick to remove any particles from the disc. If it's beyond help, take your pieces to the hardware store and get replacements. After you unscrew the spray head from the coupling, you can see if the washer underneath is worn. If it is, replace it. Now reassemble your parts in the same direction and order.

REPLACING THE HOSE

DIFFICULTY: 3

TOOLS YOU MAY NEED: Groove-joint pliers, basin wrench

MATERIALS YOU MAY NEED: Teflon tape

Like your lawn hose or your radiator hose, a faucet sprayer hose can wear out, too. To replace it, first *shut off the supply valves.* Go underneath your sink and loosen your coupling nut from the bottom of the spout shank. You'll be working in tight quarters. Although you may get your groove-joint pliers in there, you're probably going to have to use your basin wrench. After you make a couple counterclockwise turns, you can use your hand to remove it. On the other end where the sprayer connects, remove the retaining clip and pull off the coupling. When you get your new hose, you will need to slip it down into the hole of your sink and attach it to your spout shank. Wrap some Teflon tape around this spout shank before putting on your hose. Tighten down with your basin wrench by turning it clockwise. Put on the retainer clip and then the coupling. Screw your sprayer head back into place.

LEAKING UNDERNEATH THE SINK

DIFFICULTY: 3

Tired of keeping that bucket underneath the sink to catch water?

If you have water puddling underneath your sink, feel around the pipes or underneath of your sink's perimeter. Leaking water can be caused by the following:

- A breakdown of the bead of caulk used underneath the sink during installation. You may need to recaulk underneath the sink itself. See "Replacing a Sink." (page 128)

■ A loose connection of supply pipes/lines, the drain assembly, the waste pipe including the P-trap, and the rest of the many connections underneath your sink.

When to use Teflon tape, pipe joint compound, or plumber's putty: Use Teflon tape or pipe joint compound on threaded ends of pipe connections to ensure a perfect seal. I prefer Teflon tape because it's easy to use and not as messy as pipe joint compound. The trick with Teflon tape is to wrap the threaded pipe clockwise or in the direction you will be screwing on the nut. Also, especially with PVC, a slip joint nut can sometimes leak from being bumped into and break down the seal of the slip washer that lies underneath the slip nut. Use some pipe joint compound around a slip washer to ensure a tight seal. Use plumber's putty to form a watertight seal underneath the faucet before setting it in your countertop and underneath the drain assembly of the sink. *Do not* use plumber's putty on threaded pipe joints or against cultured marble surfaces.

INSTALLING OR REPLACING A SHUTOFF VALVE
DIFFICULTY: 3+
TOOLS YOU MAY NEED: Tubing cutter or hacksaw, adjustable wrench, groove-joint pliers or basin wrench
MATERIALS YOU MAY NEED: Compression ring and nut, shutoff valve, flexible supply tubes, Teflon tape or pipe joint compound, emery cloth

This project requires you to *shut off the main shutoff valve* to your home. If you don't have a shutoff valve, you will need to cut the supply pipes underneath your sink.

If you have a soldered joint, I would cut below the joint—around the middle of the length of pipe. You can use a hacksaw or a pipe cutter. I prefer a pipe cutter because it's so easy to twist it around and it makes a perfectly straight cut. A hacksaw will work; just be sure you cut it straight. When I use a hacksaw, I usually have to use a little bit of emery cloth or plumber's sandpaper to take

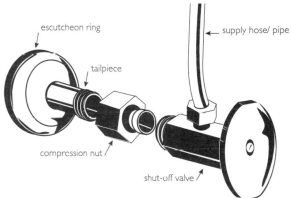

Fig 4.44- Installing a Shutoff Valve

escutcheon ring

supply hose/ pipe

tailpiece

compression nut

shut-off valve

the burrs off the end of the copper pipe. See "Cutting Copper Pipe" for a more complete guide.

Now, remove the top half of the supply pipes. With a basin wrench or groove-joint pliers, remove the coupling nuts that hold the old supply lines to the tailpieces of your faucet.

Then, install a compression nut. This makes putting on a valve very easy. No muss, no fuss! Just slide the compression nut down the existing copper supply pipe with the threads of the nut facing up, and then slip the compression ring on the pipe. Do this with the other supply pipe as well.

Install the shutoff valves. Slide a shutoff valve onto each pipe (hot and cold supplies). I like to use Teflon tape around the threads of the shutoff valve, or if you have pipe joint compound, you can use that. While you're at it, if you're using pipe joint compound, apply a small amount around the compression ring. My plumber friends will say this is going overboard, but it does help make a great seal and, let's face it, there's nothing worse than doing this work and still having a leak. Either way, when you tighten the compression nut onto the shutoff valve, the Teflon tape or pipe joint compound will ensure a good seal. Use two adjustable wrenches to tighten if you have them, or one adjustable wrench and one groove-joint pliers.

Now, install the supply tubes. I suggest using flexible supply tubes because they are so easy to install. Measure the distance from the top of the new valve to your tailpiece underneath the faucet, and add 2". Buy two flexible supply tubes when you buy your valves. Just a reminder: be sure you get supply tubes that have the right coupling nuts that fit over the threads of your valve and your tailpiece. Again, tighten all connections with your adjustable wrenches.

Finally, turn on main supply valve. After you've turned on your main supply valve, go and check your work to be sure there are no leaks and that the valves work properly.

REPLACING YOUR SINK
DIFFICULTY: 3+
TOOLS YOU MAY NEED: Groove-joint pliers, adjustable wrench, putty knife
MATERIALS YOU MAY NEED: Bucket

A sink is held in place by the sink's mounting nuts, drain assembly to the P-trap, and supply lines. You need to disconnect all of these to lift up the sink.

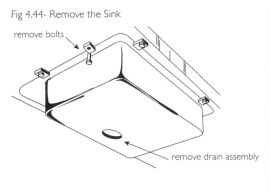

Fig 4.44- Remove the Sink

remove bolts

remove drain assembly

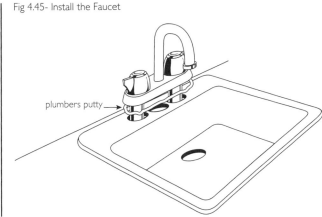

Fig 4.45- Install the Faucet

plumbers putty

Removing the old sink: *Turn off the water supply* to the sink. Turn your faucet on to drain the water left in your lines. Place a bucket underneath your sink to catch any water when disconnecting the supply lines, and use your adjustable wrench to disconnect the supply tubes. The drain of your sink has a tailpiece attached to it that leads into the P-trap and is connected by a slip nut. Loosen the slip nut with groove-joint pliers and then unscrew it by hand. Remove the bolts underneath the perimeter of the sink, and remove the sink. If you find your sink is hard to lift out, you may need to use a small putty knife around the edges of your sink to break the caulk seal. After the sink is out, you can remove the faucet. See "Replacing Your Faucet." (page 122)

INSTALLING A NEW SINK

DIFFICULTY: 3

TOOLS YOU MAY NEED: Groove-joint pliers, putty knife, adjustable wrench, screwdriver

MATERIALS YOU MAY NEED: Plumber's putty or silicone, Teflon tape or pipe joint compound, drain assembly, PVC tailpiece, flexible supply tubes if needed

You've taken out your old sink, and now you want to install the new sink. Be smart and make all the connections you can before putting the sink in place. This will save your energy and your back. For instance, put on your old or new faucet and drain assembly. Which reminds me . . . if your sink does not come with a drain assembly, you'll need to buy one.

Installing the faucet: If you're going to use your old faucet, then first install the old faucet on your new sink. Some faucets have a thin plastic or rubber gasket that the faucet base sits on and prevents any leaking. If you don't have a gasket with your new or old faucet, take some plumber's putty and roll it between your hands until you've made a long snake about a ¼" bead and place it under the perimeter of the faucet. If you're putting this on cultured marble, use ¼" of silicone caulk. Silicone caulk won't stain marble; plumber's putty will.

Press down for a good seal. Tighten the mounting nuts underneath the sink to the threaded tailpieces by hand and then turn another half turn with your groove-joint pliers. Remove any excess silicone or putty around the faucet with a putty knife. I like to wrap the putty knife with a paper towel to remove this excess. Connect your hot and cold water lines, also known as your supply tubes. I suggest the flexible ones such as the braided steel or vinyl mesh because they're very easy to work with.

Installing the drain assembly: If your sink doesn't come with a strainer and drain assembly, put it on now. Place your sink on its side. Seal the strainer flange to the bottom of your sink by applying plumber's putty under the flange of the strainer. Push into place. The putty will ooze up around the flange. From the underside of the sink, slip the rubber gasket, strainer sleeve, and locknut around the strainer, and tighten

Fig 4.47- Install the Drain Assembly

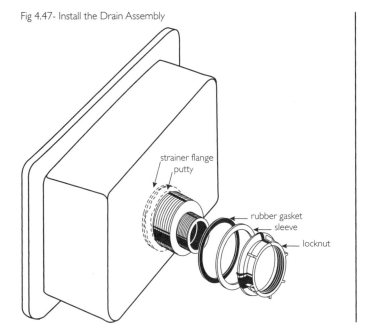

strainer flange
putty
rubber gasket
sleeve
locknut

Fig 4.48- Install the Hold-Down Bolts

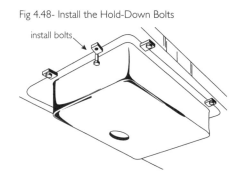

install bolts

into place with your groove-joint pliers. Because the putty will slide the strainer around a bit, tighten slowly and keep looking back into the sink to be sure it is centered in the bottom of your sink, or you can have someone help you keep an eye on it. Remove any excess putty. If you have a double sink, you will need to do this for both sides.

Installing the sink: You will either need to apply plumber's putty or silicone underneath the sink along the flange to form a seal. Always install the sink according to the manufacturer's instructions. Drop the sink into place, and push down evenly around the edge to seat it securely.

Installing hold-down bolts: Ready to go underneath the sink? Okay, get a couple towels to lean on because you need to be comfy when making your connections. I also use a gardening kneeling pad over the lip of the cabinet to protect my spine when I'm lying on my back. It has more support and less bulk than towels.

First, put the hold-down bolts in the channel underneath your sink. These will come with your new sink. Strategically place them so your sink is held into place evenly all around, and tighten all the bolts with your screwdriver.

Connecting the supply tubes: Usually, you'll connect the flexible supply tubes to the shutoff valves. Use two adjustable wrenches; if you only have one, use a groove-joint plier with the adjustable wrench. You want to tighten the supply tube as well, so with your wrenches held at a 45° to each other, push them toward each other to tighten.

Plumbing your drain assembly: You will need to add a tailpiece onto the bottom of the strainer that feeds into your P-trap. I prefer PVC pipe because it is easy to cut if necessary. The tailpiece will come with a plastic washer that fits inside the top of the tailpipe if it's a metal tailpipe. It may also come with the PVC pipe. I use it for both. Before you make this connection, ensure a tight seal by wrapping Teflon tape around the bottom threads of the drain assembly, in the same direction you will be screwing the locknut, or you can use pipe joint compound on the threads. Now, slide the metal locknut that comes with the strainer over the tailpiece, and attach it to the threaded end of your strainer. A slip nut is used for the other end that connects to your P-trap. It is called a slip nut because it has a tight washer over the tailpiece pipe called a slip washer and it allows the tailpiece to slip up and down into the connection of the P-trap. Tighten both the locknut and the slip nut with your groove-joint pliers.

Fig 4.49- Plumb the Drain Assembly

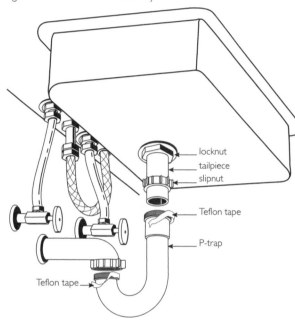

Double-sink drain assembly: If you're going from a single sink to a double sink, the plumbing for this is basically the same. Obviously, you will need two drain assemblies, but you will also need to have two tailpieces assembled with two elbows that tie into a T-fitting that leads into your P-trap. Tighten all connections with your groove-joint pliers.

Turn on your water supply: Before turning on the water supply, I like to remove the aerator at the end of the faucet's spout to allow any debris to pass through and not get caught in the aerator. See "Cleaning Your Faucet Aerator." (page 124) Tape the jaws of your groove-joint pliers with electrical tape so you don't mar the spout collar when removing. Turn your water back on at either the shutoff valves underneath your sink or your main shutoff valve.

Repairing Your Garbage Disposal

DIFFICULTY: 2

TOOLS YOU MAY NEED: Jam-wrench or hex wrench

Wanna know a secret? Since I've lived in New York City—what seems like forever without the conveniences of modern life like a dishwasher or a garbage disposal—I

Fig 4.50- Double-Sink Drain Assembly

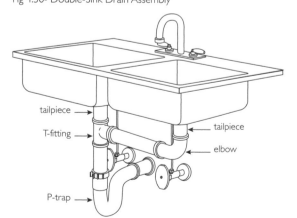

never had to repair a garbage disposal until I started doing home improvement on TV. I was surprised how easy it was.

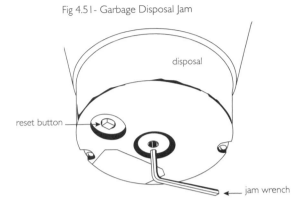

Fig 4.51 - Garbage Disposal Jam

The basics of a garbage disposal are easy. First, the disposal's motor turns a flywheel that throws whatever you put down the disposal against a shredder. The shredder does just that—shreds the garbage into pulp that is flushed down the drain into your waste line.

I always like to see if anything is in the disposal causing the problem. First, *turn off the breaker* to the switch before working on your garbage disposal. Then take a small flashlight and look into the disposal. Using tongs, take out any object that is left in the disposal. Turn the breaker back on and give it a try.

If your disposal makes a humming noise but doesn't turn, you might have a jam that you can't get to with your tongs. Be sure the on/off switch is turned off. Disposals have a hole in the bottom that accepts the hex head of a jam-wrench, which is nothing more than an L-shape Allen wrench. Often, the manufacturer will include this Allen wrench taped to the side of the disposal. Insert the Allen key into the hole, and work it back and forth. This will manually free anything obstructing the blades. You can also work from above and use a broom handle or plunger handle to push against the blade, rocking it back and forth to dislodge any object. After the object has been dislodged, remove it with tongs.

If your garbage disposal won't hum when you turn it on, then chances are the overload protection has been tripped. It has its own built-in breaker. Keep the switch to your garbage disposal off, and go underneath the sink and press the red reset button on the bottom of your disposal.

Tip: Do not put celery or grease down your garbage disposal. The celery threads will twist around the shank of the blades and slow it down or prevent it from working. To get grease off of the blades, pour some vinegar down the disposal with hot water. You can also put lemons and other citrus fruit down the disposal to make it smell fresh.

Appliances

The Refrigerator:

We take the refrigerator/freezer for granted until it stops working properly. I can't handle a less-than-cold refrigerator. I like my beverages really cold, especially milk. For

Fig 4.52- Clean Refrigerator Gasket

a refrigerator to maintain a constant temperature, it needs to be sealed properly. The seal around the door is called a gasket, which makes a suction to seal in the cool air.

If this gasket breaks down and cracks, cool air goes out and the refrigerator will turn on to cool down. Obviously, this makes the refrigerator work overtime and runs up your electric bill.

THE GASKET (SEAL):

DIFFICULTY: 1

TOOLS YOU MAY NEED: Soapy sponge

MATERIALS YOU MAY NEED: Petroleum jelly

To prevent your gasket from cracking, clean all around the gasket with a soapy sponge and dry. Then, smear some petroleum jelly on the gasket around the door twice a year to keep it lubricated. If you suspect the gasket is not sealing properly, close the door over a small piece of paper. If the paper falls down, then the gasket isn't sealing properly. You will need to call a professional to install a new gasket.

THE COILS:

DIFFICULTY: 1

TOOLS YOU MAY NEED: Vacuum cleaner

Unplug the refrigerator. Oftentimes, the reason a refrigerator will constantly run is because the coils are dirty. For some reason, these coils are like dust magnets! The coils are either behind the refrigerator or behind the front grill at the bottom. Use a vacuum cleaner with a brush extension to vacuum the coils. Do this twice a year at the same time you're cleaning your gasket.

If your coils are on the back of the refrigerator, the hardest part of this job is dancing the refrigerator away from the wall. Be sure you get a helper to move this beast. When you put the refrigerator back in place, be sure it is level—front to back

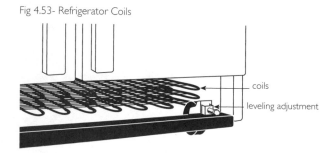

Fig 4.53- Refrigerator Coils

and side to side. You can adjust the feet of the refrigerator by screwing them up or down. You will definitely need a helper for this to gently rock the weight off of each foot while adjusting.

DEFROSTING
DIFFICULTY: 1
TOOLS YOU MAY NEED: Pot of hot water

Old refrigerators, like the one I have in Manhattan, need to have the freezer defrosted about twice a year. Okay, I really don't defrost it that much, so I usually have a literal icebox! *Unplug the refrigerator.* The best way to defrost the freezer quickly is to boil some water in a pot and place it in the freezer. I usually have to do this about four times. The ice will usually come off in big chunks. Whatever you do, *do not use an object to remove the ice.* One wrong move and you can puncture the freezer coils and then the freezer will never work properly again.

ICE MAKER
DIFFICULTY: 1+

I grew up with the old metal ice trays with the pull handle that gave you cracked ice whether you wanted it or not. They also gave you a water trail from the sink to the freezer. What they lacked in the ease-of-use factor, they made up for by being very low maintenance. Speaking of maintenance . . .

Smelly ice: Sometimes impurities in your water supply will make the ice smell or taste odd. A filter on the incoming water supply can take care of the worst of that. Charcoal filters are made specifically for ice makers and should be replaced every two to three years. The filter to your refrigerator/freezer is usually located either behind the refrigerator, in the basement, or under the sink. They are easily hooked up in-line and are easily replaced. Find the filter, model number, and brand, and replace.

Also, over time the ice bin itself can absorb odors from the freezer. Replace the ice bin either every few years or whenever it seems to have soaked up its share of smells.

Because we tend to reach for the freshest cubes on top, old cubes can sit in the bottom for months. These older cubes have had plenty of time to soak up the freezer odors and will then affect the new cubes. Chucking out the old cubes and washing

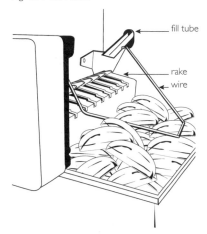

Fig 4.54- Ice Maker

fill tube

rake
wire

down the bin with warm water and dish soap every few months will do wonders.

Believe it or not, odors from the fridge will waft themselves into the freezer, so be sure to keep foods well covered.

No cubes at all: This may sound obvious, but be sure the ice maker is turned on. You will see a stiff silver wire along the right side of the ice maker. If the wire is in the raised position, the ice maker is turned off. If your ice maker has a small red plastic lever, lower it to lower the wire. If there's no plastic lever, just lower the wire by hand.

If luck is with you, the ice maker should start producing ice again. Be sure the freezer temperature is 8 degrees Fahrenheit or lower. If the freezer is too warm, the ice maker won't cycle properly.

If that didn't work, the ice maker fill tube may be blocked with ice. If so, carefully melt the blockage using a hair dryer—but be careful to not melt any plastic parts! You also want to avoid getting any moisture into the hair dryer.

Still doesn't work? Then we are off to replace the water shutoff valve or water-inlet valve—or both, if necessary. You can buy an ice maker installation kit and hardware. Be sure to follow the instructions.

The ice maker head assembly may have broken parts. Eyeball it to see if the gears are broken. Check to see if the small plastic arms that rest against the ice rake are broken. If the ice maker head assembly is modular and you've found broken parts, you can just replace it.

Cubes are too small or too few: If the cubes coming from your icemaker are too small, it may be time to replace the water filter. See "Smelly Ice." (page 135)

THE WATER LINE
DIFFICULTY: 3+

The water line runs up the back of your refrigerator from a water source. Be sure you have good water flow. If the copper tubing is bent, you will experience poor flow. You will need to replace the copper tubing. You can find this at your home center or hardware store, where it usually comes in a kit. See "Copper Pipe: Cutting and Joining Pipes." (page 101)

The water-inlet valve or water shutoff valve can be replaced. Again, buy the appropriate part and replace. See the "Copper Pipe: Cutting and Joining Pipes in the Kitchen chapter (page 101)."

Oftentimes, an ice maker can break down. Not to worry, you can call your appliance store or go online to buy a replacement ice maker that fits your model appliance. Follow the instructions that come with the new ice maker.

The Stove

I grew up in Atlanta, where we cooked on an electric stove. My mom is the Kitchen General, so we weren't allowed to cook. Therefore, I don't have a lot of experience cooking on an electric stove, because every apartment I've lived in Manhattan had gas stoves. The good news is that I do know how to maintain and troubleshoot both.

THE ELECTRIC STOVE

DIFFICULTY: 3

TOOLS YOU MAY NEED: Phillips-head screwdriver, utility knife

MATERIAL YOU MAY NEED: Replacement burner coil and receptacle

If your stove is electric, a burner might stop working or work intermittently. You can buy replacement burner coils that plug into a receptacle. When writing this book, I found them for less than $20. Find the replacement coil burner and receptacle that is suitable for your stove's name and model number, which is usually located on the back of your stove or above the stove.

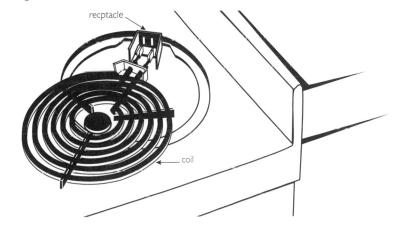

Fig 4.55- Electric Stove Burner Coil

recptacle

coil

Removing the burner coil: First, *turn off the breaker* or unscrew the fuse to the stove. Lift the burner coil up several inches, and pull it away from the receptacle. If the plug is pitted and corroded, you will need to replace both the burner coil and the receptacle.

Removing the receptacle: Lift the hood of the stove, and disconnect the receptacle. You will probably need to cut through the heat shields over the connection of the receptacle with your utility knife. Then unscrew any wiring, and using a Phillips screwdriver, remove the screw holding the receptacle in place.

Replacing the burner and receptacle: You will put the new receptacle in first and then the new burner coil. Basically, after removing these parts, you will know how to reinstall them. Be sure you follow the instructions that come with your new receptacle and burner coil.

CERAMIC GLASS COOKTOPS
DIFFICULTY: 1

These easy-to-clean cooktops have become very popular, because they are smooth on the top. The most popular of these cooktops have a radiant ribbon hidden underneath the glass top, which will heat up faster and hotter than gas or an electric coil. Aside from the radiant ribbon, some models have a quartz halogen heating system that heats up immediately, while other models use a magnetic induction that heats up the magnetic material without heating the cooktop. The upside to these cooktops is that they are sleek, easy to clean, and energy efficient. Always use a cooktop cream cleaner recommended by the manufacturer. The downside is that they can crack and break easily and can become pricey to replace. If you're having problems with a ceramic glass cooktop, look at your warranty and call a professional.

GAS STOVE
DIFFICULTY: 2

If your stove is gas, you may experience a gas flow problem. Sometimes the little holes around the burners get clogged up and need to be poked with a toothpick. Same goes with the pilot light. If you have a pilot light that keeps going out, you may need to take a little wire brush and brush off the flakes around the opening of the pilot. If you have a standing pilot light, it must be lit; otherwise, gas will escape through the pilot hole.

Safety First: If you smell gas when the stove is turned off, open your windows and *call the gas company* immediately. But it is normal to smell a little gas when the pilot light is out. No need to panic there.

Lighting a surface burner pilot light: Turn the surface burner control knobs off. Remove the grates above the burner, and lift up the cooktop. Find the pilot ports and light them using a match. Some stoves use a spark igniter rather than a pilot to ignite the gas. If you have a problem with any of these steps, I recommend contacting a professional appliance technician.

Adjusting the pilot: The flame of the pilot should be ⅜". You can adjust the pilot flame by using the pilot adjustment screw that can be found by following the pilot line back to the oven control. Using a flat screwdriver, turn the pilot adjustment screw until the flame height reaches ⅜". A smaller flame could result in the pilot going out, and a larger flame may generate too much soot underneath the cooktop.

Fig 4.56- Lighting the Pilot Light

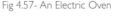

pilot line

pilot adjustment screw

THE ELECTRIC OVEN
DIFFICULTY: 2+

An electric oven usually has two elements: a bake element found on the bottom, and a broiler element found on roof of the inside of the oven. Both can be replaced from the inside of the oven.

Removing a basic bake/broiler element: *Disconnect the power.* Remove all the oven racks. Remove the mounting screws found inside and at the back wall of the oven. These hold the element mounting plate. Pull the old element away from the back wall as far as the wire will allow. Remove the screws from the element.

Replacing a basic bake/broiler element: Replace the element following the instructions provided by the manufacturer. Reconnect the leads (wires). Tuck the surplus of wire behind the insulation. Line up the holes and, using the existing screws, reinstall the new element with your screwdriver.

Fig 4.57- An Electric Oven

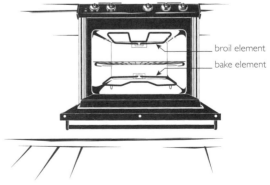

broil element
bake element

Fig 4.58- A Gas Oven

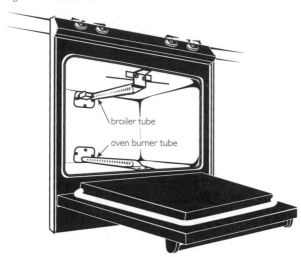

broiler tube

oven burner tube

Changing the lightbulb: Most ovens have a standard 40-watt appliance bulb. To change the bulb, remove the glass dome or shield. If there is nothing wrong with the bulb, then you may need to replace the switch.

THE GAS OVEN
DIFFICULTY: 1

Newer ovens will have two burner tubes: a broiler tube at the top, and an oven burner tube at the bottom. Older ovens will have one burner tube at the bottom, which is just above the broiler pull-out drawer. The holes in your oven's burner tubes must be free of any soot or grease. Shut off the gas at the valve, and stick a toothpick in the holes to be sure they are open. I would suggest that if your gas oven is not heating properly to call a professional technician.

Lighting the gas oven burner pilot: Turn the oven's control knob to the off position. Take out the broiler rack, and light a match, holding it in the back of the burner tube where the pilot is located. No adjustment is necessary. Replace the broiler rack.

THE STOVE'S FAN
DIFFICULTY: 1

The fan above your stove removes hot air and grease. Because the grease can clog the motor, a grease filter protects the motor, and a charcoal filter removes the odors when recirculating the air.

The filter: The grease filter is made of metal and can be cleaned in a sink of hot soapy water and/or put in your dishwasher. Be sure you dry this completely before reinstalling it. You will need to replace the grease filter every three to four years.

A charcoal filter *cannot* be cleaned and needs to be replaced every six months.

The Dishwasher

In my household, when the dishes are not getting cleaned properly, it's usually because I need a new sponge. Much like the shoemaker who goes barefoot, I'm the home improvement expert without many conveniences of the average homeowner. I seem to find homes that are so tight on space that I've opted out of a dishwasher. But for those of you who do have a dishwasher, I have a few tips for you.

The whole point of a dishwasher is to get those dishes clean; however, over time, your dishwasher's spray arm may get clogged with glass, paper, etc. To keep those dishes clean, check the spray arm a few times a year and remove any debris. If your dishwasher is still cleaning poorly, you may need a new water-inlet valve. If you hear the sound known as "water hammer" coming from your dishwasher when it is on, you probably need to replace the water-inlet valve. If this valve is defective, it will not allow water to enter your machine. The water-inlet valve is the device behind the lower access panel with a main water line feeding into it, a rubber hose attached, and two to four wires attached to it.

REMOVING A WATER-INLET VALVE

DIFFICULTY: 3

TOOLS YOU MAY NEED: Adjustable wrench, Phillips/flat screwdriver, groove-joint pliers

MATERIALS YOU MAY NEED: New water-inlet valve

Fig 4.59- Dishwasher Water-Inlet Valve

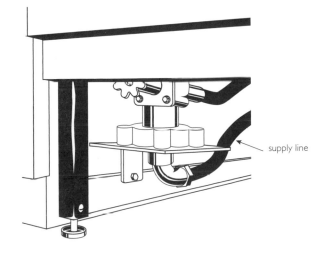

supply line

This is not a very difficult job, but it's definitely for those of you who feel pretty confident. Not that the repair itself is hard, it just requires several steps.

First, you must *turn off the circuit breaker or fuse* to the washer. Start the dishwasher just to be sure the power has been turned off. *Shut off the water supply lines*, which are usually underneath the kitchen sink or in the basement; if not, you may have to shut off the main water supply.

Locate the water-inlet valve by removing the lower access panel, which is held on by screws in the upper and lower corners.

The water-inlet valve is usually located near the front. Depending on the dishwasher, the valve will have two or four wires attached to it, along with the supply line that feeds water to the dishwasher.

Remove the water supply line from the valve using an adjustable wrench. Remove the black rubber discharge tube by using pliers to squeeze the clamp to take off the hose.

Before you disconnect the electrical wires to the valve, mark them so you know where the wires go when you connect them to the new valve.

Remove the old valve, and replace with the new valve in the reverse order: reconnect your wires, reattach the black rubber discharge hose, and reconnect the water supply line. Be sure your connections are tight! Turn on the water supply, and check for leaks. Screw the panel back on, and turn on your circuit breaker on (or screw in your fuse) and run the dishwasher.

Carpentry

The kitchen has its fair share of carpentry repairs. The countertops, floors, and walls are all subject to possible damage—if you cook like I do, that is. I tend to have a devil-may-care attitude about cooking. I rarely cook from recipes and always tend to cook in a hurry—usually when I'm about two hours past due for a meal! For someone so coordinated with tools, it's amazing how many things I can drop while I'm cooking. I guess I can attribute this to being a real hands-on chef—that is, hands on the butter, the oil, etc. So if you're anything like me, it's good to have that sponge and toolbox nearby!

Let's start with countertops.

Countertops

Many types of countertops are available: laminate, ceramic tile, butcher block, solid surface, stone, stainless-steel, or cement. Solid surface and stainless steel can be molded into decorative shapes, and sinks can be integrated into the countertop. When it comes to durability, stone and solid surface hold up the best. Solid surface and laminate come in the widest range of colors. All countertops have their trade-offs. For instance, wood or butcher block is ideal to cut on but requires sealants and maintenance. Ceramic tile looks great, but the grout can discolor and needs cleaning and sealing. Concrete can stain easily, and stainless steel looks great unless you touch it—fingerprints can easily be seen and the steel can scratch easily. The most common type of countertop is a laminate countertop, so let's start there.

LAMINATE COUNTERTOPS

Laminate refers to the thin, yet durable, material (1.2mm) that is used on the surface of countertops, furniture, and so on. For years, we in the trade referred to all laminate countertops as "Formica." But Formica is a trademarked name, like Kleenex, so we've gotten out of that habit. Many companies make very durable laminate, so you have many colors and patterns to choose from. Laminate is usually sold in sheets of 4' to 12' in length and 18" and 30" to 60" in width. Contact cement is used to adhere the laminate to the wood surface of the countertop.

REPAIRING LAMINATE COUNTERTOPS

Laminate can require repair because of the following problems:

Bubbles
Separates/comes unglued
Chips/gouges
Cuts
Burns
Stains

BUBBLES

DIFFICULTY: 3

MATERIALS YOU MAY NEED: Lacquer thinner, plastic bottle with squirt top, contact adhesive, shims, small paint brush

Laminate bubbles up in the middle because one of three things has occurred:

- There's no glue in that area.
- The laminate was put together before the glue had dried.
- There's debris underneath.

In any case, repairing laminate isn't a quick fix. Because you can't slice into the laminate and inject glue into the area, you have two options: you can install a new countertop or reglue the area.

Putting new laminate over the bubble would just re-create the same old problem. So you'll have to pull up the laminate to get the glue into the bubbled area. I have had to do this, and it's very tedious. If you want to save the existing laminate, you must work carefully.

Prying up the laminate and reglueing the area: Begin by squirting lacquer thinner under the flap where the laminate is separating from the countertop. You will be squeezing a lot and it's messy, so protect your floors. (This is *not* the time to light up a cigarette—do this in a well-ventilated area.) Work patiently and be careful not to break the laminate. This gets tricky, but even if you fail and you have to put on new laminate, you will be well on your way to removing the old laminate. Lacquer thinner dries quickly, so you will need to keep a constant thin stream underneath the laminate.

Also, because laminate is very delicate and can snap easily, I would use a very thin tool like a putty knife or a drywall taping knife to pry up the laminate while constantly squirting the lacquer thinner in between. This is best done with the help of another person.

Trick of the Trade:

I use lacquer thinner in a small plastic bottle, the kind beauty supply stores sell for applying hair dye (not that I would know about hair dye!). I make a very small squirt hole in the bottle's injector top with a push pin.

Applying contact cement: When the laminate is pried up to the bubbled area and the lacquer thinner has dried, brush the contact cement (glue) on the underside of the laminate and onto the top of the exposed wood countertop. Contact cement is very runny and viscous. As if that weren't pleasant enough, it is also a bit smelly and you'll need to do this in a well-ventilated area. You must brush contact cement on both sides and not let the sides touch

Fig 4.60- Pry up the Laminate

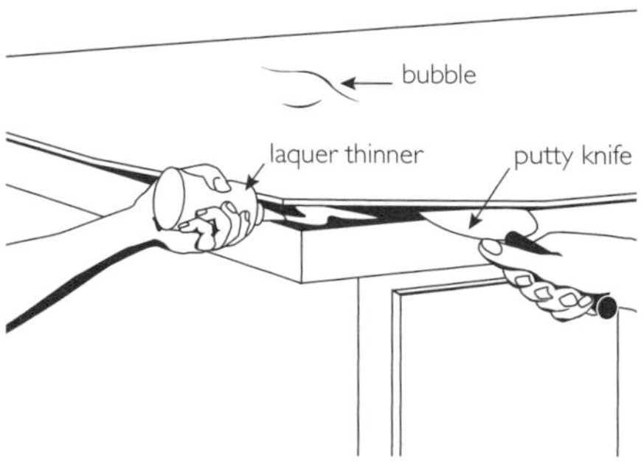

bubble

laquer thinner　　　putty knife

Fig 4.61- Apply Contact Cement

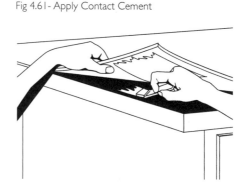

each other until it's dry. (I know, it's the only glue that requires that it be dry to stick.) You can use shims, also known as wedges, to hold the laminate up until it dries. Contact cement dries quickly. Once dry, press the laminate down. You can use the palm of your hand and press down, but I like to use a block of wood over the area and tap it with a hammer to be sure the laminate makes good contact with the countertop. Again, don't press it together until both sides are completely *dry*.

SEPARATES/COMES UNGLUED
DIFFICULTY: 2
MATERIALS YOU MAY NEED: Lacquer thinner, contact cement, wedges, small paint brush

Sometimes the countertop laminate will come unglued and separate because of improper installation, for example, if the glue isn't applied to all areas or the two sides are pressed together before the glue has dried. (These things tend to happen when work is done on Friday afternoon, eh-hem . . . for some reason.) Separating is similar to bubbling; it just happens on the ends and not in the middle. If that's the case, be sure both the laminate and the counter are entirely separated by wedges on the side before applying the contact cement with a small paint brush. You may have to squirt a little lacquer thinner like you would in the previous project. Again, contact cement needs to dry before you can put both pieces together.

CHIPS
DIFFICULTY: 2
TOOLS YOU MAY NEEDED: Fine metal file
MATERIALS YOU MAY NEED: Sandpaper, Krazy Glue®

Chipping usually occurs on the edge or near the edge on top. If you have the piece that chipped off, lightly sand the back of it with sandpaper, or use a fine metal file. Keep refitting it (dry) into the area, keeping in mind that you want to create enough room behind the chip for the chip to accept the glue and remain flush when it's put back into place. Use masking or painter's blue tape around the area before gluing so the glue doesn't get on the countertop. This is not a repair job guaranteed to last forever, by the way.

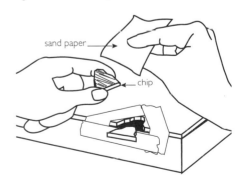
Fig 4.62- Laminate Chip

sand paper

chip

GOUGES
DIFFICULTY: 2
MATERIALS YOU MAY NEED: Clear epoxy

A gouge usually happens when something heavy falls on the laminate. This can be filled in with some clear epoxy to bring up the surface, but really, there's no great fix for a gouge.

CUTS
DIFFICULTY: 1

Even though I definitely should know better, I periodically end up slicing my laminate countertop along with my baguette if I don't keep a cutting board handy. I solved that problem a few years ago by installing a butcher block countertop. Cut laminate can't be fixed, so keep that cutting board in sight.

Minor cuts or scratches can be hidden by a self-waxing product, such as Pledge, or lemon oil. Also, you might be able to hide some deeper cuts with seam fillers, but remember, this is only temporary and will eventually wear off.

BURNS
Egads. You put the frying pan down on the countertop or someone propped a lit cigarette on the edge? Now what? Time to give up cooking or smoking? Eventually you will have to give up the countertop because burned laminate can't be repaired. Laminate can handle some heat, but prolonged heat of 140 degrees or more can cause it to come unglued or even burn the laminate itself. In the meantime, put a trivet or something decorative over the burned area.

Removing a Countertop

DIFFICULTY: 3
TOOLS YOU MAY NEED: Adjustable wrench, screwdriver or drill with a Phillips/or slotted bit, utility knife, pry bar, (rubber) hammer, safety glasses

Whatever their type, most countertops are installed in much the same manner, so the removal will require similar steps. Ceramic tile or concrete are the exceptions. Before installing a new countertop, you obviously have to remove the old one. To do so:

Step 1: First turn off the water to the sink at the shutoff valve. See "Sink Removal" in the "Plumbing" section.

Step 2: Disconnect the sink's water supply tubes at the shutoff valves with an adjustable wrench.

Step 3: Remove the screws under the sink that hold the sink to the countertop.

Step 4: Remove any screws or brackets holding down the countertop to the base cabinets. These are usually found underneath in the corner.

Step 5: If the countertop has been joined or mitered together with another countertop, unscrew the bolts that connect them.

Step 6: Using a utility knife, cut the caulk around the edge of the countertop and the backsplash. You're breaking its seal so it won't peel off any drywall or fight you in any way.

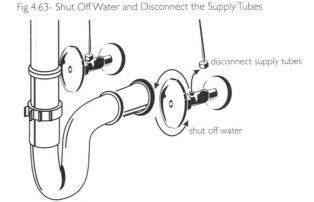

Fig 4.63- Shut Off Water and Disconnect the Supply Tubes

disconnect supply tubes

shut off water

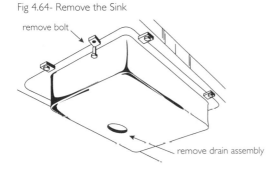

Fig 4.64- Remove the Sink

remove bolt

remove drain assembly

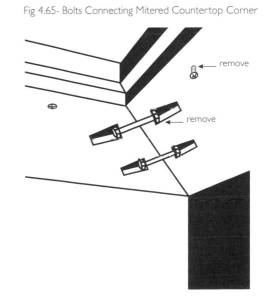

Fig 4.65- Bolts Connecting Mitered Countertop Corner

remove

remove

Fig 4.66- Cut the Caulk at the Backsplash

Fig 4.67- Pry up the Countertop

prybar→   shim

Safety First: Those safety glasses are on your head, right? Well put them over your eyes when you're demolishing things like tile. Chips are dangerous projectiles!

Step 7: Pry up the countertop with a flat prybar. I usually hit the countertop from underneath with a rubber hammer a couple times to give me room for the prybar so I don't mar the base cabinet while trying to wedge the prybar in there.

REMOVING A CERAMIC TILE COUNTERTOP
DIFFICULTY: 2+

TOOLS YOU MAY NEED: Hammer and cold chisel

Trick of the Trade:
A shim (a thin piece of wedged wood) under the prybar protects the surface from damage while you're working.

If you're removing a ceramic tile countertop, you may find that the countertop has been fastened from the top down instead of bottom up. Bottom up is the way we install things when we don't want the screw heads to be seen. If the countertop has been screwed from the top down and the tiles have been laid over the heads of the screws, chip off the tile with a cold chisel to expose the screws and unscrew the top from the base cabinets.

REMOVING A CEMENT COUNTERTOP
DIFFICULTY: 3+

TOOLS YOU MAY NEED: Sledgehammer, wet saw (a type of circular saw with a masonry cutting blade that uses water)

Fig 4.68- Removing a Ceramic Tile Countertop

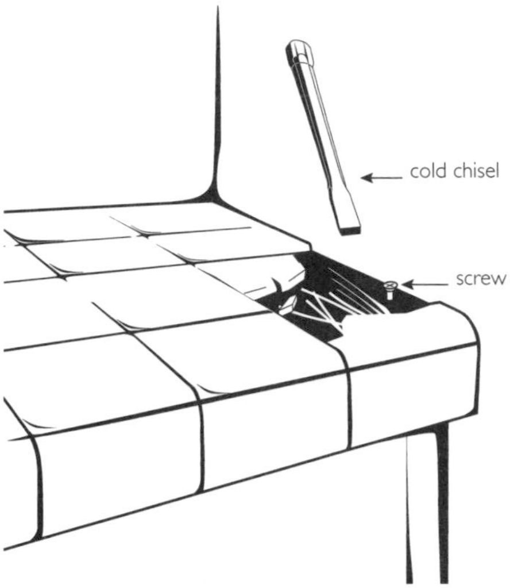

cold chisel

screw

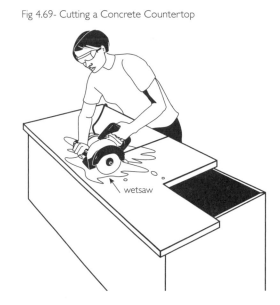

Fig 4.69- Cutting a Concrete Countertop

wetsaw

If you are removing a cement countertop (a fairly popular material these days), you may want to break it into pieces, because it might be too heavy to handle otherwise. If you have no need to protect the cabinets below, you can use a sledgehammer to break it into pieces. Or you can rent a masonry wet saw to cut through the concrete. (Do this project in lieu of this week's gym workout!)

Installing a Laminate Countertop

DIFFICULTY: 3+

TOOLS YOU MAY NEED: Measuring tape, drill, ⅜" to 12" drill bit, jigsaw (down-cutting blade preferred), fine metal file or 100-grit sandpaper, compass, hot iron, block plane or rasp

MATERIALS YOU MAY NEED: Contact cement, brush, masking tape, wood glue, kitchen caulk (silicone), and caulking gun If needed, masking tape

Measuring your countertop space: If you are going to make the countertop the same size as the one you just removed, you can use the old one as a template for measurement. Otherwise, take the measurements for the planned countertop area, keeping in mind whether or not it will be extending over your base cabinets. If so, add up to 1" on the front and possibly the side. (Measure it flush if it is meant to meet a refrigerator or stove.) If you have an "L" countertop, ask the company that will manufacture your new countertop to make the 45° cut and to mortise (cut a cavity in the bottom of the countertop) underneath to accommodate the clamps that will keep it together. (see figure 4.65)

Note: If the countertop is ready made—in the trade that's called a post-form—the backsplash will be molded right into the countertop. You can buy post-forms at your lumber store or home center in different widths and lengths. If it is custom made, you will be able to choose different kinds of edging and backsplashes. You can also make your own countertop (see "Making Your Own Laminate Countertop" [page 153]). First you will need to take the measurements.

Fig 4.70- Cut Out Area for Sink or Cooktop

jigsaw

Marking the dimensions of the sink: Keep in mind that you need to cut a hole smaller than the sink itself—usually about ⅜" to ½" less all around—otherwise, the sink would drop right through . . . d'oh! You'll be more exact if you mark from above, keeping in mind that you need space between the sink and the backsplash. If you're installing a new sink, use the template or pattern that comes with the sink. Mark the cutting line according to the manufacturer's specifications.

Cutting the sink or cooktop: With a ⅜" or ½" drill bit in your drill, make ⅜" to ½" holes in the corners of your countertop large enough to insert the blade of the jigsaw. This will help you turn the corners when you are cutting with the jigsaw. If you are cutting from the face of the countertop, be sure to use a down-cutting blade in your jigsaw. A down-cutting blade will not chip the laminate. Use the same procedure if you're cutting out space for a cooktop.

Gluing the filler piece: Ready-made countertops are sold in 3' to 12' lengths. Manufacturers leave off the end or filler piece of laminate so the homeowner can cut the countertop to the kitchen specifications. If the ends of your countertop on each side do not meet the wall, the edge will be raw and will need a filler piece.

The filler piece is the piece of wood used to "fill in" the space on the edge, creating a lip. A piece of laminate end cap on top of that will give the edge a finished look. Don't worry, the home store or lumber store that sells the ready-made countertop will also sell the filler piece and edge laminate that matches the profile of the countertop.

Use wood glue to attach the filler piece to the end of the countertop, and clamp into place. To secure the filler piece to the countertop, use a few flat-head Phillips screws, but be sure the screws are shorter than the countertop thickness! Wipe off any excess wood glue.

Fig 4.71- Glue the Filler Piece

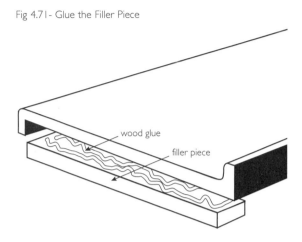

wood glue

filler piece

Attaching the end cap: If the laminate end cap is prefabricated with adhesive, set the laminate end cap in place and slowly move a hot iron above it to activate the glue. I always use a piece of paper towel in between the iron and the laminate end cap. If it did not come prefabricated, brush contact cement onto the end of the countertop and the back of the laminate end cap with a small paint brush or small paint roller. When both sides are dry, press into place.

Smoothing edges: The edge of laminate can be as sharp as a knife. To give a smooth edge, use a fine metal file held

Trick of the Trade:

Protect your new laminate with masking tape so the foot of the jigsaw doesn't mark your countertop. You can also tape the foot (bottom) of the jigsaw with masking tape to protect the surface you are cutting on.

Fig 4.72- Attach the Endcap

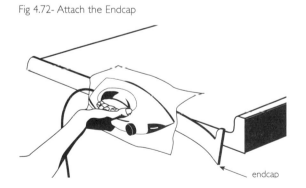

endcap

Fig 4.73- File Laminate Edges

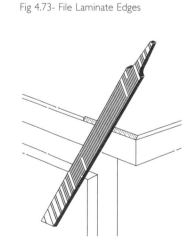

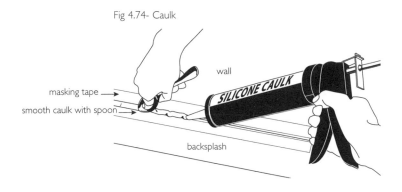

Fig 4.74- Caulk

wall

masking tape

SILICONE CAULK

smooth caulk with spoon

backsplash

at an angle. If you don't have a file, you can use 100-grit sandpaper—just wrap it around a block of wood and keep an angle to the edge when sanding it in long, even strokes.

Caulking: Silicone caulk is used to fill behind the backsplash, to hide any gaps and also, to keep water from getting behind and under the countertop. Caulk comes in a squeezable tube or a tube that fits into a caulking gun.

Trick of the Trade:

To help move the countertop in place, you may need to use a little persuasion. A rubber hammer is great, but so is a rubber-handled hammer, because the rubber handle itself can be used as a tool, if you think about it. Whatever works!

Can I Paint My Countertop?

DIFFICULTY: 2

TOOLS YOU MAY NEED: Rubber gloves, foam brushes or spray gun with compressor

MATERIALS YOU MAY NEED: Bonding primer, acrylic enamel paint, possibly 120- or 140-grit sandpaper, and TSP or ESP

As a host on *Talk2DIY* on the DIY Network, our number one question was "Can I paint my kitchen laminate countertop?" The answer *(drumroll):* yes you can, but why would you want to? You want to save money right? Of course, we all do. You can paint your laminate countertop, but eventually, you will want to replace it. A paint job on a countertop that gets a lot of use will not hold up as long as the laminate underneath because the paint is just a thin layer. For those of you set on this repair, here are the steps:

Preparing the surface: Put on rubber gloves to protect your hands, and wear safety glasses. Use a good degreaser and cleanser like TSP (tri-sodium phosphate) or ESP (Easy Surface Prep). If you want to use TSP, then I would suggest using a 120-grit piece of sandpaper lightly over the laminate countertop. This gives your countertop some "tooth" so the primer can attach itself. Then wipe it down with TSP, removing all dust, grease, and dirt. If you use ESP, all you need to do is wipe the countertop with the ESP, wait five minutes, and then wipe it off. ESP assures adhesion to glossy surfaces and eliminates the sanding process. If you have a greasy or waxy surface, soak some steel wool with ESP and scrub first, then wipe off. With TSP, once you remove it, you can prime over it; ESP needs a 2-hour wait after removing it from the surface before priming.

Priming the surface: It's important to use a bonding primer for this project. You can spread your primer or paint in three ways: sprayer, roller, or bristle brush or foam brush. I would either use either a sprayer or a foam brush to paint on the primer. You want to be sure the surface is as smooth as possible because you don't want lines from a paint brush or the roughness from a roller. With 140-grit sandpaper, lightly go over the countertop and take down any high spots from your foam brush if you have any. Go over the countertop well with a damp rag and remove *all* the dust.

Painting the surface: You will need paint with a very hard finish for your countertop. I would definitely use acrylic epoxy paint. We used the Insl-xc epoxy paint on *Talk2DIY*, and that worked very well. Insl-xc makes a two-part epoxy that is very strong. See what brands your paint store has for such a project. If you have a compressor, you can hook a spray gun to it, is ideal for this project. You can also buy a little aerosol canister that screws over a glass jar. The paint comes up through the canister, allowing the paint to be sprayed. If you don't want to spray it, I would suggest using the disposable foam brushes. Be sure you protect your floors and cabinets with drop cloths, and protect your walls if you're using a sprayer.

Making Your Own Laminate Countertop

DIFFICULTY: 4
TOOLS YOU MAY NEED: Measuring tape, table saw, laminate cutter, router with laminate trim blade, fine metal file (see Chapter 1)
MATERIALS YOU MAY NEED: ¾" particle board or plywood, laminate, contact cement, paint brush or roller, furring strips or dowels, 100- or 120-grit sandpaper

First you must determine what material you will use to make your countertop form. Your choices are particle board, plywood, or MDF (medium density fiberboard). Laminate is most commonly glued to ¾" particle board, which is cheaper than plywood.

If It Were My House:

I find that if particleboard is exposed to moisture, it will break down easily into what looks like oatmeal. Plywood will not. It may separate from itself, because it is glued in layers, but it won't break down easily. Plywood can be purchased with "one side, two sides, or no sides good." A "good" side has a smooth surface without holes or knots. Both sides good is the most expensive, of course. If it were my house, I'd use birch plywood, with at least one side good.

Fig 4.75- Make the Form

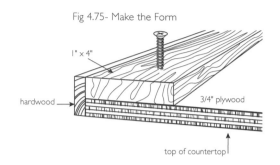

1" × 4"

hardwood

3/4" plywood

top of countertop

Making the form: Cut your form from plywood or particle board to the size you need. See "Measuring Your Countertop." (page 149) Now attach a lip or a buildup flush to the outer edge underneath and down the middle to help support the countertop. Your buildup can be made out of 1" × 4" pieces of pine. Attach this with 1¼" wood screws and wood glue. The countertop will then appear to be 1½" thick, which will give you a nicer look. I would also attach a 1½" hardwood edge made of poplar to the front edge of this form. This gives you a flat surface when laminating your front edge piece. Account for this hardwood edge when calculating your countertop's measurements.

Fig 4.76- Cut the Laminate

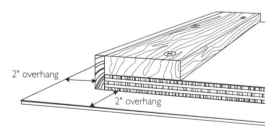

2" overhang

2" overhang

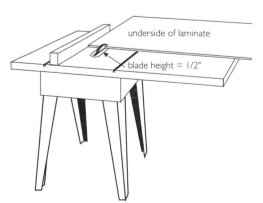

underside of laminate

blade height = 1/2"

Cutting the laminate: Always cut your laminate at least 4" longer on the length and width so it will overextend 2" all around when positioned. This will give you room to situate the laminate on your countertop form. Use a table saw to cut the laminate and make the edging strips. Set your table saw so that only ½" of the sharp blade is sticking up from the table. Cut your laminate upside down, with the good side facing down so it doesn't chip. You can also use a laminate cutter, but I have had trouble using these and prefer the table saw. Also, be sure to cut your edge pieces while you're at the table saw. You can cut your edge pieces at 2" or at least 1¾" to cover the 1½" thickness of the countertop.

Fig 4.77- Press the Laminate to the Form

Gluing the laminate: When you have your measurements (see page 154), you are ready to glue on your laminate. The glue to use is contact cement, which you spread on by brush or paint roller on both surfaces, the back of the laminate, and the countertop. *Always be sure you do this project in a well-ventilated area.* Once the glue is dry, the surfaces are ready to be stuck together. In this case, the countertop and laminate will stick together only when the glue is dry. Be sure you don't try to put them together when they're still tacky.

Before pressing the laminate to the form, put six to ten long dowels or furring strips on top of your form. This will allow both sides to dry without sticking, and they will help you position the laminate over the base countertop. Once the laminate is in place, take out the center dowel or strip and press the laminate down. Keep removing the dowels or strips and pressing down, working from the middle of the countertop outward, like pie dough, one side at a time. You can use an actual rolling pin or a block of wood to press the laminate, always working from the middle out, making sure you don't get an air pocket caught in the middle with no way to escape.

Gluing the side laminate: Before you cut off the excess, be sure you cement glue the side pieces in place. That way, when you rout the top, you won't see the brown edge of the laminate from above. Again, be sure the contact cement is dry on both sides of your form and the edge laminate before pressing them together.

Fig 4.78- Glue the Side Laminate

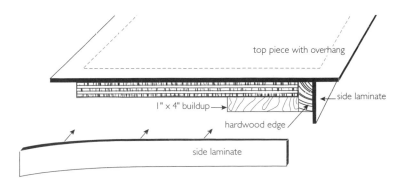

top piece with overhang

side laminate

1" x 4" buildup

hardwood edge

side laminate

Fig 4.79- Cut the Excess Laminate

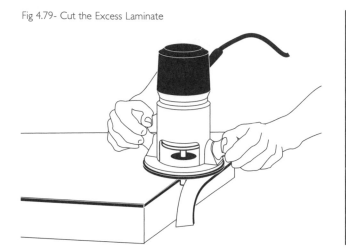

Fig 4.80- Scribe to the Wall

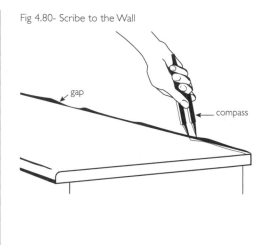

gap

compass

Tip: Be sure your countertop is sitting on sawhorses or a table supporting the middle. You don't want the weight of the countertop on the side laminate before it is trimmed off.

Safety First: An unfiled edge can cut you like a razor. Remember to file the edge at a slight angle.

Cutting the excess laminate: To cut off the excess, you will need to use a router with a laminate trim blade. Trim the excess laminate with the router by moving it counter-clockwise around the countertop. I have also been known to use a block plane to trim this. This is time-consuming and you must feel comfortable using a block plane.

Scribing to the wall: This is most definitely the hardest part. Most walls are not flat, but will have a wave to them from the taping of the drywall joints. If one end of the counter is in-tended to be flush against such a wall, you will need to *scribe* (to mark a profile line) to the wall. If you are not going to in-stall a backsplash, you will need to scribe the back of the countertop. Run a compass point along the wall to determine the extent of the bulge and then transpose the profile of the wall onto the countertop with the pencil side of the compass. This will tell you the amount you will need to cut to make your countertop come in tight to your wall. Place a piece of masking tape on your countertop so you will have a surface on which to mark a visible pencil line. Then cut that line by using a jigsaw. After cutting, use a block plane or rasp (see Chapter 1) to shave the countertop to the line neatly. If using a rasp, always stroke down, never up, or you may chip the laminate. Then remove the tape.

Securing the countertop: From underneath the countertop, screw through the corners of the base cabinets, securing the countertop to them. If a portion of your countertop is not over a base cabinet, then fasten a cleat to the wall. A cleat is a piece of wood that is fastened to the wall to give the countertop support underneath it. Then you can screw up through the cleat into the countertop to be sure the countertop stays put. I recommend doing this in a couple areas of your countertop to be sure that, with the shifting of your home, the countertop will stay flush to the wall.

Caulking the perimeter of your countertop: Even if your countertop has a backsplash, you will still need to caulk between the countertop and the wall to be sure no water gets behind and underneath the countertop, causing lots of damage. Be sure to use a silicone caulk for this.

To make a smooth and perfect caulk line, apply painter's tape to both sides of the crack, ⅛" away from the edge on the countertop and ⅛" away on the wall. Apply the caulk, and smooth it with your finger. Pull up the tape, and you will have a smooth caulk line.

Note: *Be sure the screw isn't too long, or it will go through the countertop. And you will go through the roof!*

Fig 4.81- Secure the Countertop

Backsplash

Now that you made a countertop, a backsplash is easy. You can make this out of a straight 1×4 following the same process as the countertop. If you'd like to mix things up a bit, try putting ceramic tile along the wall as a backsplash!

Ceramic Tile Countertops

I made a ceramic countertop once and loved it. Ceramic tile comes in so many different colors and patterns. I would advise against high-gloss tiles because they can dull easily and get scratches from knives. If you want to make your own ceramic tile countertop, then follow the steps above for making the form for a laminate countertop with one exception. Make sure you use ¾" *plywood* (not OSB, particle board, or MDF) and ¼" Hardibacker® board on top of the plywood, which will give your countertop a strong surface for the tile. Now, glue on ceramic tile being careful to measure your tile accordingly. Keep in mind that the edge of the tile or bull nose will need to extend over the side tile. Use a grout that won't show stains—possibly one that is darker than the color of the tile. After grouting the tile, be sure you seal the grout after it has cured.

The problems with ceramic tile countertops are usually the grout or a cracked tile.

REPLACING GROUT

DIFFICULTY: 2+

TOOLS YOU MAY NEED: Putty knife or grout removal tool or rotary saw with attachment, grout float, sponge, safety glasses

MATERIALS YOU MAY NEED: Grout

Many people who make ceramic tile countertops forget to seal the grout. That's because some grout takes a few weeks to cure before it can be sealed. However, sealing the grout is very important! Because this is the kitchen, your countertop may be exposed to raw chicken, beef, pork, and a sundry of vegetables. Therefore, you need to constantly keep the countertop clean, as the grout is a great place for germs and bacteria to settle, along with mold and mildew. Anyone with a ceramic tile countertop needs to be extra diligent about keeping the tiles and the grout clean with a cleaner that kills germs and bacteria.

Removing grout: If your grout is cracking or breaking down, you will need to remove it and regrout it. Oftentimes, the grout will be good in most areas and bad in a small area. Remove grout with a grout removal tool, a grout removal attachment on your rotary saw, or a putty knife. I have used all three of these, and they all work fine. Try a putty knife and see if the grout comes out easily. Be sure you protect your eyes with safety glasses.

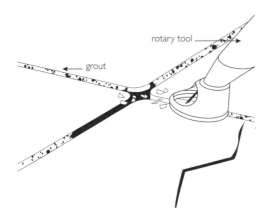

Fig 4.82- Removing the Grout

rotary tool

grout

Regrouting the tile: After you've removed the grout, wipe the tiles dry and mix up new grout to match the existing grout according to the manufacturer's instructions. You can also buy stains for grout. Pour the grout over the area, and work it into the cracks with the float. Smush the grout at an angle into the cracks, and wipe away the excess. Using a big sponge, smooth the grout and wipe away the excess. You will be left with a light haze on your tile that you can wipe away with a dry cloth. Follow the grout manufacturer's instructions allowing for the proper time to cure and then seal.

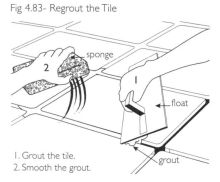

Fig 4.83- Regrout the Tile

sponge

float

grout

1. Grout the tile.
2. Smooth the grout.

REPLACING A BROKEN TILE
DIFFICULTY: 3

If you have the dropsies in the kitchen like I do, then you may have to replace a broken tile on your ceramic countertop. Just like you would replace a tile in your bathroom, you need to break up this tile and remove it. With your safety glasses on, I suggest removing the grout around the tile (see "Removing Grout" page 158) with a putty knife or grout removal tool. Now you can break the tile by using a hammer to smash it in the middle. You'll be glad you have on safety glasses, because the pieces of tile can go all over. After you take out the tile, use your putty knife to remove any grout or glue that may prevent the new tile from going neatly into place. Butter the back of the tile with tile adhesive, and tap it into place with your fist or the rubber handle of your hammer. Allow the adhesive to dry according to the manufacturer's instructions, then grout the tile (see "Regrouting the Tile" page 158).

Stone Countertops

Natural stone countertops have become quite popular. Though much pricier than other countertops, they can withstand time and never go out of style. The biggest drawback is the limit of color and lack of selection because you can only have the colors and patterns that Mother Nature produces. Always make sure your floor can handle the weight of a stone countertop.

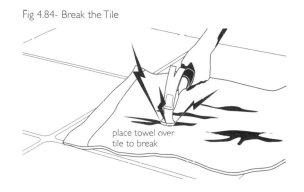

Fig 4.84- Break the Tile

place towel over tile to break

Granite: This is a high-end countertop, and the cost varies depending on thickness, quality, and type. Granite rewards you with years of use and is easy to clean, resists sharp knives, endures the heat of hot pots, handles water well, resists most stains, and is great for rolling out dough. It does need to be sealed periodically—about twice a year—to keep oils from staining it. Sealing requires a rag, the sealant, and very little time. You can get a granite sealer at your hardware store or home center.

Marble: Marble's qualities are similar to granite, but marble can stain more easily. It is important to use products specifically designed for marble, such as marble cleaner, marble sealer, and marble polish.

If you have scratches on your marble surface, try using a polishing powder that you can get from a monument or marble dealer. Sprinkle the powder over the scratched area of the marble, and, using a damp, semi-hard felt pad wrapped around a wood block, rub back and forth. After the stone is polished to your liking, spray it with a marble sealer.

CRACKED OR BROKEN CORNERS
DIFFICULTY: 4

I can tell you how to do this fix, although if it were my house, I'd hire a professional. But for those of you who want to try this, here goes.

First, rub the broken corner or crack with acetone to remove the dirt and grease from the edges (obviously, you must have the broken corner piece to do this). Buy marble repair cement from a marble dealer, or you can use an ordinary epoxy adhesive. Using a small paintbrush, cover both sides of the crack or the edge of the break and the edge of the corner that broke off. Press the edges together for the amount of time the adhesive manufacturer specifies. You can clamp it if you can get a clamp in that area. Wipe away any excess adhesive before it dries.

Filling a hole: Mix some marble dust together with a little polyester resin cement to create a paste. (You can buy marble dust and resin from a marble dealer.) Pour it into the hole and then smooth the surface.

Repairing a broken corner: (In the event you don't have the broken piece.) As when filling a hole, mix marble dust and the polyester resin cement together to make a paste. To create the new corner, you will need to create a wooden mold that will hold this paste in place. Tape two pieces of 1×3s against the edge of the countertop flush with the bottom of the sides of the countertop. Then duct tape a piece of wood or heavy cardboard on the bottom so the paste doesn't fall out of the mold. Line the mold with wax paper so the paste won't stick to the wood. Now fill the area with the paste, and let it dry overnight. Remove the mold and the wax paper. Sand the edges and the top with sandpaper—wet or dry—working down to 400 grit. Then polish.

For those of you who tackle this, I tip my hat to you!

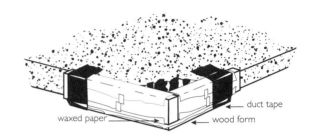

Fig 4.85- Repair a Broken Corner

waxed paper

duct tape

wood form

Solid Surface

DIFFICULTY: 5

Many people are going with solid surface countertops because, not only do they look like stone, but they can be molded to fit any layout and the choices range in color and stone effects. It's also a lot easier to work with, it weighs a lot less than natural stone, it is more resistant to stains than marble, and it is less likely to scratch than laminate. Now here's the rub: if you have a crack, chip, or bad stain, you will need to hire a professional to fix the problem. In most cases, if you look underneath your countertop, you will find the countertop's brand. That is the company that you will need to call. They will have the colors to match your countertop.

Butcher Block

DIFFICULTY: 3

Years ago, I put in a butcher block countertop because I found myself not using the cutting board and cutting on my laminate instead. I love the convenience of cutting on the board, but you have to live with the little slices and scratches that come with this convenience.

Installation of butcher block is similar to putting in a laminate countertop. Cut the block according to your dimensions, and attach cleats to your wall or L-brackets to the cabinet below.

Butcher block requires a periodic mineral-oil bath to help seal the color and luster and keep it from getting brittle. Apply the mineral oil liberally, and allow it to sit for an hour. Wipe off the excess and, with a mild detergent, sponge off the surface. Rinse and wipe dry.

You also need to be careful with food preparation, because the wood can harbor germs and bacteria. If you cut poultry or meat on it, clean it with a disinfectant cleaner, rinse with clean water, and wipe dry. You can use lemon juice to keep it smelling fresh—allow it to sit on the counter for ten to fifteen minutes.

Cement Countertop

DIFFICULTY: 4+

Durable and easily colored to any shade, cement has become a very popular surface for countertops. Most cement countertops have been sealed and need to be waxed once a month with a food-safe wax to build a protective layer and maintain a nice shine. If you have a crack or a chip and want it repaired, I would definitely call a professional who works with cement countertops.

Cabinets

Are your cabinet doors not closing right? Is one door hitting the next? Maybe the margins between the doors are all cockeyed or the door is sagging. Gravity pulls the door away from the cabinet and usually loosens the screws on the top hinge. After a lot of use, and you may get a typical sagging door. The most popular hinges on kitchen cabinets are concealed European hinges, and the fix is really easy—all you need is a Phillips screwdriver.

Tip: If your hinge is beyond help and you need to replace it, take a look at the clip. It should have the manufacturer's name on it. Bring the hinge to your hardware store; chances are good that they will carry a replacement. If not, I would suggest doing a search on the Internet to reorder the hinge.

Door Hinges

DIFFICULTY: 2

Most cabinet doors have snap-on or slide-on clips that snap or slide onto a mounting plate located on the inside of the cabinet. There are usually three adjustments on the hinge.

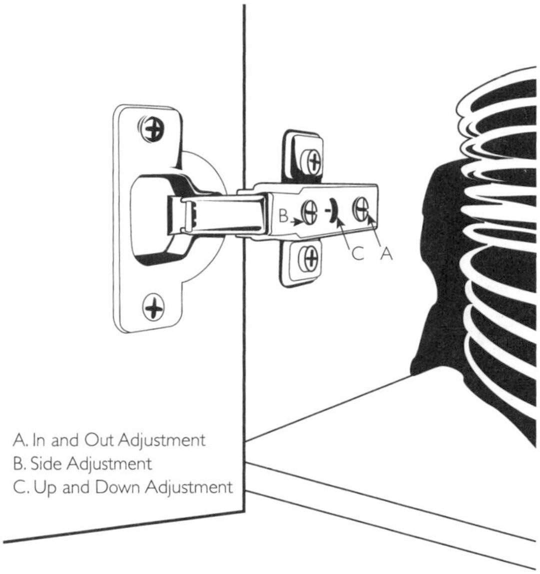

Back screw (screw A) is usually the screw that becomes loose and throws off the alignment, making the door feel like it's going to come down on you. On a slide-on clip hinge, this is the screw that allows you to take off the door and locks the door in place. There will be a groove in the hinge arm/clip that allows for the door to move in or away from the cabinet known as depth adjustment.

Fig 4.86- Cabinet Hinge

A. In and Out Adjustment
B. Side Adjustment
C. Up and Down Adjustment

Front screw (screw B) is the side adjustment for snap-on or slide-on hinge clips. This screw moves the door left or right. It usually works opposite of what you would think. If you turn the screw clockwise, it will bring the door away from the hinge. If you turn it counterclockwise, it will bring the door closer to the hinge side. This is the adjustment to keep the margin of the doors even with each other. Most cabinets are made to have a ⅛" space between the doors when closed.

Vertical screw (screw C) allows for height adjustment. Depending on your hinge, there are different locations of the height adjustment. On some hinges, this screw is found through the slot on the clip itself and allows the clip to move up and down on the base clip. Other hinges have the base plate with a groove for the screws to move up or down.

You will need to adjust both screws on both hinges to move the door up or down.

Cabinet Drawers

DIFFICULTY: 2+

Stuck cabinet drawers drive me nuts! There's nothing worse than trying to get something out of a drawer and feeling like I'm in a wrestling match to pull it open or push it closed. With time, wood can expand with humidity and, therefore, it won't fit into the opening. It used to be that to fix a sticking drawer, you rubbed some paraffin wax or soap on the side of it and it would go in easier. Worse-case scenario would be to use a block plane and shave off the wood on each side. If you have drawers in an older home or farm house, this may apply to you. Newer drawers will probably have metal slides.

WOOD DRAWERS

First, take out the drawer and inspect it. Is the drawer intact? If it's spreading or splitting, see if you can glue it together with clamps. If the drawer is beyond repair, you may need to bring it to a local cabinetry shop to have a new one made to replace it. Many times, they can use the drawer front and reconstruct the rest of the drawer.

Look underneath the drawer. Is there a wooden grooved channel in the middle of the drawer that slides into a wooden monorail in the base cabinet? If so, rub that with some paraffin wax or hard bar soap (I prefer Ivory). If you don't have a channel, the drawer probably fits into the box of the cabinet. This can be rubbed with wax, too. You may need to shave off 1/16" on each side of the drawer with your block plane. Sometimes, you can shave down the opening itself to accommodate the expanded drawer. You'll have to make that call.

METAL SLIDES

For those of you who have the metal pull-out slides, there are fixes for you, too. There are two kinds of slides: side-mounting drawer slides on the side of the drawer and monorail drawer slides underneath the drawer.

SIDE-MOUNTING SLIDES

These consist of four tracks: one on each side of the cabinet and one on each side of the drawer, which keep the drawer aligned properly. The tracks have rollers on which the drawer rides. The most common problems are loose or missing screws. Oftentimes, if the screw is stripped in its hole, you can simply screw through a different hole in the track.

Fig 4.87- Wood Drawer

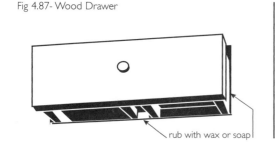

rub with wax or soap

Fig 4.88- Side-Mounting Slide

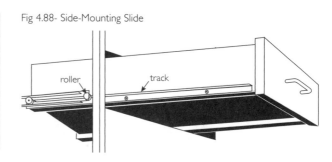

roller   track

If you don't have a choice of holes, you will need to plug up that hole with a wooden dowel. Drill in the hole with a ⅛" bit and then use a ⅛" dowel and wood glue to plug up the hole, cutting off the excess dowel with a chisel. Once dry, screw the track in place.

MONORAIL SLIDES

This consists of usually one track in the middle and a roller in the middle of the bottom of the drawer. Check to make sure all the screws are in and tight.

If you need to replace any of your drawer parts, you should be able to find them at your hardware store or home center.

Cabinet Drawer and Cabinet Pulls

DIFFICULTY: 1

Have you ever gone to pull out a drawer and the drawer stays where it is but the handle comes off in your hand? Over time, handles will loosen. This is always the time that I look at the handles and think. *Hmmm . . . maybe I should change all the handles.* Just by adding new handles to your cabinet doors and drawers, you can transform the look of your kitchen.

Handles and pulls are attached to your cabinet by a machine screw that slides through a hole in the face of your cabinet or drawer. If the machine screw strips and no longer holds, bring your handle/pull to your hardware store and find a replacement screw that fits your handle/pull. Be sure the screw is the same length, too. You don't want the screw to jut out on the inside of your door or drawer.

Also, you want to be sure that the screw slips easily through the hole of the door/drawer. Look at the screw and then find a drill bit that is just a little bigger than the screw. Place the screw right on top of the bit. If you see the outline of the bit past the screw, that is the right size bit.

Trick of the Trade:
Or you can cheat like I do. I take a few toothpicks and wood glue to plug up the hole. The toothpicks are easy to break off. Once the glue dries, you can use the screw in the same hole. Also, you can take the track off and drill another hole for the screw to go in.

Fig 4.89- Monorail Slide

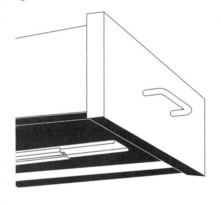

Fig 4.90- Drawer Pull

Can I Paint My Kitchen Cabinets?

DIFFICULTY: 1+

Ding, ding, ding—this is the second-most-asked question on *Talk2DIY* on the DIY Network, after "Can I paint my kitchen countertop?"

Yes, you can paint your cabinets. The trick is to take off the doors, remove the hinges and handles, properly prepare them, and paint them with the right paint. Go back and look at "Can I Paint My Countertop?" to see the steps.

I would suggest using an acrylic epoxy paint or a latex-based enamel. Whatever you choose, follow the directions on the can and lay the paint on thin. It's better to do a couple thin coats than one thick one. You will be painting vertically (up and down), and the paint will have a tendency to succumb to gravity and drip down. Thinner is better! If you get drips, not only will it look awful, but you have just signed up for more work. You will have to sand the drips down after they have dried.

Walls

The walls in your kitchen may be made of drywall, plaster, or cement backer board. On top of one of these, you may have paint, wallpaper, or ceramic tile. If you have a hole in the wall or are in need of a wallpaper, drywall, or plaster wall repair, please see the Interior chapter.

If you have a wall with ceramic tile and you need to repair a tile, please see "Replacing Broken Ceramic Tile" in the "Carpentry" section or in the "Bathroom" section. For those of you who have molding, please see "The Interior" chapter.

Painting

DIFFICULTY: 1

You will want to use paint on your kitchen walls that you can wash and scrub. Think about it: have you ever taken the cake beaters out of the bowl before you turned it off? Those of you who have know what I'm talking about. Batter *all* over the place! Now, if your walls were the flat paint you used in the bedrooms and living room, you would have to wash off the batter and probably touch up the paint.

Types of paint: The common types of paint that can be washed are high-gloss, semi-gloss, satin, and eggshell. Most people need to be able to wash their kitchen walls and keep them safe from water splatter. They also don't want the glare from their kitchen lighting on the walls, so a satin or semi-gloss finish is the most popular. Matte and flat are the same thing and most commonly used in the rest of the house because they have a softer feel and hide poor tape joints. Just recently, I noticed that Benjamin Moore has put out a matte finish that can be washed. As our technology grows, so will our choices in paint finishes. When you go to your paint store or home center, you can see samples of the different finishes. Just be sure the finish you like can be washed once it's painted.

Cleaning before you paint: The kitchen has so many spatters of oils and grease, you'll want to be sure your walls are clean before you paint. Using a degreaser or some TSP (trisodium phosphate), clean the walls well and let them dry. Also, if you have any spots or stains, be sure you use a stain killer and primer over those stains before painting. I've tried cutting corners on those stains, but there's nothing worse than having that stain bleed through your new paint job!

For painting details and techniques, see the "Paint" section in The Interior Chapter (page 41).

Fastening hardware to the wall

DIFFICULTY: 2

To fasten hardware such as paper towel holders, hooks, and other items to your wall, you must first either find the studs with a stud finder or use a wall fastener if the placement of the item doesn't land on a stud. For a more detailed account, see "The Interior" Chapter: Wall Fasteners (page 55).

Hint: Remember, when you slide a stud finder along the wall, it will light up or beep when it comes to the edge of the stud. The middle of the stud is located 3/4" past that point. You want to screw or nail into the middle of the stud.

Fig 4.91 - Finding Studs

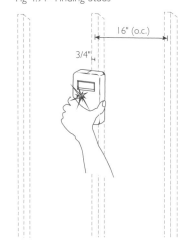

Floors

Because there is so much traffic in the kitchen, the floors take a beating. No matter if you have a cracked ceramic tile, a rip or curl in vinyl tile, or a stain in linoleum, there is a fix. Like most home repairs, we usually weigh out how much the damage bothers us against how difficult it is to fix it. Honestly, most flooring problems can be easily repaired. The hard part is finding the flooring material that matches your existing floor.

The most common types of flooring in a kitchen are sheet vinyl, vinyl tile, linoleum, ceramic tile, and laminate flooring.

Tip: If you install a new floor in your home, do yourself a favor and store at least 9 to 15 square feet of the leftover flooring material in your attic or garage. You will be glad you did if you ever need to make a repair to your floor, because you can match up the floor exactly. Ten years down the road, there's a good chance that your vinyl or ceramic tile will no longer be made.

Sheet Vinyl

Vinyl is a synthetic product made of chlorinated petro-chemicals. The two types of sheet vinyl are sheet vinyl and full spread vinyl. Sheet vinyl needs adhesive on the perimeter of the sheet vinyl and on each side of a seam. Full spread vinyl needs adhesive under the entire area of vinyl and is becoming the least popular vinyl flooring.

Linoleum

When I was growing up in Atlanta, everyone had a linoleum floor and genuine (*gen-you-wine*) Naugahyde® chairs in the kitchen. Linoleum is a term that is misused. Oftentimes, people call vinyl or sheet vinyl flooring "linoleum," but it is not. True linoleum is made of all-natural ingredients—linseed oil, pine resin, and wood flour—and forms sheets on a jute background. Linoleum lasts a long time, although it does need waxing. The colors in linoleum go all the way through, whereas vinyl patterns are printed on the surface only.

PATCHING STAINED OR DAMAGED SHEET VINYL OR LINOLEUM
DIFFICULTY: 3+
TOOLS YOU MAY NEED: Utility knife, framing square, putty knife, roller or rolling pin, clothes iron
MATERIALS YOU MAY NEED: Extra vinyl or linoleum, tin foil, masking tape, floor covering adhesive, seam sealer, mineral spirits, rag, bucket of water or heavy books for weight

Instead of replacing the entire flooring, make a repair patch. This works quite well, especially in low-traffic areas. Go up in your attic or garage and take that piece of vinyl or linoleum flooring that you saved. If you don't have any spare vinyl that matches, you can go to your flooring store and see if they still have your color and pattern. Good luck!

Fig 4.92- Cut Vinyl Patch

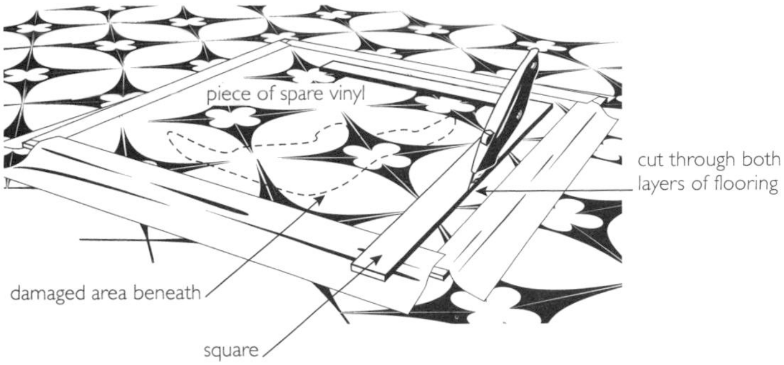

piece of spare vinyl

cut through both layers of flooring

damaged area beneath

square

If the stain is too big and you want new flooring, I would definitely hire out this job. It's definitely worth it! Cutting around the notches in your kitchen is really hard, and it's easy to make a mistake. The pros can do it in about an hour! If your floor is in good shape, they will usually lay the new vinyl or linoleum flooring over the old. My apartment in Manhattan must have at least four layers of flooring.

Start by cutting a patch. Look at the area where your stain or damage is located. Take your spare piece of vinyl or linoleum, and locate an area with the same pattern. Cut a larger square piece than you will be using, which will allow you to move it over the area until you've matched up the pattern. Once you have aligned the patch to meet the pattern, tape it down with masking tape on all four sides. Place your framing square over the area and apply pressure, holding it firmly in place. With a brand-new blade in your utility knife, cut through both the patch and the existing flooring with the blade up against the square. You will probably need to make a couple passes with your blade to cut through both. Now tape the first two sides you just cut so the patch doesn't move, and align your square to cut the other two sides. Remove the tape, and keep a little taped arrow in a direction that you'll remember to put the patch back into place.

I like to make a pencil mark on the framing square so I know where I need to stop cutting. I also like to cut my patch on a line if the flooring has lines. This will hide the patch better.

Now, remove the damaged flooring. Remove the masking tape, holding the new patch in place, and put the patch to the side. Place tin foil over the stained or damaged area and then place a clothes iron on the medium to low setting over the foil, working it back and forth to warm up the glue. With a putty knife, pry up the damaged area and remove any adhesive with the putty knife and mineral spirits on a rag.

Do a dry run with the patch. How does it look? Do you need to remove more adhesive so it sits flush with the rest of the flooring? Trim the patch if necessary. Apply

Fig 4.93- Soften the Damaged Area

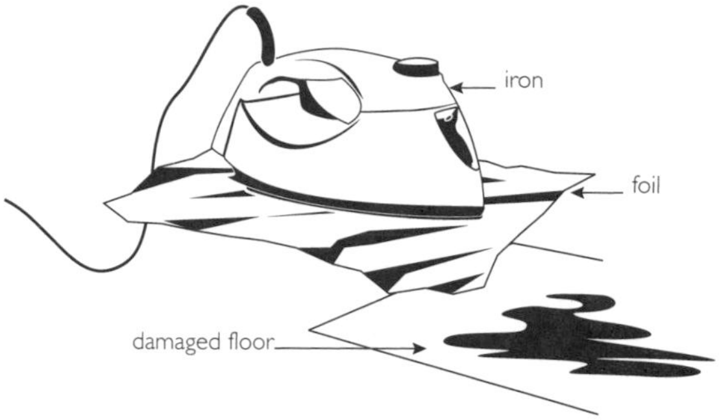

iron

foil

damaged floor

Fig 4.94- Remove the Vinyl Flooring

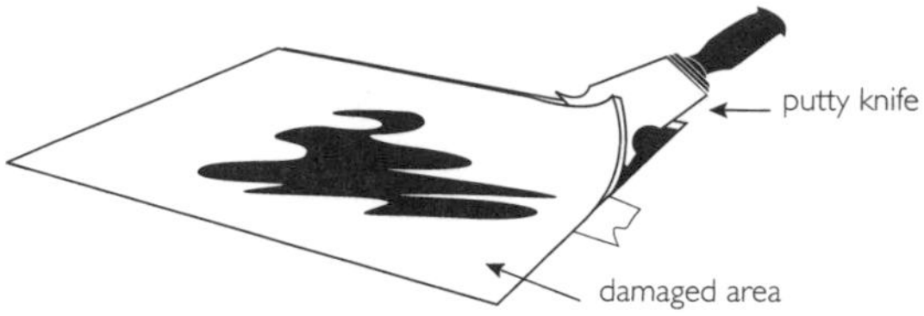

putty knife

damaged area

Fig 4.95- Test Fit the Patch

patch

Fig 4.96- Apply Adhesive

spread glue underneath
existing flooring

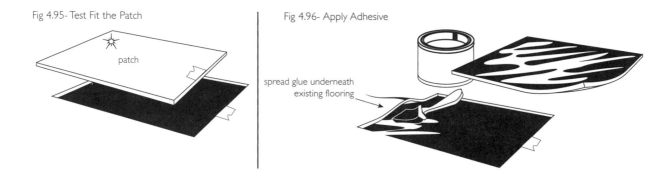

Fig 4.97- Apply Pressure over Patch

wrap rolling pin
with foil

a thin coat of adhesive on the back of the patch, and press it firmly in place. For those of you who have sheet vinyl and no glue under the area that you're making the patch, you will need to add glue under the edge of the square on the existing flooring. Do this by lifting up the area with your putty knife and working some adhesive in with another putty knife. You can use a rolling pin wrapped in tin foil over the area and remove excess glue with mineral spirits on a rag. Use seam sealer around the edges of the patch. Cover the patch with a piece of wood and put a bucket of water or stack of heavy books over it for twenty-four hours or as long as the can of adhesive instructs.

REPAIRING A LUMP/BUBBLE
DIFFICULTY: 3

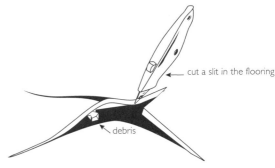

Fig 4.98- Repairing a Lump or Bubble

cut a slit in the flooring

debris

If your flooring was laid with a piece of debris underneath it, you will have a little bump in the flooring, and this may come up through the vinyl or linoleum eventually. This is an easy fix. With a sharp utility knife, make a slit through the flooring big enough to remove the debris. You may need to use mineral spirits to remove old glue. Then dab in some flooring adhesive, use a rolling pin wrapped with tin foil to adhere it to the floor, use seam sealer over the seam, and place a piece of wood over it and a heavy object like a bucket of water on top of that. It may take up to twenty-four hours to dry.

Vinyl tile

There are two types of vinyl tile. One is self-stick, and the other requires a spreadable adhesive on the back. No matter which you have, repairing vinyl tile is fairly easy, because you can take up the damaged tile and replace it with an extra tile that you have tucked away in your attic or garage. You did tuck away some tiles when you laid the floor, yes? If you didn't and you can't find a tile that matches, you can buy a vinyl floor and tile repair kit at your home store or online. These kits have color compounds that you can try to match the color of your tiles.

FLATTEN A CURLED TILE
DIFFICULTY: 2
TOOLS YOU MAY NEED: Putty knife, clothes iron
MATERIALS YOU MAY NEED: Tin foil, floor covering adhesive, mineral spirits, rag, scrap wood, buckets of water

Some tile will curl up on the edges. This is caused by lack of adhesion on the back side of the tile. If you have self-stick tiles, replace the entire tile(s). See "Replace a Damaged Tile."

Start by pulling up the corner. Place a piece of tin foil over the curled area, and

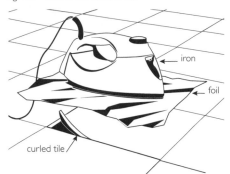

Fig 4.99- Soften the Curled Tile

iron

foil

curled tile

place a clothes iron on a medium setting over it. The tin foil helps protect the color of the vinyl and the bottom of the iron. When the tile becomes flexible, use your putty knife to pull up the corner of the tile. Scrape the adhesive off the back of the tile's corner and the floor underneath it with the putty knife.

Now, apply floor covering adhesive on the back side of the vinyl tile, and press into place. Cover with a scrap piece of wood, and use your body weight to press down. Remove any excess adhesive from the top of the tile with adhesive remover or mineral spirits. Place the scrap piece of wood back over it, and place a bucket of water or two over the area and keep it there until the glue has dried according to the manufacturer's instruction on the adhesive.

REPLACE A DAMAGED TILE

DIFFICULTY: 3

TOOLS YOU MAY NEED: Utility knife, hammer, putty knife, 1/6" notched trowel, framing square, clothes iron

MATERIALS YOU MAY NEED: Tin foil, floor covering adhesive, replacement tile(s), mineral spirits, rag, scrap wood, buckets of water

What's nice about vinyl tile is that you can replace as much of the area that was damaged fairly easily. The hard part is finding the tile that matches your existing tile unless you were smart and kept leftover tile when you laid the floor.

First, you will need to remove the tile. Place a piece of tin foil over the damaged tile(s), and place a clothes iron on a medium setting over the foil until the damaged tile is flexible. The tin foil protects the color of the floor and the iron itself.

You don't want to wedge the putty knife in the edge of the damaged tile if the tile next to it is good. This would damage the edge of the good tile. Instead, work the putty knife into the middle of the damaged tile. You may need more persuasion, so give a few taps on the end of the putty knife with your hammer until you have cut through the tile. Now you can pry the tile up. Don't worry if it comes out in pieces.

Then, remove the old adhesive under the tile. Using an

Tip: If you can't find your pattern or color tile, you can always remove a tile in an inconspicuous place . . . like in a pantry or underneath or behind an appliance.

adhesive remover or mineral spirits on a rag, work it over the old covering adhesive that was under the tile and scrape it off with your putty knife.

When the area is smooth, make a dry run fit with the new tile. Is it too big? If so, you will need to trim it down. Do this with a very sharp blade in your utility knife and a straight edge—something sturdy such as a carpenter's square.

Finally, apply adhesive and replace the tile. Place a piece of tin foil over the new tile, and warm it up with a clothes iron set at medium heat until it is flexible. Apply floor covering adhesive with a 1/16" notched trowel over the area where you will lay the new tile. Drop the tile in place with the pattern corresponding with the rest of the tile, and press it firmly into place. Remove any excess adhesive with mineral spirits on a rag. Place a piece of scrap wood over the tile, and set a bucket or two of water to hold it firmly in place until the glue has dried, following the manufacturer's instructions on the adhesive can.

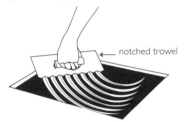

Fig 4.100- Remove the Damaged Tile

Fig 4.101- Apply Adhesive

notched trowel

REPAIR A HOLE IN VINYL TILE

DIFFICULTY: 2

TOOLS YOU MAY NEED: Putty knife

MATERIALS YOU MAY NEED: Epoxy, acrylic paint, masking tape

I've seen vinyl floor and tile repair kits online. These kits have color compounds that you can try to match with the color of your tiles. I think they would be great to fill a hole. You can also do the following:

Start by preparing the area. Remove any debris that may have been trapped in the hole. Wipe dry and use masking tape around the hole so the epoxy mixture only sticks in the hole and doesn't get on your floor.

Buy an epoxy and acrylic paint that would match your tile color at your hardware store. Follow the directions on the epoxy.

Using a putty knife, fill the hole with the epoxy/paint mixture, keeping it flush to the surface of your floor. Allow

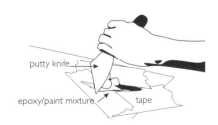

Fig 4.102- Fill the Hole

putty knife

epoxy/paint mixture   tape

the epoxy to dry according to the manufacturer's directions. Remove the tape, and you're good to go!

Ceramic Tiles

Unless you have a mosaic tile floor made of small 1" square pieces of tile, you will most likely have a floor laid with 8 × 8" or 12 × 12" tiles. Well, that's how they describe the tile, but you will notice once you put the measuring tape on the tile, they really are 7⅞" × 7⅞" or 11⅞" × 11⅞". So don't worry, you didn't get the wrong size!

> ### If It Were My House:
> And if I was renovating a room from the joists up, I would use ¾" exterior grade plywood with a ½" Hardibacker® board on top of it as my subfloor.

Oftentimes, kitchen floor tiles will crack because of settling of a house or improper installation. A ceramic floor needs to have the proper substrate. "Substrate" refers to the subfloor—the floor below the ceramic tile.

A good substrate consists of a level concrete floor (it must cure twenty-eight days before tiling), or double-layered exterior grade plywood (¾" + ½" to equal 1¼" combined thickness) with ¼" Hardibacker® board set in a bed of thinset mortar on top of that. Unlike walls, which use a ½" cement board for tiling, floors only need a ¼" cement board providing the substrate below it is strong enough.

You can see that you need a sturdy subfloor for ceramic tile. Anything less and c-r-a-c-k! Let's go back to the house that has settled. A house that settles may cause a crack in the tile. Also, if you drop your bowling ball on a tile, well, chances are good you'll need to do this fix. (Don't you know that bowling is for the living room?)

REPLACING A CERAMIC OR CLAY TILE

DIFFICULTY: 2+

TOOLS YOU MAY NEED: Flat screwdriver, hammer, cold chisel, putty knife, grout saw or rotary saw with cutting wheel, grout float, sponge

MATERIALS YOU MAY NEED: Ceramic tile floor adhesive or thinset mortar, grout, rag, grout and tile sealer

You have extra tile in the attic or basement, I hope? If not, try to find a replacement tile that will match. Now, get on your safety glasses, roll up those sleeves, and let's get started!

Removing grout around the cracked tile: If your tile is loose, you can just pry it up with a flat screwdriver. Otherwise, using a grout saw, work the saw back and forth in the grout around the damaged tile. Another option is to use a rotary tool with a cutting wheel to remove the grout.

Breaking the tile: Place a rag over the tile to prevent the pieces of tile from flying all over, and give the center of the tile a good rap with the hammer. You may have to hit it a few times.

Removing the tile: With a cold chisel or putty knife, remove the tile and dried adhesive underneath it. If your tile was installed with a mortar base, you will definitely need a cold chisel to remove the mortar underneath the tile.

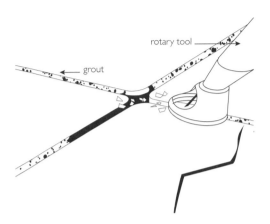

Fig 4.103- Removing the Grout

rotary tool

grout

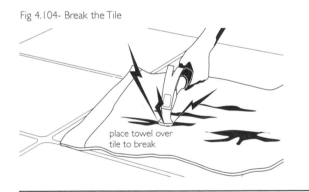

Fig 4.104- Break the Tile

place towel over tile to break

Fig 4.105- Remove the Tile

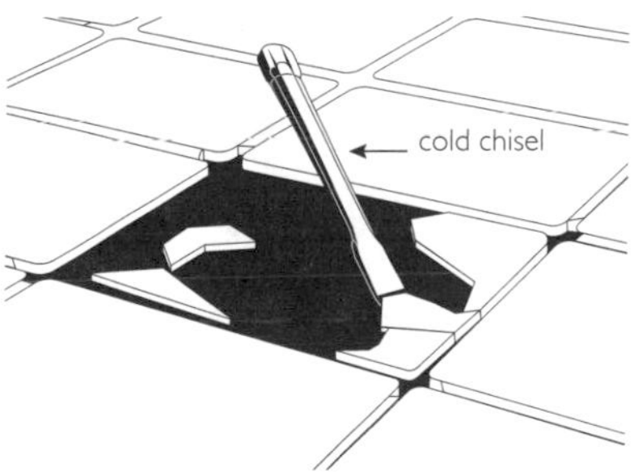

cold chisel

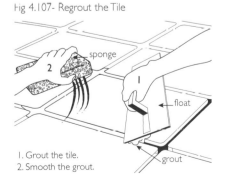

Fig 4.106- Apply Adhesive or Mortar

Fig 4.107- Regrout the Tile

sponge

2

1

float

grout

1. Grout the tile.
2. Smooth the grout.

Applying adhesive or mortar: First drop the tile in for a dry run to be sure the tile lays flush with the surrounding tile. Now take it back out and apply tile adhesive on the back with a putty knife. This is called "back buttering" the tile. If your tile floor is set in a mortar base, you will need to mix up some tile mortar instead of adhesive and spread it into the area and then set in the tile. If you put too much mortar underneath the tile, the tile will not be flush with the tiles around it. In this case, pick up the tile and remove some of the mortar underneath it.

Placing in the tile: Drop the tile into place, and apply pressure. Wipe away any tile adhesive that may squeeze up through the crack with a rag. Check the drying time on the ceramic tile adhesive, and let dry.

Grouting the tile: With a grout float, work the grout into the joints. Using a damp sponge, work the grout in evenly, and let dry.

Sealing grout and tile: Check the manufacturer's instructions on the grout, and let it cure for the specified time and then seal. You may need to seal your tile with tile sealer as well.

Tip: If you're planning on painting the molding, prime and paint before you cut the angles. That way, all you have to do is a little spot touch-up in the corners and at the joints after it's installed. This is a whole lot easier than painting it in place, being careful to not get paint on the floor.

Fig 4.108- Miter Quarter Round

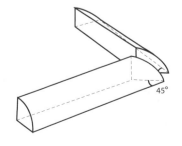

Base Molding

DIFFICULTY: 3+

Sometimes when we repair our flooring on the perimeter of the room, we have to deal with the base molding. Base molding is installed to finish out a room and to hide the gap between the flooring material and the wall.

Quarter round is usually the molding that is installed around the perimeter of a sheet vinyl or linoleum floor. The nice thing about quarter round is that it is so flexible and can follow the contours of a floor. It is also fairly inexpensive to replace when removing it.

To cut quarter round, you need to place it against the back of your miter box or your electric miter saw. At a 45° angle, hold the molding firmly in place, aligning the blade of your hand saw or miter saw against the pencil line of where you need to cut. Cut the quarter round that will meet this angle on a 45° angle from the other direction. You may want to cut a couple pieces to help you remember how to cut the angles.

Electrical

The kitchen has a lot going on in the electrical world. You may have many appliances, clocks, ceiling fans, and lights going at the same time while you're preparing one meal. This section deals with power overloads, as well as installing dimmer switches, under-cabinet lighting, fans, and telephone repairs.

You may be like me—a little wary of working with electricity. For good reason, too! I think it's healthy to have a bit of worry. If we replace worry with respect, it helps put us back in an empowered state of mind. I think of electricity like the ocean—a mighty force you can enjoy, but if you don't play by the rules of the force, it can take you down. Some people like to just wade in the ocean—pick up the phone and get an electrician to do any electrical work. There are those who like to boogie board—your beginner to intermediate do-it-yourselfer and the ones who would tackle the electrical repairs I have in this book. I'd like to think of surfers as your professional electrician. (I think I'm starting to write a philosophy book, so let me change gears and go back to your kitchen.)

If Your Power Goes Off in the Kitchen

Fig 4.109- Circuit Breaker

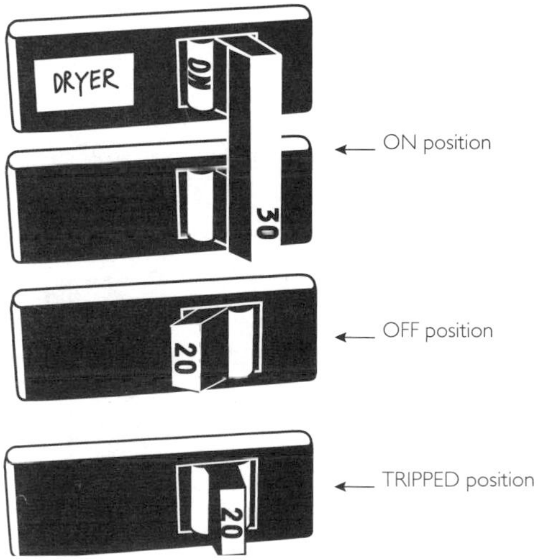

ON position

OFF position

TRIPPED position

First things first, *shut off some of the appliances* you were using. After the electricity goes back on, you don't want that mixer to turn on and fling cake batter all over, do you? Plus, you don't want to keep tripping the breaker or blowing the fuse.

Next, locate the breaker box or fuse box. Refer to the "Electrical" section of "The Interior" chapter.

If you have a fuse box, the fuse that services the kitchen has blown and needs to be replaced by a fuse with the same amperage. If you have a breaker box, then trip the circuit breaker that feeds your kitchen. You will notice the tripped breaker because

Good to Know:
It's always good to have a telephone in your house that is not wireless and is plugged directly into the phone jack for a situation like this. If your power goes out, your phone will still work.

Tip: You can always spray a little WD-40 on the base of the bulb. This will allow you to easily remove it next time you need to replace the bulb.

it is in between the on and off settings. Flip it off first and then flip it on.

If Your Power Goes Off in the Whole House

Refer to the "Electrical" section of "The Interior" chapter. (page 82)

Lightbulbs

A BROKEN LIGHTBULB

DIFFICULTY: 1

TOOLS YOU MAY NEED: Safety glasses, leather gloves, paper bag

MATERIALS YOU MAY NEED: Lightbulb

If you have track lighting, high hats, florescent lights, or a lamp in your kitchen, you may experience a bulb breaking at some point or another. Turn off the breaker or unscrew the fuse to that light fixture. Of course, if it's a lamp, then just unplug it. Put on your safety glasses and some leather gloves, and keep a paper bag close by. Unscrew the broken bulb, toss it in the paper bag, and take it out to your garbage can.

A STUCK METAL LIGHTBULB BASE

DIFFICULTY: 2+

TOOLS YOU MAY NEED: Carrot, needle-nose pliers

MATERIALS YOU MAY NEED: Lightbulb

Fig 4.110- Broken Lightbulb

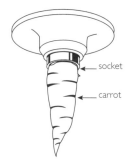

socket

carrot

Sometimes the metal threaded base will expand in the socket from the heat, the glass part of the bulb can twist right out of the metal base and you're left with getting the base out. First, *shut off the power at the breaker box or fuse box.* To remove the base, take a carrot and fit it in the socket. If the carrot doesn't catch and make the base turn, use needle-nose pliers and turn it out of the socket. Once, I had to use two needle-nose pliers to get that thing out of the socket. Once the base is out of the socket, replace with a new lightbulb.

A Flourescent Fixture

Fluorescent bulbs: Some kitchens have overhead fluorescent bulbs. You may also see these in garages and basements. They deliver great light inexpensively. When a bulb starts to flicker or doesn't work at all, see if the problem is the bulb. Take it out by turning the bulb a half-turn. This will align the prongs to drop out of their sockets. Put the bulb in a fixture that is working properly. Be sure the prongs on the end of the bulb are connected properly. If it doesn't turn on, replace with a new bulb. If that doesn't fix the problem, you will need to replace the starter or the ballast.

REPLACE THE STARTER
DIFFICULTY: 1

Older fluorescent fixtures have a small gray metallic cylinder that is plugged into a socket, which is attached to the frame of the fixture. It sends a shot of high-voltage electricity to the gas that lies within the fluorescent lightbulb. This makes the gas ionized so it will conduct electricity. The starter is located under the bulb, and you must remove the bulb to gain access to the starter. If you have a newer fluorescent fixture, you will *not* have a starter and will need to proceed to the next step. Remove the starter by pressing it in and turning it counterclockwise. Take it to your hardware store, and replace with the same type. If that doesn't fix the problem, then replace the ballast.

REPLACE THE BALLAST
DIFFICULTY: 3

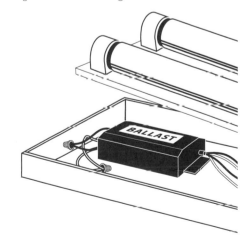

Fig 4.111- Fluorescent Light Ballast

A ballast is a charging device for starting and regulating a fluorescent lightbulb. It "jump-starts" the gas inside the lightbulb to make it glow. If you absolutely *love* your fixture, then replace its ballast; otherwise, buy a new fixture, because a new ballast may be almost as expensive as a new fixture.

To replace a ballast, *turn off the power* to the light fixture. Remove the cover to the light fixture and the bulb.

The ballast looks like a small black box at one end of the fixture. Disconnect the wires to the ballast, and remove any screws or nuts holding the old ballast in place. Take your old ballast to your hardware or electrical supply store, and buy a replacement of the same size and exactly the same wiring. Ballasts are either magnetic or electronic. The magnetic ballast are less expensive but cause that hum from the fixture. An electronic ballast will cost more but won't hum!

Did you remember how the old ballast came out? Put the new ballast back using the nuts and screws to keep it secure.

Finally, connect the wires. The new ballast should have the same color-coded wires as the old, so match wires color to color. Fortunately, most ballasts will either have a wiring diagram on the body of the ballast with the wire colors marked clearly on it or have instructions in the box. With wire strippers, strip the plastic insulation off of each wire about ½". Twist the pair of color-coded wires together, and tighten a wire nut securely over them. Tuck the wires back in the fixture, replace the bulb and cover, and turn the power back on.

Poor Lighting

Call me crazy, but I think it's important to see in a room where you use machinery and knives! I can't stand poor lighting. Wanna know a great fix? Under-cabinet lighting! It's great because it's hidden underneath your cabinets so it doesn't blind you as it lights up your work. You can find an assortment of under-cabinet lighting. You can buy single-light units and multi-light units with halogen bulbs or fluorescent bulbs that either plug into your outlet or can be hard-wired directly in your outlet. Another great choice is the "xeon" lightbulb, which runs cooler. These are installed on the surface or recessed on the underside of the cabinet. This system needs a transformer that converts the 110 volts to 12 volts. You can place the lights where you want. You need to keep in mind that if you have 12 bulbs at 10 watts, the total equals 120 watts, and you will need to get a transformer that is at least 120 watts. You can also put these on dimmers. Be sure to follow the manufacturer's directions, and always shut off your power when working with electricity!

Another choice is to surface-mount flexible rope lighting underneath your cabinets. These come in kits and are very easy to install. You can also buy a dimmer for these.

Replacing or Installing a Dimmer

I love to have my kitchen nice and bright when I'm preparing a dinner and cooking, but once I have things under control, I like to dim the lights and create a mood! A dimmer switch is great for that! Only use dimmers if you have an incandescent bulb. If you have fluorescent lighting, you will not be able to use a conventional dimmer switch. See "Replacing or Installing a Dimmer" in the "Electrical" section in "The Interior" Chapter (page 89).

Installing A GFCI Receptacle

DIFFICULTY: 3
TOOLS YOU MAY NEED: Screwdriver, needle-nose pliers, circuit tester
MATERIALS YOU MAY NEED: GFCI outlet, wire nuts

A GFCI is a ground fault circuit interrupter. In all new construction, a GFCI must be installed if the receptacle is within six feet of a sink in kitchens, baths, and unfinished basements and garages. If you have an older home, it's important to replace your receptacles with a GFCI in those parameters. A GFCI has its own circuit breaker built in the receptacle. So heaven forbid you plug something in the receptacle with soaking wet hands, it will trip the circuit before you get shocked. If there is too much power going through the receptacle, it will also trip the outlet. Ever use a hair dryer that tripped a GFCI? You must push the "reset" button for the receptacle to work again. Replacing an outlet with a GFCI is really easy!

Turn off the power! I like to plug a radio into the receptacle and turn up the volume loud enough so I can hear it shut off when I shut off the power at the breaker or fuse box.

Fig 4.112- Test for Power

It's always a smart move to be sure you turned off the correct breaker or fuse and use a circuit tester. Place one end of the probe of your circuit tester in one slot of the receptacle and the other prong in the other slot. If the power has been shut off, the light will *not* go on.

Now, using your screwdriver, remove the cover plate and remove the two screws holding the receptacle in place. Pull the outlet out of the box.

Fig 4.113- Disconnect the Existing Receptacle

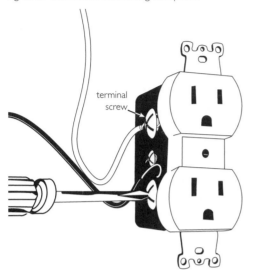

terminal
screw

Then, disconnect the wiring with your screwdriver and release the screws a few turns to allow the wires to slip off the terminals. Remove the old receptacle.

GFCI receptacle at the end of a series of receptacles? This means there are no other receptacles tied into this circuit on the other side of it. When you take out your old receptacle and you see that there are two wires plus a ground wire coming out of the electrical box through one cable, then your receptacle is at the end of a series of receptacles and the connection is easy.

Wiring end-of-the-line receptacle: Look on the back of the new GFCI receptacle. You should see the word *LINE*. The brass screw (terminal) is where the black (hot) wire needs to be screwed. Now do the same with the white (neutral) wire to the silver screw on the other side of *LINE*. Your wires should have ½" of exposed wire on the end. Take your needle-nose pliers to make a little hook, and install the wires in the clockwise connection. Now connect the green ground wires. You will probably have to pigtail a wire to the other green wire or wires out of your electrical box. Screw the ground wire into the green screw terminal on the receptacle and then attach the other green wire(s) in the electrical box securely with a wire nut. Your ground wire may be green coated or bare copper coming out of the electrical box.

GFCI receptacle in the middle of a series of receptacles? When you have two cables coming into your electrical box (top and bottom) with two wires and a ground wire coming out of the top and two wires and a ground wire coming out of the electrical box, the receptacle is in the middle of a series of receptacles. This is when it's good to work with a helper because you need to figure out which two wires (one black, one white) are coming out of the breaker box. To do this, spread the wires apart, not allowing them to touch anything. Try testing the black and white wire coming out of the top part of the electrical box first. Have a helper turn that breaker back on. Now with your circuit tester, test which wires are hot.

Now shut the breaker off again.

Fig 4.114- GFCI: End of the Line

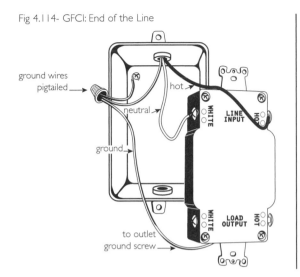

Fig 4.115- GFCI: Middle of the Line

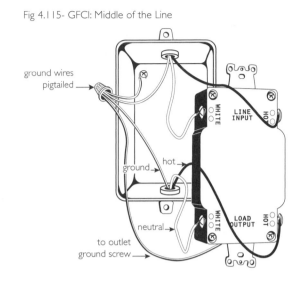

Wiring in the middle of a series of receptacles: These two wires coming from the breaker/fuse box are the two that you will need to attach to the GFCI terminals marked *LINE* (see "Wiring End-of-the-Line Receptacle"). Attach the black (hot) wire to the brass screw/terminal and the white (neutral) wire to the silver screw/terminal next to the word *LINE*. Now attach the other two wires. The black wire will go on the same side of the other black wire but next to the word *LOAD*. Again, attach the black wire to the brass screw/terminal and the white wire to the silver screw/terminal on the other side of *LOAD*. Your wires should have ¾" of exposed wire on the end. Take your needle-nose pliers to make a little hook, and install the wires in the clockwise connection. Screw the ground wire into the green screw terminal on the receptacle and then attach the other green wire(s) in the electrical box securely with a wire nut. Your ground wire may be green coated or bare copper coming out of the electrical box. You may need to pigtail a green ground wire to these other ground wires.

Fig 4.116- Wrap with Electrical Tape

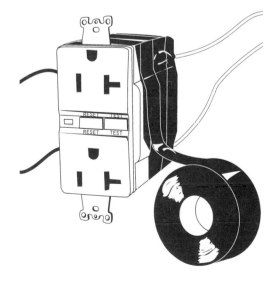

Wrapping with electrical tape: I like to be sure the outlet is well insulated in the electrical box by wrapping electrical tape around the side of the outlet three times.

Screwing the receptacle into place: Push the wires neatly into the box, making sure you don't pinch them when screwing the receptacle in place. Tighten the screws, holding the receptacle in the box, and replace the cover plate. Turn on the electricity, and press the "test" button to be sure it works properly. You should hear a click. Now press "reset," and you're good to go. You can also plug an appliance into the outlet, turn it on, and press "test." The appliance should go off. When you press "reset," it will turn the appliance back on.

The Telephone

I've always had a telephone in the kitchen until recently, when cordless phones seem to have taken care of a phone in every room. I'm going to admit to something I'm a little embarrassed about—my small, 600-square-foot apartment in Manhattan has four phones in it. That's what happens when your dad worked in the phone industry his whole life like mine did!

Out of all the household injuries I've had, I think most of them have happened in the kitchen. That is why I'm a big believer in having a phone in the kitchen. On the upside, I like to kill two birds with one stone (isn't that a brutal metaphor? I'd never kill a bird with a stone!), by catching up with friends or family members while preparing dinner.

STATIC ON THE LINE:

If you are experiencing static on the line, try another phone on that jack. If there's no static on the line when you use a different phone, you will need to investigate the kitchen phone itself. If you still have static, then you may have a cord problem. You can find an extensive explanation in the "Telephone Repair" section of "The Interior" Chapter.

Difficulty Key:

1 Beginner

2 Confident
beginner

3 Intermediate

4 Advanced

5 Professional

Chapter Five

The Bathroom

If something goes wrong in the kitchen, you can always eat out. But if you have only one bathroom and you have a problem with the eh-hem . . . toilet, you can only do the pee-pee dance for so long! That's why plumbers can name their price. And why is it that the toilet only overflows when you have company? Blame it on Uncle Sal!

For those of you who have paid a plumber for a job that took him/her only ten minutes to fix, you probably gave that bill a double-take! Imagine being able to fix the problem yourself and use that $150 for Pilates classes or some new tools instead!

In a room where there is so much water, there is a greater chance for damage and repair than say, your bedroom. This is why the bathroom and kitchen chapters are such hefty chapters. All areas of construction, plumbing, carpentry, and electrical lie within the small area of your bathroom. I will take you through the steps of the most common repairs in a bathroom. You will notice that sometimes you will be referred to the kitchen chapter, because many plumbing, carpentry, and electrical problems are common to both rooms.

Plumbing

Plumbing is so wonderful in the respect that it is so linear, methodical, and logical. Water comes in, and it needs to drain out. Easy, right? Well, in theory, yes. Watch how much damage and chaos can ensue when we have a clog or a leak. Let's start with the toilet.

Fig 5.1 - The Toilet

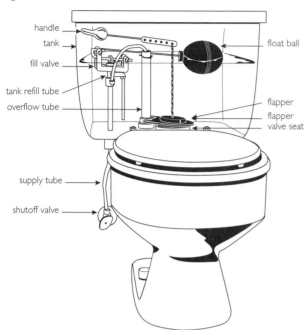

handle
tank
fill valve
tank refill tube
overflow tube
float ball
flapper
flapper valve seat
supply tube
shutoff valve

The Toilet

The john, loo, privy, lavatory, water closet (W.C.) and alas . . . the toilet. Call it what you want, but this plumbing fixture, invented in 1898, has made our lives more comfortable ever since. Although I had heard for years that Thomas Crapper, a plumber in England who held many patents of his own, invented the toilet, according to my research it was actually his employee, Albert Giblin, who got the patent for the Silent Valveless Water Waste Preventer—Patent No. 814. We all thank Mr. Albert Giblin!

Years ago, I was eating lunch with a friend of mine who was telling me that she knew nothing about home improvement and if her toilet started overflowing, she wouldn't know what to do. I know, nothing like having a potty mouth while eating, but I asked her if she knew where her toilet shutoff valve was. She looked at me puzzled, "Shutoff valve?" she said. I then explained to her that if the toilet ever started looking like it was going to overflow, the first thing to do is turn off the shutoff valve. She called me about a year later and told me that this knowledge saved her life! Not really, but it did save her bathroom from flooding, which is pretty good, too. She had since shared the knowledge with many of her friends.

THE SHUTOFF VALVE

The shutoff valve is a small knob that is commonly located on the wall behind the toilet. If you have a hard time turning this valve, try putting a rag around it for a better grip. A little lubricant spray can help you turn the knob if it is still being stubborn. If you have an older home, you may not have a shutoff valve at your toilet. You will need to shut off the water supply at the main valve to the house.

If you have a leak at the valve itself, first try tightening the nut on the valve using your adjustable wrench. If that doesn't fix the problem, you may have to replace the shutoff valve.

Replacing a shutoff valve: See "Installing or Replacing a Shutoff Valve" in the kitchen chapter.

LEFTY LOOSEY, RIGHTY TIGHTEY:
You turn the valve or nut left to unscrew or open the valve and turn right to tighten it.

A RUNNING TOILET
DIFFICULTY: 1 to 3
TOOLS YOU MAY NEED: Screwdriver, adjustable wrench
MATERIALS YOU MAY NEED: Bucket, sponge, chain, flapper, float, ballcock or fill valve assembly, emery cloth or scrub brush

The sound of a running toilet drives me nuts, but what really drives me crazy is throwing away money and not being environmentally conscious. I've read several different statistics on how much water a running toilet wastes, and the highest number was 4,000 gallons. I think the "Niagara Falls" leaky toilet is just a wee bit of an exaggeration, but if you don't fix the leak, you will definitely feel it in your wallet.

A toilet runs because water either leaks in or leaks out. Over time, parts will wear out. The rubber breaks down from the minerals in the water, and different parts made out of copper and even plastic tend to break down from sediment in the water of the tank. Take the lid off the tank and take a look inside.

A Word to the Tired:
If your toilet is running and it's driving you crazy, turn off the water at the valve. This will stop the sound of water running in. If water is running out, you will need to flush the toilet after you shut off the valve. Obviously, you will have to turn the valve back on when you want to use it again.

Water coming in the tank? Is water coming out of the refill tube into the overflow tube? The refill tube is that little rubber hose that goes from the intake or fill valve (on the left) to the overflow tube (in the middle). You may need to unclip the refill tube from the overflow tube to see if water is coming out of it. If it is, your toilet tank is **leaking in**, and you will need to replace the fill valve, (ballcock), or float ball. Seriously! That's what it's called—I couldn't make that up!

Water leaking out of the tank? If the refill tube isn't dispelling water in the overflow tube, your toilet tank is **leaking out**. In this case, you will need to fix either the lift chain or flapper. Easy, right?

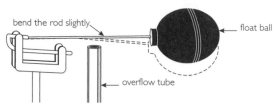

Fig 5.2- Adjust the Float Ball

bend the rod slightly

float ball

overflow tube

THE FLOAT BALL

Before you go and buy a new ballcock or fill valve, try pulling up on the float ball. If it stops the water from running, then you need to adjust the float ball. You can make a slight bend in the arm to keep the ball down lower. This will keep the water at a lower level as well. The water level should be at least a ½" to 1" below the top of your overflow tube.

REPLACING THE BALLCOCK, A.K.A THE FILL VALVE
DIFFICULTY: 2

If you have water coming out of the refill tube into the overflow tube, you will need to replace the ballcock or fill valve (which looks like a tower on the left-hand side of the tank). Recently, I've been hearing the term as "fill valve" or "intake valve" rather than the term I've always heard, "ballcock." Is the FCC monitoring plumbing, too?

Whatever you want to call it, they all do the same thing: control the water coming into the tank.

This is an easy fix! First you will need to *turn off the water supply* at the valve. Then, flush the toilet and let the water drain out of the tank. Remove any excess water with a sponge, and keep the floor dry so you don't slip and fall.

If It Were My House:
I would get a float cup fill valve or a floatless ballcock, which does away with the big, cumbersome float ball.

Now, remove the ballcock or fill valve. With your adjustable wrench, remove the retaining nut holding the water supply tube from the bottom of the tank. With the same wrench, remove the retaining nut to the (fill valve) ballcock or underneath the tank. Ballcock assemblies have the arm attached to the float ball. Keep a bucket below this hole to catch the leftover water draining out. Remove the refill tube from the ballcock or fill valve assembly, and lift it out of the tank. If you have a float ball that you will be reusing, take that off as well.

Replacing the ballcock or fill valve: Whatever type of ballcock or fill valve you buy, you will need to put the tailpiece in through the hole and tighten the retaining nut underneath the tank. If you bought a ballcock assembly with a float ball, screw the float ball on the arm of the ballcock and tighten using your screwdriver with the screw provided. Then align the float arm so it passes just behind the overflow tube. Always follow the directions with your particular assembly.

Adjusting the water level: You will either have a ballcock assembly with a float ball, a float cup that slides up and down on the body of the fill valve, or a floatless fill valve that sits on the bottom of the tank. If you have a float ball, you can bend the arm (see "The Float Ball"); otherwise, you will need to adjust the float cup on the fill valve or the adjustment screw on the floatless fill valve.

Float cup fill valve adjustment: This assembly usually has the ability to twist the entire assembly up or down. If you are removing this kind of fill valve, adjust the replacement valve to the same height. You lengthen it by turning the top to the left and shorten it by turning it to the right. It will come with instructions. You can adjust the float that slides up and down on the fill valve by pinching the spring clip located on the pull rod. I usually adjust the bottom of the float cup to about an inch or more below the top of the overflow tube. (Always follow the manufacturer's directions.) Turn on the water supply at the shutoff valve, and flush the water. See where the water line is after it fills up. You want the water level about ½" to 1" below the overflow tube.

Floatless fill valve: This fill valve does not have a long tower, but rather it sits on the bottom of the tank. The adjustment mechanism on this fill valve is a screw at the bottom of the assembly. With your screwdriver, turn the screw to the left (counterclockwise) to lower the water level, and right (clockwise) to raise the water level. I leave these where the factory set them first and turn the water supply back on. If I need to

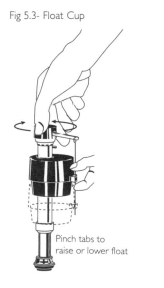

Fig 5.3- Float Cup

Pinch tabs to
raise or lower float

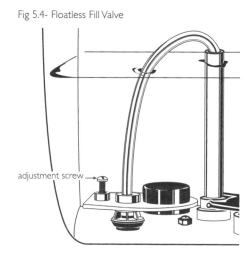

Fig 5.4- Floatless Fill Valve

adjustment screw

make any adjustments to the screw, I do it with the water in the tank. Wipe dry your screwdriver so it doesn't rust!

REPLACING THE CHAIN, FLAPPER, OR TANK BALL
DIFFICULTY: 2

Usually, the problem of water leaking from the tank lies with the chain or the flapper.

The chain: Take a look at the chain. It attaches the arm of the flush handle to the flapper. This lifts the flapper, allowing the water to drain out. Is it gnarled up? Sometimes when we flush the handle hard, the link chain will do a loop-dee-loop, causing a kink in the chain. This, in turn, keeps the flapper lifted just enough for water to continuously leak out of the tank. Simply unravel the kink. If you're replacing a chain, be sure you leave just a little bit of slack on it to allow the flapper to settle over the hole. *(See illustration at the beginning of chapter.)*

The flapper: This is the item most commonly replaced. This little rubber flapper wears out with time. Remember, the toilet gets used a good bit, and this flapper goes up and down a lot. Between the wear and tear and the minerals in your water supply, it will break down the rubber, causing the water to seep in around the flush valve—there's your running water sound. Your flapper may be hooked on the side, or it may slip over the overflow tube. Look at your old flapper and how it is attached. Place it in a resealable bag, bring it to the hardware store, and replace it with the same or a similar flapper. These days you can find a flapper that will fit either configuration. They adjust to suit the hardware on your overflow tube.

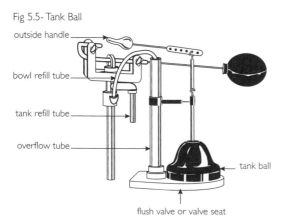

Fig 5.5- Tank Ball

outside handle

bowl refill tube

tank refill tube

overflow tube

tank ball

flush valve or valve seat

The tank ball: Those of you who have a tank ball, it looks like a plunger on a wire. These do the same thing as a flapper. The tank ball screws onto a guide wire and is held on the end of the handle arm by a lift wire. If the tank ball is not directly over the valve seat or flush valve, it will allow the water to seep through. Be sure you align it directly over the valve seat by making adjustments on the guide arm to the tank ball. You can replace these, but honestly, I'd go with the newer flappers if they fit your valve seat. Bring the tank ball to your hardware store and have someone help you. If you need to replace the tank ball with the same kind, screw the new tank ball back on the guide wire and you're done.

CLEANING THE VALVE SEAT
DIFFICULTY: 2

Feel around the hole, also known as the valve seat, flush valve, or ball seat. If you feel it needs to be cleaned, use an emery cloth for a brass valve seat or a scrub brush for a plastic valve seat.

LEAKING UNDERNEATH THE TANK
DIFFICULTY: 3
TOOLS YOU MAY NEED: Adjustable wrench, basin wrench or ratchet wrench, level
MATERIALS YOU MAY NEED: Spud washer, old towels or drop cloth

If you have a leak in between the tank and the toilet, you will need to *shut off the water* either at the valve below the toilet or at the valve at your home's main water supply. Then flush the tank a couple times to remove the water. Be sure this isn't a sweating tank. You will be able to determine this because the water will be beaded up all around the tank. If this is your problem, see "Tank Sweating."

This leak is caused by a broken-down gasket called the spud washer between the tank and toilet at the valve seat. Before you do anything, try tightening the screws holding the tank to the bowl. Don't overtighten them, as you could crack the tank. If the screws were a little loose, see if that fixes the problem. If not, then you will need to repair the gasket. Many of you may opt to call the plumber. I understand, but honestly, this is not a hard fix, so you may want to keep reading.

After you have flushed the water, soak up any remaining water in the tank with a sponge, removing it completely. Always have some old towels around to clean up any water on the floor so you don't slip!

Replacing the spud washer: Using your adjustable wrench, unscrew the water supply tube that hooks up to your intake valve or ballcock. To unscrew the tank from the bowl you will need your adjustable wrench. Behind and under the back of the tank you will see brass tank-mounting bolts. Turn the nuts counterclockwise (left) to unscrew them. You may need to put an adjustable wrench on the nut below the tank

Fig 5.6- Remove the Water Supply Tube

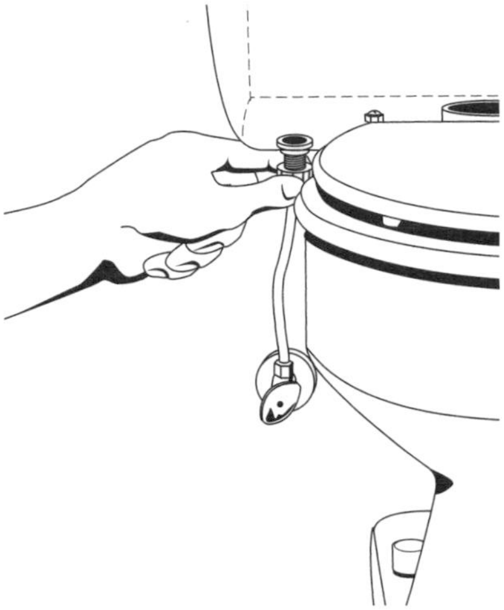

Fig 5.7- Remove the Screws on the Inside of the Tank

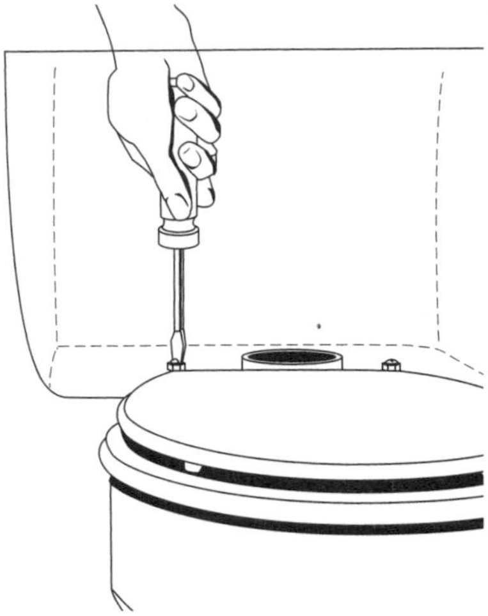

Fig 5.8- Lift off the Tank

Fig 5.9- Replace the Spud Washer

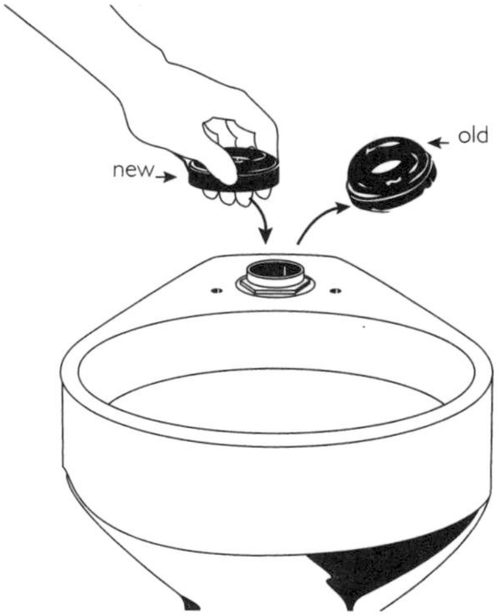

new→   ←old

to keep it from spinning. It's a tight area to move around, so be patient. Remove the screw and lift the tank up and away from the bowl. You may need a helper to lift the tank off the bowl. Turn the tank upside down, and remove the spud washer. Set the new rubber spud washer neatly into the seat valve opening with the beveled side facing out. This cushions the tank on the bowl, sealing the water within.

Securing the tank to the bowl: Set the tank on the bowl. Place the brass bolts down through the corresponding holes, and screw the washer and retaining nut back on each bolt. Hand tighten and then tighten with your adjustable wrench, compressing the spud washer. You may not be able to move your adjustable wrench, so if you have a basin wrench or a ratchet wrench that fits over your nut, use it instead; it will be easier and faster to tighten your retaining nut. Place your level across the top of the tank, and be sure it is level while you are tightening the nuts.

Fig 5.10- Replace the Tank

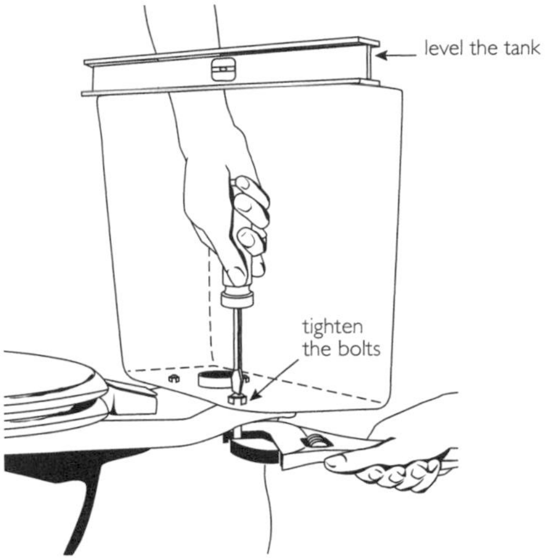

level the tank

tighten the bolts

LEAKING AT THE FOOT OF THE TOILET
If you have water coming out from under your toilet, you will need to lift the toilet off and put a new wax ring beneath it. You want to do this repair as soon as possible, because water can do a lot of damage to your floor and subfloor and, eventually, the ceiling below.

REMOVING OR REPLACING YOUR TOILET BOWL
DIFFICULTY: 3+
TOOLS YOU MAY NEED: Flat-head screwdriver, utility knife, adjustable wrench, hacksaw
MATERIALS YOU MAY NEED: 3-in-1 oil, old towels, wax ring, Johnny bolts, masking tape, silicone caulk

Removing the water supply tube: Shut off the water supply at the valve under the toilet or the main water supply valve, disconnect the supply tube to the tank, and flush the toilet a couple times to remove the water out of the tank. You will also need to use a sponge to soak up the remaining water in the tank. Remember, you will need to turn the tank upside down, so definitely get all the water out.

Removing the nuts: You will notice on your toilet that the nuts holding your toilet bowl to the floor on each side of your toilet are covered by a plastic dome or, in older toilets, ceramic. These are usually stuck on the base of your toilet with double-sided tape, and the covers just snap on. A flat-head screwdriver will help to pry off the caps. They can also be caulked on, so you may need to use your utility knife to cut underneath these domes. When you get them pulled off, use your adjustable wrench to remove the nuts. You may need to drop some penetrating oil, such as 3-in-1 oil, on top of the nuts to help them along. The worst-case scenario I've run into is that the nut gets stuck on the bolt and then spins around with the bolt. If this happens, you will need to cut it off with a hacksaw. Cut the bolt underneath the nut, being careful to not break the toilet. Most of you will not experience this, so don't worry!

Lifting the toilet off the bolts: These bolts are referred to as "Johnny bolts"— makes sense, right? Some toilets are caulked at the bottom where the toilet meets the floor. You may need to cut through the caulk around the base of the toilet with your utility knife. If you have any back issues, it's time to call in that favor from the friend you helped move last year. Toilets are heavy. By slowly rocking it back and forth until it is free from the caulk and wax ring, lift the toilet off the bolts. Place the toilet on old towels or a drop cloth to protect your floor. You will definitely get water on the floor, so have a sponge and towels around to wipe up to avoid any slip and falls.

Safety First: Be sure you stuff a rag in the toilet flange opening to keep those awful sewer gases out of the house, as well as to keep anything from falling into the waste pipe.

Tip: Those of you who have wanted to install a new valve or paint behind the toilet . . . seize the moment now!

Removing the wax ring: The wax ring seals the discharge outlet at the bottom of the toilet to the waste pipe flange. Remove the old wax from the flange on the floor and the bottom of your toilet with a putty knife. A lubricating spray can help work up old wax from the toilet and flange. You can also use a degreaser to clean up the area.

Replacing the wax ring: There are two types of wax rings: a plain wax ring and a wax ring with a plastic funnel sleeve. Both are good, although I prefer the one with the plastic funnel sleeve because it helps prevent water from leaking out even if the seal gets broken. With the toilet on its side or upside down, install the wax ring around the "horn" of the toilet. The horn is the discharge outlet or hole. Set the wax ring with the smooth side facing out or the plastic sleeve facing out, and press it into place enough so it sticks and doesn't drop off while you're setting the toilet into place.

Replacing the flange bolts or Johnny bolts: These bolts are connected to the flange—hence the name flange bolts—but in the trade we call them Johnny bolts. Those of you who think you may want to just reuse the existing Johnny bolts, think again. Seriously, you definitely want to replace these bolts, too. They're very inex-

Fig 5.11- Remove the Nuts

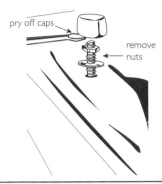

pry off caps

remove nuts

Fig 5.12- Lift off Toilet

Fig 5.13- Remove the Wax Ring

LUBRICATING SPRAY

remove wax ring from the bottom of the toilet

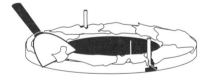

remove wax from the flange

stuff a rag into the flange to block sewer gasses

Fig 5.14- Place the New Wax Ring

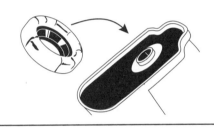

Fig 5.15- Replace the Flange Bolts and Toilet

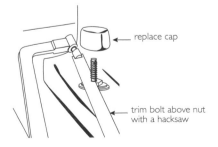

toilet

old flange bolt

new flange bolt

flange

masking tape to guide toilet placement

Fig 5.16- Tighten and Trim Bolts

replace cap

trim bolt above nut with a hacksaw

pensive and will make the next few steps easy. Take the old Johnny bolts off and throw them away. Slide the new Johnny bolts underneath each side of the flange, and slide the plastic keeper over the bolt on top, snugly against the flange. This keeps it in place. The flange needs to be ½" off the floor.

Put a piece of masking tape on the floor on each side of the toilet with an arrow pointing to the middle of the bolt. This will make it much easier to place the toilet properly over the bolts. Trust me—with a heavy toilet in your hands, you don't want to be messin' around!

Setting the toilet in place: Again, get help lifting the toilet. If you have a bad back, then get two people to help and you help guide them over the bolts. This is the hardest part of the job because the bolts stick up and if you don't lift the toilet high enough over the bolts, you may push them over. Gently align the holes in the bottom of the toilet over the Johnny bolts and let it rest on the flange.

Now sit on the toilet. Hey, hey, hey . . . keep your pants on! You just want to distribute equal weight on that wax ring. Gently rock back and forth and side to side until the toilet is touching the floor.

Tightening the nuts on the bolts: Place the metal washer and the plastic washer that holds the cap in place over the bolt. Now place the nut on the bolt and tighten using your adjustable wrench. Tighten a little on one side and then tighten the other side. Do this back and forth until it is even. After all that work, don't be overly aggressive and break the cast-iron flange or the porcelain base.

Cutting off the excess bolt: With your hacksaw, cut off the bolts directly above the nut. If this loosens up the bolt, be sure you tighten it again before sawing it off.

Snapping the caps in place: Snap the plastic caps back in place. If they don't snap down properly, you can always put a dab of caulk underneath the cap.

Caulking the base of the toilet: Apply a bead of silicone caulk between the toilet and floor. It will probably be hard to caulk the back of the toilet, so don't stress it. If you have a leak in the future, you'll want to spot it quickly so it doesn't damage your floor or your subfloor.

TANK SWEATING

DIFFICULTY: 2

TOOLS YOU MAY NEED: Utility knife

MATERIALS YOU MAY NEED: Tank liner

If your tank or toilet is sweating, then don't make it work so hard . . . bah, dum, bum! . . . thank you and don't forget to tip your waiters and flush! Seriously, this is caused by the water in the tank being colder than the air outside. Think of your iced tea glass. Notice how it sweats on the outside of the glass? Well, the same goes for the toilet tank/bowl.

You can pick up a foam rubber liner that will pad the inside of your tank's walls. First, you will have to remove all the water from the tank by turning off the water supply at the valve, flushing a couple times, and then removing the remaining water with a sponge. You will need to let the inside dry so you can glue the liner to the inside walls of the tank. Cut the foam rubber pads with your utility knife and, using the glue that comes with the kit or suggested by the manufacturer, glue the liner to the inside walls, letting it dry according to instructions. Turn the water back on and see if this fixes your problem. If not, I would suggest hiring a plumber to install a tempering valve that will mix some hot water with the cold water when it enters the tank.

THE HANDLE

DIFFICULTY: 2

TOOLS YOU MAY NEED: Adjustable wrench

MATERIALS YOU MAY NEED: Lubricating spray or petroleum jelly

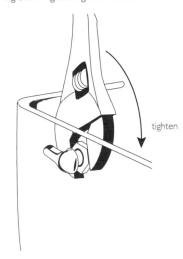

Fig 5.17- Tightening the Handle

tighten

At some point, you may need to replace every part inside your tank. The handle is very easy to replace. If it is sticking, first see if the handle's mounting nut needs to be cleaned. If it does, remove it with an adjustable wrench and use steel wool if it's metal or a scouring pad if it's plastic. For ease of screwing it back into place, dab a little petroleum jelly or lubricating spray on the threads, and tighten into place. This will make you feel a little dyslexic if you're not already, because to tighten the retaining nut, you have to turn it to the left (counterclockwise); to loosen it, you'll need to turn it to the right (clockwise)—just the reverse of how screws and nuts normally fit together.

REPLACING THE TOILET SEAT

DIFFICULTY: 1

TOOLS YOU MAY NEED: Screwdriver, groove-joint pliers

MATERIALS YOU MAY NEED: New toilet seat with mounting bolt hardware, rubber gloves, soft scrub sponge

You've just moved into your home and you want a brand-new toilet seat. Yes? Please say yes! Or maybe your seat is cracked or a bit worn out. Replacing a toilet seat is very easy to do.

Removing the old toilet seat: Drop the lid down on your toilet seat and look behind it. Do you see those little caps? You will need to pry them up with a flat screwdriver. Underneath those caps are usually plastic bolts that have a retaining nut underneath the bowl, holding it down. Place your screwdriver in the head of the bolt and turn counterclockwise to remove the bolt. Oftentimes, this will spin the entire nut and bolt assembly, so you may have to hold the nut below the bowl with some pliers while you unscrew the bolt.

Fig 5.18- Replacing the Toilet Seat

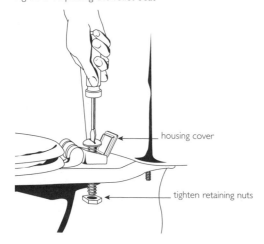

housing cover

tighten retaining nuts

Cleaning the top of the bowl: Put on your rubber gloves, and take a soft scrub sponge and clean the top of the bowl, especially around the holes where the bolts go in. Wipe dry.

Installing your new toilet seat: Your new toilet seat will come with new mounting bolt and nut assembly. Some have a peel-and-stick piece of foam that you will stick on the bottom of the hinged bolt-head housing. Place the toilet seat on the bowl, aligning the holes of the bolt-head housing to the holes on the toilet bowl, and drop your mounting bolts through. Hand tighten the retaining nuts, and eyeball the seat, making sure it sits evenly around your toilet bowl. From above, snug the two bolts with your screwdriver, but not so tight that you risk cracking the bowl. You just want to be sure it doesn't slide around when you have a seat. Close the housing covers over your mounting bolts, and you're done!

A CLOGGED TOILET

DIFFICULTY: 2
TOOLS YOU MAY NEED: Plunger, toilet auger (a.k.a. snake), safety glasses, rubber gloves
MATERIALS YOU MAY NEED: Bucket

Maybe your toilet got a little toy army soldier stuck inside? Or perhaps a visitor decided to flush too much toilet paper down. Whatever the case may be, fixing a clogged toilet is a fix that you will surely want to know about.

Some clogs happen because people have trouble flushing the waste down with enough water and then it keeps getting added to until the pipes get clogged. First, take off the lid of the tank and look inside as you flush the toilet. Watch the flapper or tank ball. If your flapper or tank ball doesn't stay up long enough to give a good flush from the tank, check its chain or wire. Flappers and tank balls needs to have no more than ½" of slack, because if you flush the handle and it barely picks up the flapper, it won't allow enough water to flow out of the tank and into the bowl. If the chain/wire is fine but the flapper or tank ball still closes too fast, you will need to replace with a new flapper. See "Replacing the Chain, Flapper, or Tank Ball." Some toilets are low-flow toilets and have such low water pressure they require a couple flushes before everything goes down the toilet, but it has nothing to do with the flapper.

Call a Pro: If you're having trouble with water flowing down your toilet drain, you may have a vent problem. Pour a bucket of water down your toilet drain. If it causes a normal flush, then the drain vent is probably fine. If you don't get a normal flush, then you probably have an obstruction in your drain vent. You'll need a professional to run a plumber's snake down the vent from your roof.

Plunging your toilet: You definitely want to have a plunger in your bathroom or at least nearby. This is the fix if your toilet is *not* overflowing or rising to the top. Take your plunger and give it ten to fifteen up-and-down pumps. A little bit of water in the bottom of the bowl will help give you a good suction or vacuum. After plunging, pull it away quickly to let it "pop" or dislodge the object. You will probably need to do this several times. Wear safety glass and rubber gloves. Fill a bucket of water and

Fig 5.19- Using a Closet Auger

pour it into the toilet bowl until the bowl clears or until it gets close to overflowing. Keep plunging. Hopefully, this will remove the clog. If not, read on.

Toilet or closet auger: A toilet auger is also called a closet auger. You have most likely heard it referred to as a "snake." This auger has a bent tip to fit in the toilet's built-in trap. This will help catch most paper clogs and pull them up and out of the toilet.

Lifting the bowl off the flange and checking the trap: If you have a little toy, comb, or something of the sort caught in the toilet trap, then you will need to lift the toilet off the flange. This will require you to *turn off the supply valve.* See "Removing or Replacing Your Toilet Bowl." I've had to use a toilet auger up through the bottom of the drain into the toilet to catch something in the toilet's trap. This is also a good time to look into the toilet drain for any objects. If the toilet's trap is clear, the clog is underneath in the drain system.

Obstruction in the drain underneath the toilet: To clear this, you will need an electrically powered snake, so it might be best to pick up the phone and call the plumber.

Word to the Woman of the House:

Especially in older homes, the plumbing has a hard time with tampons. Some tampons can expand, and between that and the toilet paper, your older system might get clogged, especially if the old clay sewer pipes have tree roots growing through. Newer homes don't generally have this problem, but you still might want to be careful and not throw tampons down the toilet. Never put sanitary napkins, kitchen napkins, or paper towels down the toilet, either!

The Bathroom Sink

There are differences in your bathroom sink and your kitchen sink. For instance, you're not going to have a garbage disposal in your bathroom sink. At least I hope not! Your bathroom sink will have an overflow hole in the front and a pop-up stopper, whereas your kitchen sink will not. And although food and grease may cause a lot of clogs in your kitchen, your bathroom sink gets clogged by H-A-I-R!

Fig 5.21- The Bathroom Sink

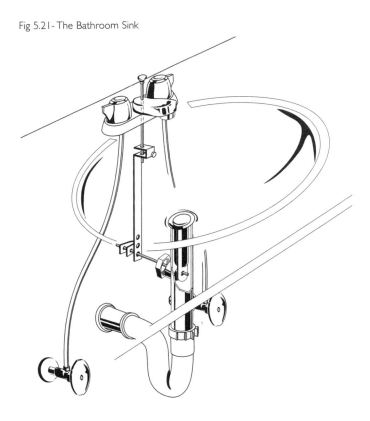

UNCLOGGING A SINK

DIFFICULTY: 2+

TOOLS YOU MAY NEED: Plunger, pipe wrench or groove-joint pliers, drain auger or plumber's snake

MATERIALS YOU MAY NEED: Old rag, petroleum jelly

I think we have all experienced that queasy feeling when pulling up a wad of soapy hair out of a clogged drain. *Br-rrreeeckk!* I tend to brush or comb my hair over the sink because the mirror is usually on the wall over the sink, and, you guessed it, the hair goes into the sink. If I don't have a strainer or my stopper isn't closed to catch it, then down it goes. Enough hair down a drain will create a nest that will eventually create a bigger nest that can clog your drain. Wanna save $80 or more? Then put down that phone to the plumber and unclog your sink yourself.

Where Is Your Home's Sewage Drain Cleanout?

In a house I was renting, I had a toilet that not only got clogged but started to back into the tub. *Yuck!* So I immediately got on the horn and got a plumber to fix it. First the plumber went into the bathtub drain and then he lifted up the toilet and went into that drain. Because we noticed that the sink in the bathroom was having trouble, he snaked that drain pipe, too. Two hours later, I had the same problem. This time that plumber was off duty and I had to call someone else. This plumber went to the sewage drain cleanout that was located on the ground next to the house. I recall it to be about a 4" black ABS plastic pipe with a rubber cover over it. (Be sure you know where this is to your home!) He used this super-duper heavy-duty electrical snake with cutting blades on the end and slid it in the sewage drain cleanout. He worked it back and forth for about 45 minutes to an hour. When he pulled it out, he removed a huge barrel of tree roots. The whole mess looked like a pile of cable or a scary sci-fi creature! No wonder my plumbing got backed up! He explained that years ago the sewer pipes were clay, and eventually they crack and tree roots grow inside. He said it was too expensive to replace sometimes, and most people will just call a "rooter" company to remove the roots from time to time. Go figure!

Fig 5.21- Plunging the Sink

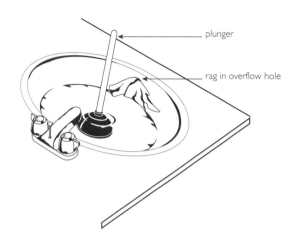

plunger

rag in overflow hole

Fig 5.22- Remove the P-trap

P-trap

Trick of the Trade:

Place a little petroleum jelly around the rim of the plunger to help give it a solid seal and vacuum.

True Story: When I was about eight years old, my family rented a cottage in Florida for a family fishing trip. I guess this cottage hadn't been inhabited for a while, because there must not have been any water in the P-trap, which causes a seal. When we got to the cottage it was late at night and I went to brush my teeth. Much to my surprise, the water had disturbed this scorpion that came scurrying out of the drain and into the sink. Fortunately, my dad, who doesn't flinch about such things, was nearby. To this day, I make sure I run the water in the sink at any "rustic" little cottage I rent to form that seal in the P-trap!

Removing the pop-up stopper: Before you plunge the sink, remove the pop-up stopper. Otherwise, your plunging may cause the stopper to go up and down. Pull up the stopper lever to the upright position. Go underneath your sink, and with your hand or your pliers, remove the retaining nut that secures the pivot rod in the hole at the bottom of the stopper. Now pull the rod out of the drainpipe, releasing the stopper. Pull the stopper out of the sink. The stopper will snare hair, so you may be pulling up the beginning of the clog. Clean the stopper of any hair and goo. With the stopper out, don't forget to replace the pivot arm back into the pivot seat and screw it back together with the retaining nut; otherwise, you will plunge water into your sink's cabinet. After the sink has been cleared of the clog, re-install the pop-up stopper.

Plunging the sink: Put a rag in the overflow hole so when you start plunging, the water doesn't go up through the overflow hole and splash you in the face. With a little water in the bottom of the sink, start plunging up and down, about ten to fifteen strokes, ending with abruptly lifting it off the drain, creating a little slurping "pop." Do this several times. You might want to wear some safety glasses, because this can spray water out of the sink. If this doesn't free the clog, then proceed to the next step.

Checking the P-trap: Traps are curved to "trap" an object that may fall down the drain and "trap" water, so that gases from your waste system won't come into your home. The curve of the trap holds water to seal out those smelly gases and to keep little crawling creatures from entering into your home from the sewer line.

Turn off the water supply just in case you accidentally turn on the faucet with the P-trap removed.

Place a bucket underneath the P-trap to catch the water in the trap. Unscrew the slip nuts at each end of the P-trap with your groove-joint pliers or pipe wrench. If you see the obstruction, remove it and replace the P-trap. Tighten the slip nuts with your pliers, turn on the water supply valve, and check to see if your water is flowing well. If there is still a clog, you will need to use a plumber's snake or auger.

Using a drain auger or plumber's snake: This is different from your toilet auger. Use a plumber's hand snake to go directly into the drain pipe that returns into the wall underneath your sink. If you have an S-trap, your drain is leading directly in to the floor. For a more detailed account of using your plumber's snake, see "Snaking the Waste Pipe" in the kitchen chapter under "The Clogged Drain." If you come up to the clog and break it up, then reassemble the P-trap and tighten the fittings with your groove-joint pliers.

FIXING A LEAKY FAUCET

I've noticed that most sinks have a two-handled faucet, also known as a compression type. You can save yourself a

Tip: Some P-traps will have a hex or square plug on the bottom of the bend. You can clean out any debris from the trap if you unscrew this plug. Be sure you have a bucket underneath the P-trap to let the water drain out. Bend a wire hanger at the end, and push it into the hole to try to grab the debris.

Fig 5.23- Using a Drain Auger

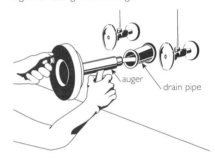

auger   drain pipe

Call a Pro: If you don't want to go into the drain or if you have gone into the drain and still have a clog, it's time to pony up the money and call a plumber.

Safety First: Do not use a caustic drain cleaner. Many times these chemicals can cause worse problems in your drain by eating away at your drain pipes. Or worse, you may put your body and eyes at risk, because if it doesn't unclog the drain, you will need to plunge or use a plumber's snake, possibly getting those chemicals all over the place.

pretty penny by fixing these faucets yourself. Most of the time, you need to replace a little washer on the end of the spindle. A detailed illustration and the steps to do this repair are in the "Sinks" section in the "Plumbing" part of the kitchen chapter.

REPLACING YOUR FAUCET

At a certain point, you may want to replace the entire faucet. Over time, your faucet may look awful from water corrosion, and you may want to replace the entire fixture. Pick out the faucet of your choice, and follow the steps from the manufacturer. Also, see the steps to replace your faucet in the "Sinks" section in the "Plumbing" part of the kitchen chapter.

LEAKING UNDER THE SINK

The biggest difference between your bathroom sink and your kitchen sink is the shape, size, and the pop-up stopper. A loose pop-up stopper can be the cause of leaking under your sink.

REPAIRING OR REPLACING A POP-UP STOPPER

DIFFICULTY: 2

TOOLS YOU MAY NEED: Groove-joint pliers

MATERIALS YOU MAY NEED: Plastic bag or bowl, plumber's grease

Fig 5.24- Replacing a Pop-Up Stopper

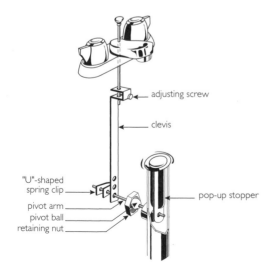

adjusting screw

clevis

"U"-shaped spring clip

pivot arm
pivot ball
retaining nut

pop-up stopper

If your sink is draining slowly, maybe you need to open up your pop-up stopper by going underneath the sink and adjusting the screw on top of the clevis. The clevis is that flat thin bar with holes in it that connects to the pivot arm. One of the holes will be where the pivot arm goes through, and a U-shaped spring clip holds it in place. As far as other problems, the problem is usually with the pivot nut, which is located underneath the sink and holds the pivot arm to the pop-up stopper. If the pivot nut becomes loosened, the arm can come out of the hole of the pop-up and prevent it from working properly.

Unscrew the retaining nut from the pivot seat on the tailpiece, and pull out the pivot arm. Be sure you keep all your parts together in a little plastic bag or a plastic bowl. Take the stopper out and examine it to see if it needs to be replaced. Also, you want to be sure that you align the hole on the bottom of the stopper with the middle of the hole on the tailpiece where the arm goes in. This is much like threading the eye of a needle. Tighten the retaining screw with your hand and then use your groove-joint pliers to be sure it's snug.

The pivot arm now needs to go through one of the holes of the clevis (that metal strap with holes in it). I usually put it through the second-to-last hole from the bottom and then slide on the clip by pinching it together to hold it in place. Loosen the screw on the top of the clevis, push the pivot arm all the way down, and push the rod of the lever (from below) up and tighten the screw on top of the clevis. You may have to do a couple adjustments until you get it just right. Just remember, you pull up on your stopper lever to stop up the drain and push down on the lever to open up the drain.

> **Trick of the Trade:**
> Oftentimes, the rotating ball can get a little stuck from buildup of the minerals in the water, so clean the ball off and butter up the rotating ball with some plumber's grease before putting it back into the pivot seat. I keep a little bit of plumber's grease in my toolbox just for this kind of project. (Petroleum jelly works well in a pinch!)

If you need to repair parts or the entire assembly, follow the manufacturer's directions. Remember, sometimes you may only need to replace the stopper itself. Bring your old stopper with you to get a similar one.

REPLACING YOUR SINK

DIFFICULTY: 3+

TOOLS YOU MAY NEED: Basin wrench, adjustable wrench, utility knife, ratchet wrench, screwdriver, drill, prybar, stud finder, drywall keyhole saw, hammer

MATERIALS YOU MAY NEED: Bucket, a couple 2×4s, plumber's putty, silicone caulk, drywall screws, green board or cement board

At some point, if you've lived in your home long enough or if you buy an older home, you may want to replace the sink in your bathroom. The nice thing about doing this job yourself, aside from the money you save, is that you can put the sink at any height you'd like. A very dear friend of mine, whom I call "Pop," recently renovated his home. He's a tall man whose home was previously owned by a Girl Scout leader who had built a countertop low enough for the girls to gather around. For Pop, this height was great if his knees needed washing, but in general, it just didn't work out. So when he renovated his home, he lifted the island to a comfortable level.

I'm 5'6" and have had a major back pain in some older homes just brushing my teeth in a sink that was too low. If this is going on at your home, replace the sink or lift it up. Go to a bathroom specialty store to get a feel for what height would fit you best. Then you can figure out what type of sink you want. The sink in the bathroom is different from the sink in your kitchen. Your choices are a pedestal sink, a wall-mounted (free-standing) sink, or one dropped into a base cabinet or countertop. If you're going to reuse your sink, depending on what kind of sink you have, you'll either have to relocate the wall-mounting brackets or replace the cabinet and then replace a tailpiece pipe underneath.

See also "Replacing Your Sink" in the kitchen chapter.

Removing the supply tubes: *Turn off the water supply* at the shutoff valves or the main valve. Underneath the sink, unscrew the coupling nuts with a basin wrench. These nuts hold the supply tubes to the tailpieces of the faucet. (In a pinch, you can use an adjustable wrench, but there's not much room, and it will take you longer!)

Tip: Those of you who are removing the sink and the countertop do not have to remove the sink. You can remove the entire countertop with the sink in it. Don't forget to disconnect the supply tubes and plumbing connections first.

Removing the P-trap: Slide your bucket underneath the P-trap to catch the water in the trap, and remove the slip nuts at both ends.

Faucet mounted on countertop: If your faucet is mounted on the countertop, remove the retaining nut holding the horizontal pivot arm to the sink's tailpiece underneath the sink. If you don't do this, you won't be able to lift out the sink.

Removing the sink: After you have removed the plumbing connections from the sink, you can now remove the sink. Those who would like to keep the sink but replace the countertop need to remove the sink first, then the countertop. See "Removing a Countertop" in the carpentry chapter. The title of sink you have determines how you remove the countertop.

Self-rimming: These sinks have a rim that sits on the countertop or base cabinet. They are usually caulked under the rim. You will need to cut through the caulk with a utility knife or a sharp putty knife. After this seal is broken, lift the sink straight up and out.

Rimless sink: These are fairly rare, but they are out there. The sink is in a counter-top but doesn't have a rim. Instead, it is supported by a piece of wood, a wire, and mounting clips. I like to get someone to hold the sink below while I slice through the caulk with my utility knife and then detach the wire, and mounting clips to lift it out.

Pedestal sink: The plumbing, pedestal, and wall brackets hold this sink into place. First, cut a couple 2×4s so they will wedge snuggly underneath the sink to the floor and hold the weight of the sink. With the sink secure, disconnect the bolts holding the pedestal to the sink with your adjustable wrench. Now lift the sink off the wall brackets.

Wall-mounted sink: Check the back of the sink where it meets the wall. If there is caulk, you will need to slice through it with your utility knife to free the sink. In many cases, the sink will lift right up. If not, then look underneath the sink at the bracket. There might be some lag screws or wood screws holding the sink into place. Get a helper to hold the sink or wedge a couple 2×4s underneath. See "Pedestal Sink" above. Use a ratchet wrench to remove the lag screws and a screwdriver or a drill with a magnetic bit holder with the appropriate tip for the screw. After you have removed the screws, lift the sink out.

Integral sink and countertop: This may be a solid surface sink where the sink and the countertop are molded together. To remove this from the cabinet, first take a look underneath your cabinet. In the corners, you will notice mounting hardware and screws. With your screwdriver or drill with a magnetic tip, remove all the screws holding the countertop in place. Just underneath the countertop, with a sharp blade in your utility knife, break the seal of caulk or construction adhesive from the top of the cabinet. You may need use a prybar to help pry this off the base cabinet. If you have any caulk on the back of your backsplash, cut through that seal as well.

Replacing an integral sink and countertop: This is an all-in-one installation. Make it easy on yourself and attach the faucet and the drain assembly to the sink before installing it. Use plumber's putty underneath the drain flange unless your sink is made of marble. Plumber's putty will stain a marble sink, so use silicone caulk instead. If you're keeping your base cabinet, you will need to apply a bead of silicone caulk or the manufacturer's suggested adhesive to the top of the base cabinet and then set the countertop.

Trick of the Trade:

To find the correct size bit to drill a pilot hole, place the drill bit over the screw you will be using. When you find the drill bit that matches the "shank" of the screw (not including the threads), that is the correct size to use for making your pilot hole.

Installing a pedestal sink: If you're installing a pedestal sink, you will need to set it in place. Be sure you cut a couple 2×4s to help with the weight and stability of the sink while you're putting it together. Mark around the sink where it meets the wall, and mark around the holes on the bottom of the pedestal where it meets the floor. Now place the sink and pedestal in a safe place while you're preparing the area.

Adding blocking in the wall: With your stud finder, locate the studs behind the marked area around the sink on your wall. You will probably notice that where you need your sink, you will not find studs or have too few supports to screw into. If that is the case, find your studs near the area you want to mount the sink and cut out a square area so you can get in a 2×4 blocking between the studs. Use a drywall keyhole saw to cut into the drywall. You can hammer the keyhole saw into the wall and then start sawing, keeping the blade at an angle, almost lying on the drywall, so the blade doesn't cut through any wires that may be behind the wall. Measure the distance between studs, and cut a 2×4 to this measurement. Screw this blocking to the studs by "toe-screwing" it in.

Repairing the wall: Measure the thickness of your existing wall, and buy that thickness in "green board" drywall or cement board. Both are water resistant. For complete details, see the "Walls" section in "The Interior" chapter.

Fig 5.25- Adding Blocking

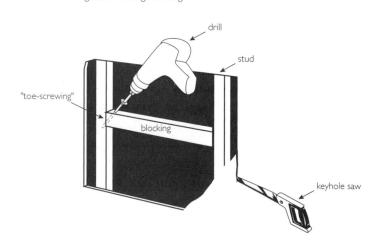

Drilling the pilot holes: Drill the pilot holes in the floor and wall. If you had to add blocking, you will need to put the sink on the pedestal and mark the holes under the sink to the wall. Remove the pedestal and sink, and drill pilot holes in the marked holes. A "pilot" hole is a hole that is slightly smaller than the screw you will be using.

Securing the sink and pedestal: Using the lag screws or whatever screws came with your pedestal sink, secure the sink to the floor and wall. Use a ratchet wrench to tighten the lag screws.

Attaching the plumbing: You will need to add the drain assembly, making sure to put plumber's putty underneath the drain flange. Use silicone under the drain flange if your sink is made of marble. For a detailed account of plumbing your sink, see the "Installing Your Drain Assembly" section in the Kitchen Chapter (page 130).

Installing a drop-in sink: See the "Installing a New Sink:" section in the Kitchen Chapter (page 129).

D'oh! Make sure you don't over-tighten the screws. That could crack the sink or pedestal.

The Bathtub

The bathtub is a wonderful luxury . . . until it's time to move it out of your bathroom! It's anything but luxurious to move a bathtub. For this reason, if you would like to

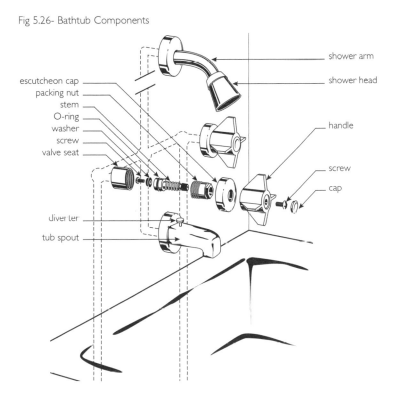

Fig 5.26- Bathtub Components

shower arm
shower head
escutcheon cap
packing nut
stem
O-ring
washer
screw
valve seat
handle
screw
cap
diverter
tub spout

replace your bathtub and you are a beginner to intermediate DIYer, call the plumber. Those of you who may know how to replace a bathtub will probably also want to call the plumber. Sometimes you can save yourself money by hiring a professional. In my opinion, this is one of those times. You can shop around for the bathtub and fixtures you would like and show pictures and measurements to your plumber. This will help expedite the job and will ensure that you will get what you want for a savings if you do your homework.

This next section deals with clogs, cleaning, adjustment of tub drains, and replacing caulk around your tub.

THE CLOGGED TUB DRAIN
DIFFICULTY: 2+
TOOLS YOU MAY NEED: Screwdriver, plunger, needle-nose pliers, drain auger/hand snake
MATERIALS YOU MAY NEED: White vinegar, baking soda, scrub brush, towel/rag, wire hanger, petroleum jelly

You know the deal: you finish taking a bath or shower and you reach down and pick up the rubber hair catcher over your drain. What? You don't have one? Then you are part of the majority of people who suffer time to time from a slow-draining tub. The culprit? Soap and H-A-I-R! We let this problem go on too long because who really wants to fish out all that ick? But often the fix is just inches away and will help the turnaround time on your household bathers.

First establish what kind of drain you have: a pop-up or a plunger type drain. Look at the round metal cover plate on your tub and flip the lever. If your metal stopper goes up and down as you flip the lever, you have a pop-up drain. If you have a strainer over the drain opening, you have a plunger drain assembly.

A POP-UP DRAIN
DIFFICULTY: 2+

The pop-up literally pops up and down, stopping the drain.

Homemade Drain Cleaner:

I'm not a promoter of commercial drain cleaner. Not only can it hurt your pipes, but also if it doesn't fix the drain, you will be plunging or snaking toxic chemicals that may get on you while you're working on the pipes. There's really no need for a drain cleaner if you take the proper steps to find the clog. But for those of you who are hell-bent on using something, try this safe drain cleaner: heat up about 1 cup white vinegar. Pour the vinegar down the drain and add a few tablespoons baking soda. You will see it foam up. Let it sit until the foaming stops and then rinse with h-o-t water. Hopefully, this will clear your drain.

Remove the pop-up by turning and raising the lever on the cover plate to lift the stopper and pull it out. This may take a little wrangling to get it out, and it may have a good bit of hair and soap attached to it. Clean this and throw the gunk into the garbage . . . not down the drain! Place the pop-up stopper back in the drain with the bend in the rocker arm facing down. "Rocker arm" is the term used for the lower part of the pop-up assembly, which actually rocks in the hinge underneath the drain. If it's still draining slowly, remove the cover plate's two screws from the overflow drain opening and lift out the drain assembly. On the end it will have a striker spring, which can be an excellent trap for catching hair. Clean this off with a scrub brush. Run *hot* water. If the drain flows well, put the assembly back into the overflow hole.

If you still have a clog, try using a plunger. See "Plunging the Clog." (page 212)

D'oh! Be sure you don't lose any of your assembly pieces down the drain. Always put a towel over the drain. This will also prevent your tools and materials from scratching the bottom of your tub.

Hint: Sometimes you may need to allow more water to go through your drain and adjust the plunger by raising the rod about ⅛". Unscrew the locknut on the threaded rod to make this adjustment. When the rod is raised, tighten the locknut. Put the assembly back into the overflow drain, and tighten the screws on the coverplate.

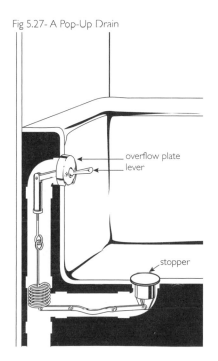

Fig 5.27- A Pop-Up Drain

overflow plate
lever

stopper

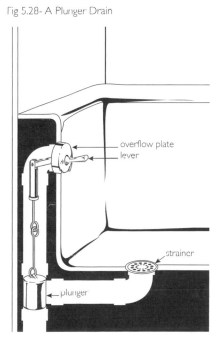

Fig 5.28- A Plunger Drain

overflow plate
lever

strainer

plunger

A PLUNGER DRAIN
DIFFICULTY: 2+

This type of drain will have a little strainer in the drain. Turn this counterclockwise with needle-nose pliers. Can you see a cobweb of hair?

Using needle-nose pliers and a coat hanger or piece of wire, make a small hook to catch this furball. You may need to use your needle-nose pliers for a better grip when it gets closer to the opening. While you're at it, take off the cover plate to the overflow drain with your screwdriver and lift out the assembly. The cover plate will be attached to a couple rods called the trip waste linkage and will have the plunger on the bottom of it. Remove any hair and soap scum with an old toothbrush or cleaning brush. Run *hot* water. If the drain flows well, put the assembly back together. If you still have a clog, try using a plunger.

Safety First: Be sure to protect your eyes with safety glasses when plunging. Also, you can use some petroleum jelly around the rim of your plunger to give yourself a good seal when plunging. Just be sure when you're done you wipe the petroleum jelly off the tub thoroughly with a little tub cleaner. Otherwise, the next time you step in for a bath/shower, you may have quite the slip.

PLUNGING THE CLOG
DIFFICULTY: 1

If you've taken out the drain assembly and the tub is still slow moving or clogged, put an old, wet rag in the overflow hole. (You don't want any waste coming up into your face, especially if you've used any chemicals!) If you have a strainer in your drain, remove it with your needle-nose pliers by twisting it counterclockwise (left). Be sure you have a little water in your tub so when you put the plunger over the drain it will create better suction. Now plunge up and down ten to fifteen times, pulling away from the drain and popping it out on the last plunge. Do this a few times.

Still clogged?

AUGER THE DRAIN LINE
DIFFICULTY: 2

The auger or plumber's snake is really the best way to get out a clog. You can buy the kind that either you attach to a drill or turn by hand. The plumber's snake looks like a flat,

Fig 5.29- Plunging the Tub

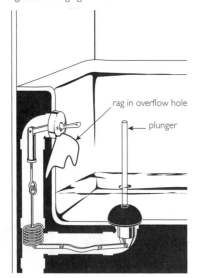

rag in overflow hole

← plunger

disc-shaped gun with a crank handle on the back of it. You have to feed the coil out of the disc by hand down into the drain, but when you crank the handle, the spiral coil at the end rotates. If you have the kind that attaches to the drill, you still need to feed it by hand, but the drill will turn the coil for you. The coil then grabs onto the hair or whatever is clogging the drain line, and you retrieve it by feeding the line back into the disc-shaped gun. It's really that simple. You should invest in one of these for your home and save yourself a plumber's bill. At the time I wrote this, I found a hand snake for less than $16 and one that attaches to the drill for less than $35.

The trick with the auger or plumber's snake is that you *don't* put it down your drain on the floor of the tub. Instead, you put it down the overflow hole, which in turn will feed down into the drain line. With the drain assembly out of the overflow hole, insert the snake down into the hole and start pushing the coil in. When it stops going down, you have probably hit a bend in the pipe. Give yourself at least 6" or 7" of extra cable, and set the lock, which may be a screw to hold the cable in place. Start turning the crank clockwise until it gets past the bend and keep feeding it in the hole. When you do get to the clog, turn the crank clockwise. If you can push it through, it was most likely a soap clog. You'll have to do this back and forth a few times. If you get to a hair clog or an object, give yourself 6" or 7" of cable, lock down the cable, and turn the crank clockwise. Release the lock and start pushing the cable into the snake housing while you turn the crank. This will help you get past the bend in a pipe and hold on to the obstruction. Remove the object or hairball. Do this again to be sure you have everything, and flush with *hot* water. If you still have a clog, I would suggest picking up the phone to call the plumber, but most times you will have fixed the problem yourself!

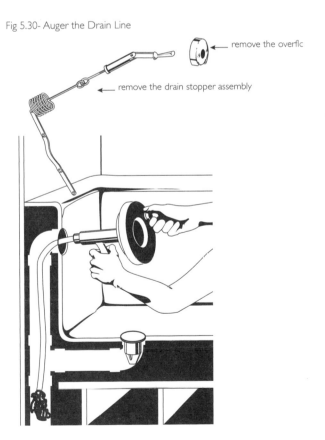

Fig 5.30- Auger the Drain Line

remove the overflo

remove the drain stopper assembly

THE CLOGGED SHOWER DRAIN

DIFFICULTY: 2

TOOLS YOU MAY NEED: Screwdriver, plunger, plumber's snake

MATERIALS YOU MAY NEED: Wire hanger

Basically you will need to go through the steps in "The Clogged Tub Drain." First, pry the strainer cover off with a slotted screwdriver. Check to see if you can see any hair or an object. You may be able to place a wire hanger in the drain to pull up the clogged item. If you don't see anything, use your plunger. See "Plunging the Clog" (page 212) for the tub. If that doesn't fix it, use the plumber snake as suggested above. The snake will go directly down your shower's drain. Good luck!

A LEAKING SHOWER OR TUB

DIFFICULTY: 2

TOOLS YOU MAY NEED: Caulk-removing tool or utility knife, putty knife, caulking gun

MATERIALS YOU MAY NEED: Silicone caulk, mold fungicide, paper towel, plastic spoon, blue
painter's tape

If you are experiencing a leak underneath your tub or shower, you may not have sealed the area properly with caulk. Caulk will break down over time and needs to be replaced. If the problem isn't sealing around the tub or shower, you probably have a leak at a fixture in the wall or a plumbing connection. This will require removing sections of the wall to get to the problem. Yes, this can be quite a mess, but you don't have any options, because water leakage can cause you a lot more financial headache if left alone. Remember, mold and mildew need moisture, and the longer you have a leak, the longer you may have a mold and mildew problem.

Caulking around the tub/shower: First, look at the caulk around your tub or shower. Is it lifting off the wall or porcelain/fiberglass? If it is, it needs to be replaced. Is it black or gray in color? If it is, you have mold and mildew starting to grow.

Removing the caulk: You can buy a little plastic caulk-removing tool that looks like a boot, or you can just use

Mold and Mildew:

For years I had used bleach to kill mold, but from the new reports I'm reading, it is not enough to actually kill the mold. Instead, get a mold fungicide. Spray it on and follow the manufacturer's directions. It is key that after you have killed the mold, you let the area dry before you recaulk. You can also visit www.epa.gov/iaq/molds/index.html for more information on mold in your home.

your utility knife. I use a utility knife with a sharp blade to cut through the caulk and remove it with a putty knife. If you have any spotty or gray caulk, you need to remove the caulk and kill the mold in that area with a mold fungicide. If it looks really bad, you may need to tear out a section of your wall to remove mold that has grown behind the wall. This is why you want to do this project ASAP so you don't have to tear out walls.

Trick of the Trade:

To get a smooth caulk line, use painter's blue tape about ⅜" from the center on each side of the seam where you will be caulking. Apply the caulk, smooth with the spoon, and lift up the tape after you've finished. When lifting the tape, lift it at an angle away from the center of the caulk.

Recaulking around the tub and shower: Now that you have removed the caulk, killed any mold or mildew, and let the area dry completely, you're ready to caulk the area. Be sure you use a silicone caulk. Caulk is sold in the large tubes and small tubes the size of toothpaste. There are many silicone caulks made just for your bathroom and kitchen. Slice the tip of the caulk off at an angle. You may need to puncture the seal in the tube. If you have a large tube, place it into a caulking gun and slowly squeeze out a bead of caulk while moving the gun in the seam around the tub or shower. Have a paper towel in one hand, and use the back of a plastic spoon to fan out the caulk, making it look like a nice bead. Wipe the excess on the paper towel while doing this. Allow the caulk to dry according to the manufacturer's directions before using the bath or shower, usually twenty-four hours.

The Shower: Tub, Faucets, Handles, and Heads

Similar to your sink's faucet, your shower and tub are basically the same. The difference is that when you have a tub and shower combined, you will have a diverter. The diverter is what directs the flow of water into either your tub spout or your showerhead. The diverter is either a pull lever on top of the tub spout or a handle that looks like your faucet handle. If you have a handle diverter, you probably have two faucet handles, giving it the look of three faucet handles. If you have a gate diverter or a pull lever, you either have a two-handle faucet or a single-handle faucet.

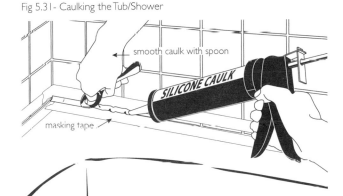

Fig 5.31 - Caulking the Tub/Shower

smooth caulk with spoon

SILICONE CAULK

masking tape

LEAKY FAUCET

DIFFICULTY: 3

TOOLS YOU MAY NEED: Adjustable wrench, groove-joint pliers, screwdriver, bath socket
wrench, wire brush, utility knife, Allen key (hex key)

MATERIALS YOU MAY NEED: Rag, lubricating spray, electrical tape, silicone caulk, heatproof
grease, pipe compound or Teflon tape

If a drip, drip, drip is keeping you up at night, it's best to fix it as soon as you can.
Not only can those drips cost you a good night's sleep, but they can also hit your
pocketbook when you get your water bill. Get out your adjustable wrench, screwdriver, and groove-joint pliers, and roll up your sleeves. My suggestion is to tackle
this project early on a Saturday after everyone has bathed. You will probably be
making a run to your hardware store for replacement parts, so leave yourself enough
time.

First, determine if the water that is leaking is cold or hot. This will let you know
which handle needs fixing.

Turn off the water at the valve in the bathroom or the main valve to the house.

Three-handle faucet: This fixture has a hot and cold handle in addition to a handle
in the middle that diverts the water either to the shower head or to the tub spout. All
three handles are valves. If the spout is leaking hot water, you need to fix the hot
side. Cold water means the cold water handle. Usually you will need to replace the
washer on the bottom of the stem assembly. With the water turned off, remove the
"H" or "C" plastic cap on the handle. This will expose the screw. Remove this screw
with a screwdriver, and pull the handle off the stem. This may take some effort. I like
to place a rag around it to pull, but you may also need to use some lubricating spray
and a handle remover if it's really stubborn. Take off the escutcheon—the round
chrome plate. Your stem assembly may be deep set and require you to remove a
round escutcheon (flange) around the handle and one that looks like a tube covering
the stem. Use your groove-joint pliers with electrical tape wrapped around the jaws
to protect the finish of your plated escutcheon.

You may want to take a look at the "Plumbing: Leaking Faucet" section in the
Kitchen Chapter (page 111) to see the difference between a compression-type faucet
and a cartridge. You will need to replace a cartridge-type stem assembly, but you can
fix the compression-type faucet. Here's the fix on the compression-type faucet.

Removing the stem assembly: The hard part of this job is removing the stem assembly, because after years of water deposit buildup, it can seem almost welded on. You may be able to remove the bonnet nut with an adjustable wrench. If the bonnet nut is behind the tile or is hard to move, then buy a bath socket wrench, which slips over the stem assembly. These look like a spark plug sleeve—which re-

Tip: If you have a lot of space around the tile and the fixture, apply some silicone caulk to be sure no water gets behind the escutcheon cap and into the wall.

minds me, if you have a deep-socket wrench, you can use that, too. Use a little lubricating spray so you don't loosen the solder joints. You may have to chip away at the tile a little to get your wrench in place. Wear safety glasses if you do.

Replacing the washer: The washer is found on the end of the stem assembly and is held on by a screw. Again, you might need to spray the screw with lubricating spray to remove it from the assembly. Your washer may look worn with a dip in the middle. Check the seat by sticking your finger in the hole and feeling the seat that the washer pushes up against. If it feels worn, you will need to replace that, too. Of course, it never hurts to replace both. Take the stem assembly to your hardware store to be sure you buy a washer that fits.

Fig 5.32- Replace the Washer

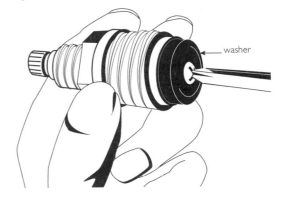

Cleaning the brass stem assembly: Check the stem assembly by unscrewing the retaining nut from the threaded spindle. You have to unscrew it by turning it clockwise. Take out the old packing washer with a flat screwdriver. Clean any deposits or

Fig 5.33- Stem Assembly

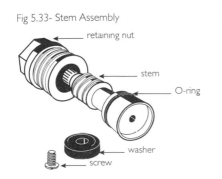

Fig 5.34- Clean the Stem

Fig 5.35- Replace the O-ring

Fig 5.35- Replace the O-ring

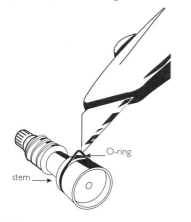

sediment buildup with a wire brush, coat with some heat-proof grease, reassemble the packing washer, and screw the retaining screw back on counterclockwise. (Just opposite of how things usually screw on.) If it looks awful, replace the entire stem assembly.

Checking the O-ring: You may have an O-ring on your stem assembly that needs to be replaced. This is easy to cut off with your utility knife and replace.

Replacing the seat: There's a special L-shaped seat tool that fits neatly into the center of the seat. Place it in the seat, and turn it counterclockwise to remove the seat. Take this seat to the hardware store to replace the same seat.

Be sure to use some pipe compound or Teflon tape on the threads of the seat valve and the thread on the end of the retaining nut. Do *not* tape the inside threaded spindle. Use some heatproof grease for the threads in the spindle.

Fig 5.36- Replace the Valve Seat

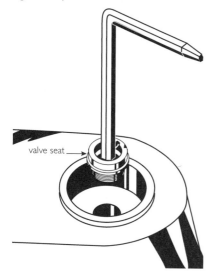

REPLACING THE DIVERTER VALVE
DIFFICULTY: 3

The fix for the diverter valve is the same as the hot and cold handles. At some point, these wear out, too. You will know when the diverter valve needs some attention when you turn it to have the water come out the showerhead and it comes out the spout, too.

SINGLE-HANDLE SHOWER
DIFFICULTY: 3

Turn off the water supply at the valve. Similar to the compression valve, remove the handle and escutcheon to get to the bonnet nut. Remove the nut with your groove-joint pliers or your adjustable wrench—whichever fits the fitting—and remove the cartridge assembly. With this type of valve, I would suggest replacing the entire cartridge assembly. It's worth it.

REPLACING A GATE DIVERTER
DIFFICULTY: 2

The gate diverter is the little knob or lever on the tub spout. When you pull up on it, it stops the water going out to the spout and diverts it up to the showerhead.

Replace the diverter by removing the screw located under the spout in a notched area. This is where you will put in the Allen key (also called a hex key) into the hex-head screw inside this access slot. Turn it counterclockwise to remove the screw. Place a towel over the drain to prevent losing any pieces of the assembly.

Insert a screwdriver into the spout for leverage and unscrew it counterclockwise. The spout is threaded on a nipple (yes, that's what they call it), which is a small pipe sticking out of the wall. Spread pipe compound or wrap Teflon tape around the threads of the spout nipple. If you use tape, wrap it clockwise about three times. Now install your new tub spout with the diverter snuggly onto the nipple until the spout faces down.

LEAKING SHOWERHEAD
DIFFICULTY: 2+
TOOLS YOU MAY NEED: Adjustable wrench, groove-joint pliers
MATERIALS YOU MAY NEED: Electrical tape, pipe compound or Teflon tape, heatproof grease

If your showerhead is leaking, determine where the leak is coming from. If it's behind the head itself, you may need to tighten the head or replace an O-ring. If it's leaking at the wall, you will need to tighten or spread pipe joint compound on the threads.

Sometimes you can reach up and unscrew the showerhead from the arm by hand. More often you will need to use an adjustable wrench to unscrew the nut holding the head to the arm. If the arm moves with it, wrap your groove-joint pliers with electrical tape to hold on to the arm while you are unscrewing the nut with your pliers. Look inside at the O-ring (the black rounded rubber ring), if it looks worn, replace it.

Whether you're going to replace the head or not, wrap pipe joint compound or Teflon tape

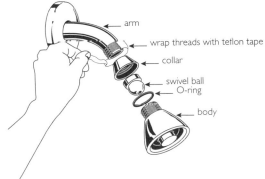

Fig 5.37- Replace the Showerhead

arm
wrap threads with teflon tape
collar
swivel ball
O-ring
body

around the threads of the arm clockwise before you install the head. It's not a bad idea to put a little plumber's heatproof grease on the O-ring. Screw the showerhead back onto the arm, and tighten using your adjustable wrench.

Some showerheads may need a new size thread on the end of the arm. Bring your old arm to the hardware store to be sure you buy one that will fit into the pipe in the wall and the other end into the head. Always wrap Teflon tape clockwise around the threads of both sides of the arm. Turn the arm until the bend faces the head down.

Carpentry

The fixes in your bathroom will be similar to your kitchen, so I will refer you to the kitchen chapter when necessary. This section will focus on the repairs that are particular to the bathroom. With a sink, a tub, and a toilet, the bathroom has to deal with an enormous amount of moisture and possible water damage from any of these fixtures. The first thing you must do is find the location where water is coming in and fix it immediately. Investigating a leak may lead to some demolition. Between the demolition and any damage you might uncover, you may have to deal with the repair of walls, tiles, floors, and ceilings, not to mention cabinets.

Mold and Mildew

Mold and mildew are used interchangeably. I appeared on CNNfn's *Flip Side*, where they featured a mansion that had to be torn down because removing the mold would cost more than removing the house! Mold can be a serious problem. Not only can fixing a leak save you money in the long run, but it can also save you a medical problem. Granted, some people are more susceptible to mold allergies than others, but if you want to sell your house, you better get rid of the mold!

FIGHTING MOLD AND MILDEW
DIFFICULTY: 1
TOOLS YOU MAY NEED: Water extraction vacuum, dehumidifier, space heater
MATERIALS YOU MAY NEED: Mold test kit

First, clean up the water within twenty-four to forty-eight hours after you have water damage or a leak. Remove the water with a water extraction vacuum and dry out the area. If your walls are wet and you have any insulation that is wet, remove it and replace it once the area is dry. To help remove the moisture, use a dehumidifier and fans or a heater. Open up a window to vent the moisture.

Identifying Mold: Mold looks spotty black or gray. When it's really bad you can smell the musty odor associated with it. If you are not sure if you have mold, you can get a mold test kit at the hardware store. Mold spores are found in the air and in your basic house dust. The mold spores can't grow unless moisture is present. The bathroom, with all its moisture, lends itself to a wonderful breeding ground for mold. With that said, it is extremely important to have your bathroom well vented. I strongly urge you to install a fan in the bathroom if you don't already have one. See "Installing a Fan" in the electricity section.

REMOVING MOLD
DIFFICULTY: 1 or 5
MATERIALS YOU MAY NEED: Mold fungicide

First you need to determine how much mold there is. Generally speaking, the average person can remove a ten-square-foot section of mold themselves. Anything bigger should be handled by a contractor who is experienced in mold cleanup. Be sure you check the contractor's references and that they follow the government's guidelines of mold removal in your area. See www.epa.gov/iaq/molds/moldcleanup .html for more information and recommendations.

Kill the mold with a fungicide—an indoor mold killer. If you have any drywall that has mold on it, remove it to the point where there is no mold. Remove all caulk that is lifting up or has the spotty gray area in it. It's mold! Let it dry before working on it.

Repairing your walls, floors, and ceilings: Now you will need to make any repairs to your walls, floors, or ceilings. The degree of damage will depend on how deep you need to go.

Walls

Your Bathroom Walls

Because the bathroom gets a lot of moisture you want to be sure you have the proper materials on your walls. The drywall for the rest of your house doesn't work in the bathroom. Instead, use a material that is moisture resistant. You have a couple choices: green board drywall, or cement backer board. Cement backer board is also called "backer board" and Wonder Board™. It is cement sandwiched between fiberglass cloth. This cement board has been a contractor's and home owner's dream for tiling because it's impervious to water. Because it is much heavier, it comes in 3×5' and 4'×5" sheets. You would use ½" thickness on your wall. If you are going to tile, you can use either green board drywall or cement backer board. I would use cement backer board for the floor and walls if tiling. If I was going to paint and not tile, I would use the green board.

Those of you whose bathroom walls are not made out of one of these materials may notice that your walls aren't holding up too well. Maybe when you press in some areas of the tile, the wall shifts. This means that moisture has broken down the wall and eventually it will need to be replaced.

Choosing your wall material: If you are going to tile your bathroom, I would suggest using ½" cement backer board around the tub and green board drywall for the areas away from the tub and shower that will be painted and tiled. Remember, you can tile on green board, too.

REMOVING OLD WALLS
DIFFICULTY: 2+
TOOLS YOU MAY NEED: Claw hammer, drill with magnetic Phillips #2 bit
MATERIALS YOU MAY NEED: Heavy-duty garbage bags, drop cloth, safety glasses

After you've had your breakfast and coffee, turn on some music and get ready to remove the old damaged walls. Get some heavy-duty bags and/or waste containers, put a drop cloth on your floor, put on those safety glasses, and start removing the damaged wall(s). The best place to start is at the damage, where you can get your hammer's claw into the wall and start to pull the wall off the studs. You may need to use a drill to remove any drywall screws securing the wall to the studs. Pieces will usually come off in sections. I like to pack the pieces in the bag as soon as I get them down. This is when it helps to have someone with you to pack up the demolition as you're doing it. Some people l-o-v-e demolition, so just be careful to not get overexuberant and hurt your helper!

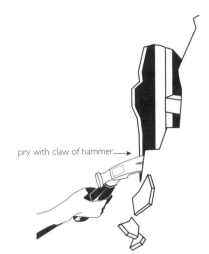

Fig 5.38- Demolishing a Wall

pry with claw of hammer

REPLACING YOUR DAMAGED WALLS

DIFFICULTY: 3+

TOOLS YOU MAY NEED: Drill with screwdriver bits, 2" or 3" putty knife, drywall jacks (for ceiling repair), utility knife or carbide-tipped backerboard scoring knife, trowel

MATERIALS YOU MAY NEED: Green board drywall or cement backer board, drywall screws or cement board screws, fiberglass mesh tape, joint compound or polymer modified mortar, silicone caulk

Green board drywall: This drywall is green in color and has a chemically treated face paper to resist moisture. Usually the core of the gypsum is treated with a moisture-resistant compound. Because it is not waterproof, I suggest using this in the area of your bathroom that will be away from the shower and tub such as the ceiling and walls without tile. Although it is green in color and slightly heavier, it cuts and looks like regular drywall and comes in 4'×8' sheets. You install it the same way as drywall by using drywall screws, fastening it to the studs every 8 inches vertically up the studs. Use 1¼" drywall screws for ½" green board and 1⅝" drywall screws if you are using ⅝" green board. If you are tiling over the green board, you will not have to tape and compound the joints, or the heads of the screws. The area that you will be painting *will* need to be taped properly. Use 2" fiberglass mesh tape over the joints, and apply joint compound over the taped joints and screwheads. For details on installation and cutting of drywall, see Chapter 3.

> **Tip:** Leave a ¼" gap between the green board and the shower pan or tub. Green board has gypsum in it that will wick water into the core of it and eventually deteriorate it. Be sure you use a silicone caulk at the ¼" gap before installing your tile.

If you use green board for your ceilings, be sure the framing is no more than 12" o.c. for ½" green board and 16" o.c. for ⅝" green board. "o.c." or "on center" means from the center point of one joist to the center of the next joist. Those of you who want to tackle hanging a ceiling, be sure you get at least one helper and make a couple of drywall jacks, or a "deadman" as we call them in the trade. See "Walls" in the "Interior Chapter" for more detailed information on installation.

Cement backerboard: There are two types of cement backerboard. Wonder Board™; which is a name brand of a cementous material sandwiched between glass mesh that I worked with a good bit in the, 80s and 90s and comes in 3' × 5' sheets. Hardibacker® board (name brand) comes in 4' × 5' sheets and has become very popular today by many builders for tiling. Both require a thickness of ½" for the walls. After the insulation has been put in between the studs, I would suggest stapling a moisture barrier on the studs before you screw the backerboard on them because there is so much moisture in the bathroom. You can use 6 mil. polyethylene plastic or 15 lb. roofing felt.

Cutting cement backerboard: Cutting cement backerboard is just like cutting drywall. You will measure your piece, score one side, and snap it. It will hang over until you score the other side and snap it off. Use a utility knife for Wonder Board™ to score through the fiberglass mesh cloth. You will need a carbide-tipped backerboard scoring knife for the Hardibacker® since it is tougher to cut. For Wonder Board™, I just use a utility knife and buy extra blades, because cement board dulls the blades easily. You will also need to make more than one pass with your utility knife in most cases. Remember, you're cutting cement, and when the board breaks, you may need to get some pliers to take off some rough points on the cut side.

Securing backerboard to studs: You should stagger the joints of the board and secure to the studs with 1¼" to 1 ⅝" cement board screws that have an alkali-resistant coating. Place cement backerboard screws every 8" to the studs, making sure your studs are no more than 16" apart on center (o.c). Leave ⅛" gap at the joints for expansion.

Fig 5.39- Taping the Joints

Taping the joints: Using a trowel, spread a polymer-modified mortar (bonding material for cement backerboard) over the factory tapered edged joints, and lay 2" fiberglass mesh tape over the joint and into the bonding material. If you have to cut two sheets of backerboard and butt them together, spread a larger 6" layer of bonding material over the joint and fiberglass tape. Apply the same bonding material to any ends and corners.

REPLACING BROKEN CERAMIC TILE

DIFFICULTY: 2+

TOOLS YOU MAY NEED: Grout saw, rotary tool with grout-cutting blade, putty knife, hammer, flat screwdriver, five-in-one putty knife, tile cutter or glass cutter

MATERIALS YOU MAY NEED: Rag, safety glasses, tile adhesive, grout, grout sealant, sponge, grout float, nail

FYI: Most people do not have tiled ceilings so you wouldn't want to install cement board on the ceiling. If you do want tiles on the ceiling, be sure the ceiling joists or furring channels that you would be screwing the backerboard into are no more than 16" apart o.c.

I went into depth about this project in the kitchen chapter and basically, it's the same steps to fix it here. Usually in the bathroom, you will have 4¼" × 4¼" ceramic tile on the walls. That is standard. These tiles are so easy to replace. The only hard part is finding a tile color that matches. That's why I always suggest keeping some extra tile in your attic or basement when doing a project just in case ten years down the road a tile cracks; you can then replace it with the same color.

Removing the grout: Before you try to lift out the tile, remove the grout. This way, if you need to break it up more, you will have a little more room. The last thing you want to do is create more work by cracking other tiles around it. Use a grout saw, as it is sized specifically for this purpose, working it back and forth around the grout of the broken tile. You can use a rotary tool with a grout-cutting wheel on it to help this process along.

Fig 5.40- Removing the Grout

Removing the tile: If your broken tile is on the end, you will have an easier time getting to it than if it is in the middle. If it's on the end, just slip a putty knife underneath the tile and tap the end of the handle with a hammer—it may lift off. If it's loose in the middle, you may be able to pry it up with a flat screwdriver. Otherwise, put on your safety glasses, put a rag over the tile, and give it a good hit with the hammer. You want it to crack in a few pieces so you can work the flat screwdriver in to pry the entire tile

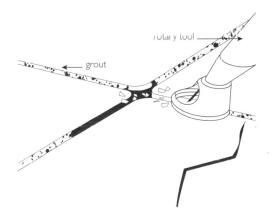

Fig 5.41 - Break the Tile

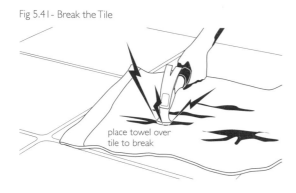

place towel over
tile to break

up. I always have a five-in-one putty knife to help remove any old mastic (glue) from underneath the tile.

Applying adhesive to the tile: Using tile adhesive and a putty knife, "back butter" your tile, or smear the adhesive onto the back of the tile. Place the new tile in place, and let it dry according to the adhesive manufacturer's directions. Just eyeball it to be sure the tile sits in with the same amount of space around it. You can also put in spacers or roll up a small piece of cardboard to act as a spacer.

Regrouting the area: If you're only replacing one tile, I'd suggest buying the premixed grout in a small container. Work the grout into the joints with a damp sponge, and wipe away any excess. If you're going to replace a good amount of grout, get a float to work the grout into the joints.

Sealing the grout: This is very important, but unfortunately, it is a step many people skip. After the grout has cured according to the manufacturer's directions, you need to seal the grout. This will help prevent water damage down the road.

Tip: If you need one or two tiles cut, often home centers will cut your tile to the desired measurement.

Cutting the tile: If you need to cut a tile and you have ¼-inch-thick ceramic tile, you can either use a tile cutter or a glass cutter and nail. If you want to keep the cost down, use a glass cutter and score the tile to the measurement you need. Place the scored line over a nail, and press on the edges. The tile will snap in two. For more on tile cutting, see "Cutting Tile" under "Laying Out a Tile Wall."

TILING A WALL
DIFFICULTY: 3+

TOOLS YOU MAY NEED: Measuring tape, level, tile cutter or glass cutting wheel, notched trowel, screwdriver, rubber mallet, wood block, china marker, tile nippers, grout float, grout sponge, caulk gun, notched trowel

MATERIALS YOU MAY NEED: Tile, tile adhesive, grout sealer, grout, silicone caulk

For those of you who are doing a remodel or have had to repair an entire wall, you will need to start tiling from scratch. After you have repaired or patched any damage to your wall(s), the first thing you need to do is to pick out the tile. Tile comes in various sizes of ceramic, porcelain, and stone. I would suggest using cement backerboard as a substrate under the tile. See "Replacing Your Damaged Walls." I would say that the majority of the people in our country have the standard 4¼" × 4¼" tile on their walls, although this is changing. More and more people are adding stone tile and marble to update and renovate their homes. No matter which you pick, you will need to do a bit of planning first.

Take measurements: After you've chosen your tile, take the measurements of the tile itself. Then measure your wall. You will need to find out the square footage of the wall (see below). Then you need to figure out if you will be using bull nose, edging tile, or base tile with a cove on the bottom. These are all considerations before tiling.

- Square footage = height × width (for instance: 8-foot-tall wall × 6-foot-width wall = 48 square foot)
- If your tile is 4¼" × 4¼", you would need 9 tiles for 1 square foot.
- For a 48-square-foot wall, multiply 48 × 9 = 432 tiles needed for project.

Always buy extra tile for mistakes and breakage and to tuck away for years down the road when you may need to replace one or two tiles.

Choosing your tile: After you've decided on the tiles, determine how you want the edge of the wall to look. Instead of having tile all the way to the top of the ceiling, you might want to end the tile halfway up the wall. Be sure you buy bull nose tile for a finished look on the ends. If you have an exposed corner, buy a corner tile that will have two bull nose sides and a rounded corner. You may also want to pick out border tiles. These borders are longer and narrower than the rest of the tiles and have a bull nose. There are many different ways of laying out tile. You can pick the one you like the best.

The Layout:
Method #1:

1. Find the middle of the wall, and make a mark.
2. Using two tiles, butt one tile up to the middle line, and butt the other tile next to it. Keep leap-frogging the tile (moving them hand over hand), butting each next

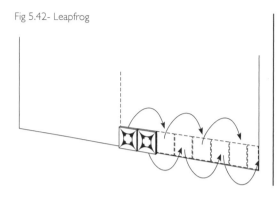

Fig 5.42- Leapfrog

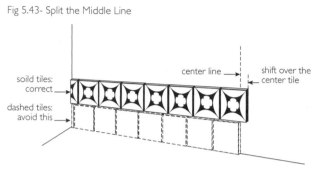

Fig 5.43- Split the Middle Line

soild tiles:
correct

dashed tiles:
avoid this

center line →

shift over the
← center tile

to each other horizontally until you see how the end tile lays out. More than likely you will have to cut the end pieces. If you notice that you have a sliver of a tile you will need to cut at the end, go back to the middle and put the center of the tile on the center point of the wall and leapfrog the tiles to the end of the wall. You will notice that by splitting the center line of the wall, you will be left with bigger end pieces.

Method # 2:

1. Using a 1" × 2" layout stick, mark off the tile and the space between tiles on the stick. Use the stick to help you lay out the wall.
2. Find the middle of the wall, and make a mark.
3. Use the stick as a guide to show how the tile will lay out off the middle of the wall.
4. If you don't like the way it lays out, adjust the stick accordingly.

Method #3:

1. Mark the size of the wall on the ground/floor.
2. Lay out one horizontal line and one vertical line to see how it lays out.

Whichever method feels most comfortable for you, don't forget to calculate the spacers if they're not already tabbed on your tile.

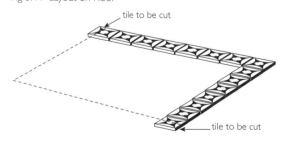

Fig 5.44- Layout on Floor

tile to be cut

tile to be cut

Horizontal layout: To get a perfectly plumb (a line straight up and down) tiled wall, you must be sure your horizontal tiles are level. Check to see if your floor or tub is level. If it is, you can start from the bottom and work your way up. Oftentimes, the floor and tub aren't perfectly level. If it isn't level, I

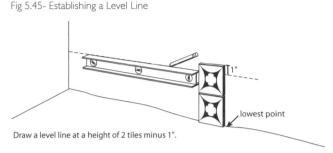

Fig 5.45- Establishing a Level Line

1"

lowest point

Draw a level line at a height of 2 tiles minus 1".

suggest establishing a horizontal layout line by measuring at the lowest spot. Place a tile up against the wall at the lowest spot. Place another tile on top of that tile against the wall so you are two tiles above the low spot. Make a mark 1 inch below the top of that tile. That will be the line you will start to lay your tile. You do this because you want to be sure the tile is level consistently throughout the bathroom. Because you will need to cut the tile to the slope of the tub or floor, you want to allow yourself enough tile to cut.

Vertical Layout: With the horizontal line established, go to the center line of the wall. If you decide to lay out the tile to the center line, you will need to plumb that line up the wall. This will be the layout line that will guide you to keep the joints perfectly plumb. If you are going to install the tile in the middle of the center line of the wall, make a mark on the edge of the tile once it is placed over the center line and plumb that line with a level.

Installing the tiles: If you will be tiling more than one wall, always tile the widest wall first, using the kind of mastic or thinset cement mortar the tile manufacturer suggests. Starting on one side of the vertical line and working up from the ledge and using a notched trowel, spread the adhesive evenly on the wall with the flat side of the trowel. Go over it again with the notched side, and comb it into ridges. Only apply adhesive to an area that you can work in about ten minutes. Otherwise, the mastic will start to set up and create a film on the top, which will not allow the tile to stick properly.

I like to alternate on one side of the vertical line to the other side, so I continue to

Trick of the Trade:

I always install a ledge on this horizontal line. This is made up of a straight piece of 1" × 4" (or scrap wood) that is screwed into the width of the wall. This acts as a shelf for the first row of tiles. Just be sure it's straight by looking down the edge of the board from one end to see that it's straight. I have noticed that mastic or cement mortar that holds the tile can allow the tile to sag a bit before it sets up. This ledge will stop that and be sure your tiles are perfectly level, providing you screw the ledger level. After you have laid all the tiles above the ledge, remove it and lay the rest of the tile below it.

Fig 5.46- Ledger Board for Tiling

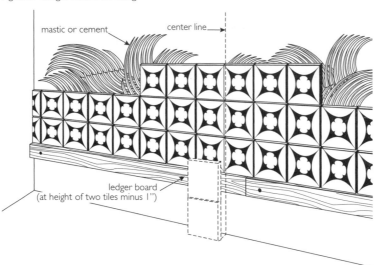

mastic or cement

center line

ledger board
(at height of two tiles minus 1")

Trick of the Trade:

Keep the tile about ⅛" to ¼" above the tub or shower pan. Use silicone caulk instead of grout in this gap. This will ensure a watertight seal around the tub and shower.

go up the wall evenly. Just be sure you don't apply the mastic right on the vertical line, because that is your guide. I usually like to make all my cuts at the end of the job.

When you place your tile on the wall, give it a little twist to ensure it adheres well to the wall. Also, keep a block of wood and a rubber mallet handy to tap the tiles into place, making them even unto themselves.

Don't forget to use the spacers in between your tile, unless tabs are already on the tile themselves, such as with most ceramic tile. This will be the space for your grout.

Install the trim tile or the edge tile where needed. You may need to back butter the tiles individually if you don't have the adhesive on the wall in those areas. Back buttering means applying the adhesive on the back of the tile before placing it in. I like to use the edge of the putty knife or trowel and make a few lines in the adhesive. This gives the adhesive some smushing room when it's tapped into place.

Fig 5.47- Types of Tile Profile

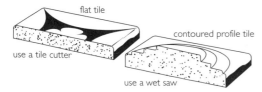

flat tile

contoured profile tile

use a tile cutter

use a wet saw

Cutting tile: If you are cutting flat ceramic tile without a profile, then by all means buy a tile cutter. If you are cutting tile that has a profile or is made of stone, then rent a wet saw. I suggest making all the cuts at the same time. This way you will only need to rent a wet saw for a day or two.

Cutting flat tile: Measure the area with your measuring tape, and use a china marker to transfer this measurement to the tile. Put the tile mark in the center of the (nonpowered) tile cutter, and keep it placed against the top plate on the cutter. Lift the handle of the tile cutter, and score the tile on the mark. Only score once. Place the wings of the cutter ½" from the top or bottom of the scored tile, and press down on the handle firmly until the wings break the tile. You may be surprised at how lightly you need to score the tile to be able to break it.

Cutting around pipes: A handheld tile cutter will help you cut shapes on the edge of the tile. Score with a glass cutting wheel, and use tile nippers to break the tile at the score mark. If you have rented a wet saw, you can make a series of cuts before smoothing it out with the blade. To make a hole in the tile, use a tile-cutting hole saw bit if you have one. Another way to cut around pipes is to cut the tile in half and use your nippers to cut out half the circle in each tile.

Removing the spacers: If you are using spacers, once the tile starts to set up, remove the spacers. I usually remove them about an hour or two after I install the tiles.

Grout the tiles: Allow the tile adhesive or mortar to dry according to the manufacturer's directions. For ceramic tile that have a small grout line, use a nonsanded grout, as it won't scratch the glazed finish of the tile. For stone or other tiles with a thicker grout line, use a sanded grout. Mix up enough grout that you can use up in thirty minutes. Mix the grout following the directions on the grout

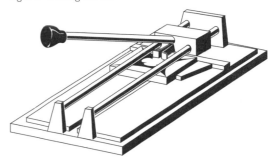
Fig 5.48- Cutting Flat Tile

Trick of the Trade:

Instead of measuring the tile for your cut-in, try placing the tile you need to cut directly over the last full tile, then butt a tile up to the wall over that tile and mark the edge of this tile onto the tile for your measurement. Works like a charm.

If It Were My House:

I only use nippers to break off corners, because I never have a glass cutter handy when I'm tiling. Nippers are great to cut corners of a tile and some shapes if you tackle little bits at a time.

Fig 5.49- Tile Nippers

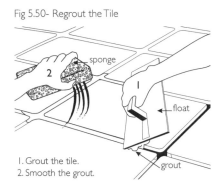

Fig 5.50- Regrout the Tile

1. Grout the tile.
2. Smooth the grout.

package unless you buy premixed grout in a bucket. Most grout is required to slake or stand for about fifteen minutes before you use it.

Spread the grout with a grout float. A grout float is a rectangular piece of rubber with a handle on it. Work the grout holding the float at a slight angle to the joints. You will notice that you can smear on a good bit of grout with one pass. Just take your time working it into the joints.

After you've pushed the grout into the joints, remove the excess grout with the float. Use a large grout sponge to smooth the grout lines. In my opinion, this is the tedious part of the job, because if you're a bit of a perfectionist, it can make you cross-eyed. Just keep the joints smooth and consistent as best you can. You will want to wear some rubber gloves, because you will dunk the sponge into the water bucket enough times to prune your fingers.

You will notice that a thin film of grout will remain on the tiles. Remove this film with a soft, dry cloth.

CAULKING AROUND THE TUB AND SHOWER PAN
DIFFICULTY: 2

Be sure you use silicone caulk between the tile and the tub or the tile and the shower pan. This is the area where the most water will sit, and silicone caulk will guarantee no water will get behind the wall.

To get a smooth caulk line, use painter's blue tape about ⅜" from the center on each side of the seam where you will be caulking. Apply the caulk, smooth with the spoon, and lift the tape up after you've finished. When you're lifting the tape, lift it at an angle away from the center of the caulk.

Sealing the grout: You went through all that trouble, now don't forget to seal the grout. Some grout takes twenty-eight days to cure—so mark your calendar! The last thing you want is for water to get behind the tile. Wipe any sealer off the tile.

Sealing the tiles: Glazed tiles do not need sealing. The glaze is the sealer. Most stone and clay tiles generally need sealing. Be sure you follow the tile manufacturer's instructions.

Painting Your Bathroom Walls

DIFFICULTY: 1

Similar to the kitchen, you want to be sure you use a paint in your bathroom that you can wipe down and won't be affected by water. Whether you choose a semi-gloss, eggshell, or satin, always add a mildew-resistant additive to the paint. Ask someone at the paint store to add it for you before putting it in the mixing machine. Some paints already have the mildew inhibitor mixed into the paint.

For more information on painting see the "Paint" section in "the Interior" Chapter.

FASTENING HARDWARE TO THE WALL

DIFFICULTY: 2
TOOLS YOU MAY NEED: Stud finder, Phillips head screwdriver or drill bit extension, tape measure, drill
MATERIALS YOU MAY NEED: Screw-in anchors or toggle bolts

Drywall or plaster? More than likely, wherever you want to put a towel or toilet paper holder there's not going to be a stud to screw into. That's Murphy's Law, folks! Determine where you want to have your hardware. Place the stud finder on the wall, and push the side button to allow it to calibrate; then slide it over your wall. You may find that you are so close to a stud that it would be worth it to move the fixture a little to catch the stud. For more information on wall fasteners, see the "Carpentry" section in "The Interior" chapter (page 55).

Drywall: If your wall is made of drywall, I would suggest buying screw-in anchors. These are made of plastic or metal and fit on the tip of your Phillips screwdriver or drill bit extension. These are what I use, because they are very easy to screw into drywall and the thickness of your wall doesn't matter. If you use the plastic anchors with the wings, buy the anchor that will fit the thickness of the wall. Your drywall will either be ½" or ⅝" thick depending on what part of the country you live. If you don't know, try to look at the cutouts around the pipes in the drywall underneath the sink. Take the tape measure, catch the back of the drywall, and measure the thickness. It's important to know the thickness of the drywall to buy the proper anchors.

Plaster: It is a little harder to detect the studs behind plaster walls because they are about 1" thick including the lathe. You will need the stud finder set on deep scan to detect the studs because a regular scan will pick up the lathe rather than the stud. I recommend using a toggle bolt in a plaster wall. These are metal bolts with a wing that screws onto the bolt. The wing acts as an anchor behind the plaster. You need to drill a hole in the plaster big enough for the toggle to fit through when it's squeezed. The trick with these bolts is to fit the wing on properly so the flat part of the wing sits up against the back of the plaster. You will then need to pull the anchor toward you as you turn the screw. A little awkward, I know.

If It Were My House:

I have lived in homes or apartments with plaster walls my entire adult life, and this is what I do: I determine the location of my hardware that will be mounted to the wall, and I screw it into place to see if I catch some lathe behind the plaster. Many times the lathe behind the plaster is enough to hold what I'm putting up. Although if I'm installing a shelf holding a good bit of weight, I'd put in a toggle anchor.

Tile: I don't know how many homes I've been to where I'll go into the bathroom, and as I'm unrolling the toilet paper, the entire toilet paper holder starts to come out of the wall. Have I been to your home? Don't worry, the problem is that the hardware was installed using expanding sleeve anchors, which work well for masonry but are not really intended for use on a tiled wall. Toggle bolts work better for this installation. The only problem with toggle bolts is that the hole you need to drill through the tile to allow the wing to fit through is so big that the hardware sometimes won't cover the hole. Just recently, I found anchors that are perfect for these tiled walls. They are made of plastic and go in like an expanding sleeve but have wings that flip out the sides when you insert the screw. They also come with a gauge that fits into the hole and catches the back of the wall so you know the depth of your anchor. Once you determine that, you will need to buy a masonry bit that is the thickness of the shank of the anchor. Drill through the tile and drywall or plaster, insert the anchor, and screw in the screw.

Countertops

Countertop repairs, removal, and installation are the same as for the kitchen's countertops. The home centers have made it very easy for you to buy a replacement laminate countertop complete with backsplash. For information on all types of countertop repairs and installations see "Carpentry: Countertops" in the kitchen chapter.

Here's an idea: How about using a piece of antique furniture for a sink cabinet? When I was a host on HGTV's *The Fix*, we showed how to use an antique cabinet for a sink cabinet in the bathroom. This is a great idea if you have a home with antiques. Because this is an antique, you want to do your homework before cutting into it. Those of you who like antiquing will enjoy shopping for your cabinet. Basically, you will cut in the top of the cabinet for the sink just like you would cut in to a countertop. What you

> **Tip:** If you're doing a bathroom remodel, lay your flooring down first before you set in your cabinets.

may have to do, depending on your antique, is to take off the face of the top drawer, remove the drawer part, and attach the drawer face permanently to the cabinet, giving it a faux look of a drawer. The other drawers may have to be shortened in depth to accommodate the plumbing.

Cabinets

DIFFICULTY: 3

TOOLS YOU MAY NEED: Level, drill, stud finder, tape measure, screwdriver, clamp, countersink drill bit, drywall saw, jigsaw, pliers, hacksaw

MATERIALS YOU MAY NEED: Shims, quarter round molding, 1×1s, screws, 2×4s

You may find yourself wanting to upgrade your bathroom by replacing a top cabinet or base cabinet, or you may have to due to years of water damage. If you go to the home stores, you will notice that there are quite a few base cabinets to choose from. If you're a tall person, I would suggest buying a taller base cabinet to ease your back.

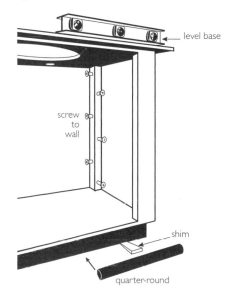

Fig 5.51 - Base Cabinet

level base

screw to wall

shim

quarter-round

Securing the base cabinet: Once you establish where the cabinet is going, level it into place, checking the level side to side and back to front. You can do one of two things: scribe the bottom of the cabinet to fit the floor, or shim the cabinet level and then install quarter round molding on the bottom of it to hide the shims. I would shim it.

If you make your own cabinets, you can use the wall as the back of the cabinet. In this case, secure the cabinet to the wall by attaching a cleat (1×1) on the wall next to the

Fig 5.52- Secure Cabinets to the Wall

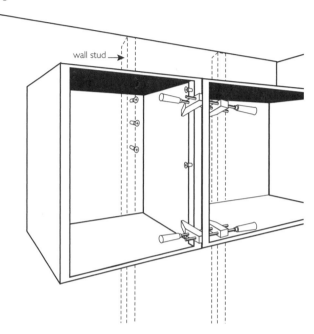

wall stud →

inside of the cabinet. Drill three holes going through the 1×1 cleat and three other holes going through the other way. One set of holes is for the screws to attach to the wall, and the other set of holes is for the screws to go through and secure the cleat to the cabinets.

Securing the top cabinets: Establish where you would like the cabinets to go, and find the studs of your walls. Make a level line at the bottom of the cabinet location. Measure from the point where your cabinets will begin to where the center of the studs are, and write down that measurement. Take the doors off the cabinets, then measure the back of your first cabinet, starting at the side. Transfer the location of the studs to the back of the cabinet. Drill a pilot hole through the hanging rail or cleat of the cabinet at those measurements—not through the ¼" backing. Get a helper to hold the cabinets in place on the level line when you're mounting them to the wall, being sure to catch the studs. When you have two cabinets in place, secure the cabinets together with a clamp, making the faces flush with each other. Then drill a pilot hole through one cabinet and countersink the holes so the head of the screw is flush to the surface. A countersink fits onto your drill and is funneled in shape with fluted cutting blades that will remove the wood in a V groove so the head of the screw will lay flush to the cabinet. Now, secure a screw holding both cabinets together, making sure your screw is shorter than the depth of the two cabinets. Keep going until all the cabinets are in place.

D'oh! Be sure your screws are the correct size and don't go through the side of the cabinet.

MEDICINE CABINETS

Medicine cabinets come hinged (or with pivoting doors) or with sliding doors. There are two ways to mount a medicine cabinet. One way is to install it between the

Trick of the Trade:

When I want to recess a medicine cabinet into a plaster wall, I use a jigsaw. With the saw un-plugged, I place the blade inside the jigsaw and use pliers to pull the blade out as far as it will go while still secured into the saw. Measure from the bottom of the foot of the saw down 1" on the fully extended blade, and make a mark. I take the blade out of the jigsaw and cut that mark with a hacksaw and then put the stubby blade back into the saw. I slowly plunge the blade into the wall until it lies flat on the wall and I cut around my cutout lines. By doing this, my blade only cuts the plaster wall and lathe behind it, and I don't have to worry about cutting any electrical or plumbing lines because my blade doesn't stick out that far. I do this with drywall, too, although you have to cut ⅝" away from the footing on the blade because drywall is a lot thinner than plaster.

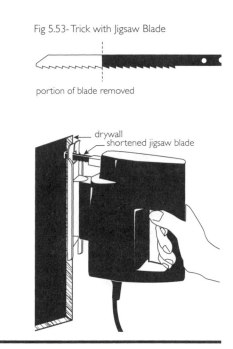

Fig 5.53- Trick with Jigsaw Blade

portion of blade removed

drywall
shortened jigsaw blade

studs—recessed in the wall. The alternate way is to surface-mount it on the finished wall.

If you have a recessed cabinet and want to upgrade it to a surface-mounted one, patch the wall before installing the new cabinet. Because a lot of medicines and products are stored in the cabinet, be sure you screw the cabinet into the studs through the hanging rail on the top and bottom of the cabinet. Use your stud finder to find the location of the studs. If you have a plaster wall or cement tile board, I would recommend using a surface-mounted medicine cabinet.

If you want to mount a recessed cabinet, measure the back of the cabinet and transfer the measurement to your wall, keeping the lines level and plumb. Use your drywall saw and cut through the drywall, being careful not to cut through any electrical wires or plumbing lines. If you have a stud finder with an electrical detector and a metal detector, use it in this area to be safe. You will most likely need to cut through a stud for the medicine cabinet to fit in place. Use a jigsaw to cut through the stud. Frame around the cabinet cutout with 2×4s, and secure them into the existing wall studs. Push the cabinet into this framed-out hole, and screw through the sides of the cabinet catching the studs.

Adjusting cabinet doors: I have detailed how to make these adjustments in "Carpentry: Cabinets" in the Kitchen Chapter.

Replacing handles: See "Carpentry: Cabinets" in the Kitchen Chapter (page 165).

FYI: The mesh tape, screws, thinset, and bonding material will all be sold with the backerboard at the home center. A lumber store will also sell the proper materials that work with the brand of backerboard you buy.

Lay Out Your Floor:

Similar to laying out your wall, figure out how you want your tile to lay on the floor. You may want to have a handful of tiles to see how they look on the floor. When you determine how you want your tile, snap a chalk line in the middle of the floor. Either use a framing square or bisect the line perpendicular to the original line, and snap that chalk line, too. This will be your guide to laying out the tile. Remember to allow for spacers for the grout lines when measuring. And keep the lines where you want to have a tile joint.

Flooring

DIFFICULTY: 3+

TOOLS YOU MAY NEED: Utility knife, notched trowel, chalk line, framing square, tape measure

MATERIALS YOU MAY NEED: Cement backerboard, thinset, screws, mesh tape, tile adhesive or mortar, tiles

Bathroom floors usually have ceramic tile or sheet vinyl because the floor is susceptible to a lot of water from the bath and shower. If your floor is made of different material, check "Flooring" in the Kitchen Chapter or The Interior Chapter for more information.

Underlayment: I suggest using cement backerboard in the bathroom especially under tiles because it is unaffected by water. The proper thickness of the underlayment and the subfloor under a tile floor is $1\frac{1}{8}$" thick. If you have a $\frac{3}{4}$" subfloor, install a $\frac{1}{2}$" backerboard. If your subfloor is already $1\frac{1}{8}$" thick, install $\frac{1}{4}$" backerboard. Cut the backerboard with a utility knife to the size that will fit your floor. Stagger the joints, and don't have the joint of the backerboard line up with the joint of the subfloor underneath it.

Before you screw down the cement backerboard, you need to spread thinset over the subfloor with the flat side of a notched trowel. Comb the thinset with the notched side, and lay down the cement backer board. Leave $\frac{1}{8}$" gap between the joints and the edges, and screw down using the screws sold with the backerboard every 8" and no closer than 2" from the edge of the backerboard. After you have screwed down the floor, use an alkali-resistant mesh tape over the joints and apply the backerboard bonding material or thinset over the taped joints with the flat side of a trowel.

Trick of the trade: bisecting a line: I learned this very early on in my apprenticeship as a union carpenter in Manhattan. This is such an easy method and a sure-fire way to get a 90° bisecting line to cross another line. Let's say I want to cross a perpendicular line through the middle of a room.

Find the middle of the room: First, measure from one wall to the other, and divide that measurement by 2. If your measurement is 12 feet, it's 6 feet to the middle of the room. You want to draw a line directly down the middle of the room, so measure 6 feet out from the wall and go to the other end of the wall and measure 6 feet out. Take your chalk line, hold it taut past both lines, and snap the line. (The chalk line is a piece of string in a metal or plastic housing with dry, loose chalk in it. When you pull out the string, it has chalk on it. When pulled taut when you're holding it to the ground and then snapped, you will have a perfectly straight chalked blue or red line—depending on the color of chalk.) Next, take the measurement between the other two walls. If the measurement is 20 feet between the walls, half of that is 10 feet. Measure 10 feet from the other wall on the snapped line, and that is the center of the room. Now you have to bisect that line.

Bisect the line: From this middle mark on the line, measure anything you want, say 2 feet from the middle, and mark each side from the middle of the line 2 feet. Go to that 2-foot mark and extend the tape measure 3 foot (again, this number is arbitrary as long as you hold the same measurement for all the arcs). Hold the 3-foot mark of the tape on that point, and stretch your arm to mark the end of the tape with your pencil. Slide the tape back and forth, making an arc—make that arced mark to the side of the middle point. Do this on each side of the snapped line. Now, go to the other 2-foot mark and do the same thing, keeping the same 3-foot distance and mark the arc until it bypasses through the other arc line on both sides.

Snap the bisecting line: With the chalk line, stretch the line so it is taut and directly over the two bisecting arcs and snap the line. You will notice that the line will go directly over the middle point. Your room is now laid out perfectly square. You can use these lines as base measurements for laying out your floor.

Tile floors: Spread the adhesive or mortar with the flat side of a notched trowel, and comb the adhesive with the notched side. Leave the layout lines showing to keep the tiles straight and square. Usually, the trowel notch size is the depth of the tile. Only

Fig 5.54- Bisecting a Line

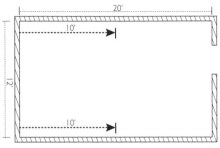

Step 1. Measure an equal distance
from a wall in two places.

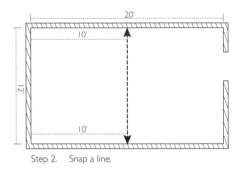

Step 2. Snap a line.

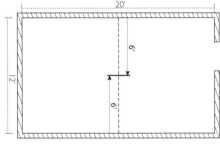

Step 3. Find the middle of the line.

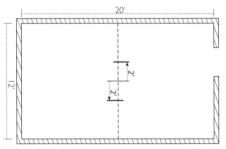

Step 4. Measure an equal distance from
the middle point.
(Example: 2' from center on
each side.)

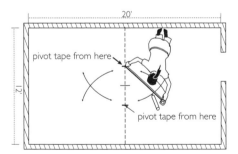

Step 5. Hold an equal distance from step 4's
mark with tape measure. Keeping
the measurement on the mark,
swing the tape back and forth to the
side of the middle mark, and mark
the arc on each side.

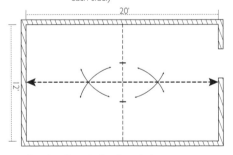

Step 6. Snap the line through the arcs.

comb enough adhesive or mortar that you can lay tile on in fifteen minutes. You don't want the mortar to set up or film over before the tiles are laid in. The 1" mosaic tiles come in sheets that are all stuck to a fiberglass paper. The tiles are set apart to allow for the grout and are very easy to install and very easy to cut around tubs and toilets. Other ceramic or stone tile can be applied the same way.

Vinyl tiles, linoleum, sheet vinyl, and stone tile: Repairing, replacing, and other repairs, see Carpentry: Floors in the Kitchen Chapter.

Electrical

This section will focus on the electrical fixtures that are made for the bathroom, such as exhaust fans and lighting over a medicine cabinet.

EXHAUST FANS/LIGHTS
DIFFICULTY: 4
TOOLS YOU MAY NEED: Stud finder, screwdriver, drywall saw, drill, reciprocating saw, tape measure, tin snips, flashlight
MATERIALS YOU MAY NEED: Stainless-steel screws, drywall screws, scrap 2×4s, silicone caulk, expandable foam, insulation, metal foil duct tape

If you don't have a fan in your bathroom, go out this Saturday and buy one! This will help remove the moisture and combat mold and mildew. Remember, mold grows in moist areas. Without moisture, the mold spores that fly around in the air cannot grow. Buy an exhaust fan with a light.

Installing an exhaust fan duct is similar to installing a dryer vent duct.

First, *turn off the power* to the light fixture.

Determining the location: The best location for the fan is where there will be the least bends in the duct and where the existing light is located. Every bend in the duct increases the resistance to the air flow. With your stud finder, find out where the overhead joists are located. In the best-case scenario, you want to run the duct between the joists rather than cutting through the joists. Take the existing light out and disconnect the wires.

Fig 5.55- Cut for Duct

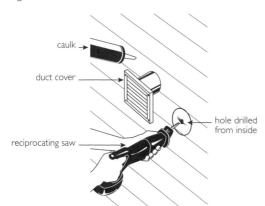

Removing some of the ceiling: If you can get to the bathroom from the attic above, you won't have to remove the drywall except for the place where the fan will go. If you have another floor above, you will have to remove the ceiling drywall or plaster to get into the area. Use a drywall saw to remove the drywall. You can keep the same drywall piece and replace it. You will need to screw in some scrap pieces of 2×4s to the joists to screw the drywall back into place.

Cutting through the outside wall: Most exhaust fans will require a 4" duct. After you locate the area between the joists on the outside wall, make a pilot hole in the middle of the location of the duct from the inside, breaking through the outside of the rim joist. Go outside and use the duct to mark around it. Use a drill bit big enough to slip the blade of the reciprocating saw through. Just be double-sure you're not going to cut through any pipes or electrical wires when you're cutting.

Installing the duct cover: Slip the duct part of the duct cover in the hole, and screw the cover in place, making sure the cover sits flat against the outside of the house. Use silicone caulk around the cover, and screw into place with stainless-steel screws.

Fig 5.56- Running the Duct

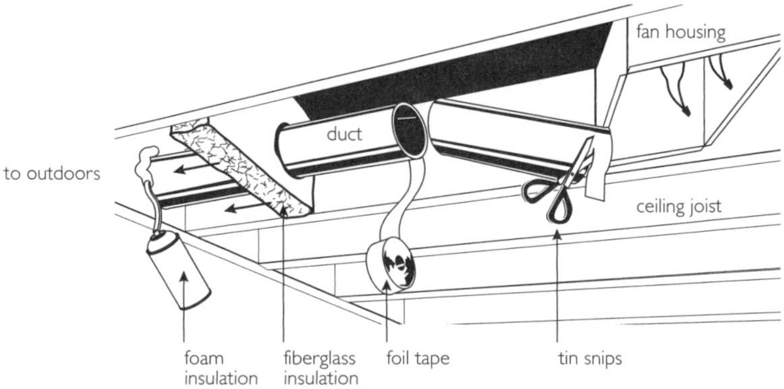

Insulation inside: I like to use expandable foam around the inside of the rim joist and then place insulation around the duct against the rim joist on the inside.

Running the duct: Measure the distance between the fan and the outside duct. Give it a dry run first. You may need to cut the duct using tin snips and use metal foil duct tape for all the joints.

Securing the fixture to the joists: The framing bars that come with the light fixture can be secured with drywall screws to the joists on either side of the fan.

Wiring the exhaust fan: You may get up to this point and call your electrician in to make the connections. That's fine, too. You will have saved yourself a lot of money just making the cutouts and running the ducts.

Those of you who feel confident with electrical projects will notice that the motor may have an electrical plug. Many fans will have a removable motor that plugs into the outlet that is built right into the fan housing. You will want to tie this fan/light into the existing light switch, so use the same wiring of the old light fixture. With the power off, you may need to use a flashlight to make the connections. Your fan will have the instructions for proper wiring installation. Please follow the directions. Remember, the black wire is the hot wire, the white wire is neutral, and the green wire is the ground wire.

GFCI Outlets: All bathroom remodels must install GFCI outlets. A GFCI is a ground fault circuit interrupter, which is basically an outlet with its own circuit breaker. Because there is moisture in the bathroom, the outlets within six feet of sink and baths must be GFCI so if you plug something in with wet hands, the circuit trips before you get hurt. They have a reset button built into the outlet. For installation on a GFCI outlet, see "Electrical" in the Kitchen Chapter (page 181).

For more information or projects about electrical wiring, see "The Interior" chapter.

Difficulty Key:

1 Beginner

2 Confident
beginner

3 Intermediate

4 Advanced

5 Professional

Chapter Six

The Basement

I grew up in Atlanta in a house that had a basement, which was my first introduction to construction. Years after we moved in, my folks decided to "finish" half of the basement. I got to see how central air, electricity, and paneling are installed. I also got to see my folks panic when the creek behind our house rose and our basement filled with water. For me, it was exciting, but what did I know? I was a kid. Now I get what all the fuss is about. Water can be such a damaging element to a home.

This chapter will go over the steps of moisture problems, water removal, waterproofing, drainage, and basement conversions. I will also address the water heater and air conditioning maintenance. Those of you who don't have a basement may want to skip to the water heater and air conditioning section.

Moisture Problems

Water in the basement is a serious ordeal, and I suggest hiring a professional whose business is waterproofing a home. But first, it's always a good idea to do your own investigating of the problem, so read about the causes and your options before you make that call. The majority of moisture problems are caused by the following:

- Improper grading around the house
- Improper drainage
- Structural cracks

- ▪ Problems with gutters and downspouts
- ▪ Improper installation of window wells

IMPROPER GRADING
DIFFICULTY: 5

We all know that water flows downhill, and if your home's landscape is sloped or graded toward your home, then guess where all the water will end up? That's right, inside your home. Usually in the lowest point—the basement. If your home suffers an improper slope, I would recommend calling a landscaping company to help you. Also see "Drainage Systems." (page 248)

IMPROPER DRAINAGE
DIFFICULTY: 3

If your sewer system is above the basement floor, you won't be able to have a drainage system because water drains down, not up. In this case, you will need a sump pump. A sump pump is usually installed in a sump pit that collects the water in the basement or crawlspace and then pumps the water from your basement to the outside.

STRUCTURAL CRACKS
DIFFICULTY: 3 to 5

Most homeowners with poured-in concrete foundations will have to deal with cracks in a basement wall. It's a fact of life due to drying, thermal movement, and shrinkage. Minor cracks are not usually a structural problem, but over time, they can get wider and not only compromise structural integrity but also provide a great source for water to leak in. I would recommend hiring a contractor or structural engineer to take a look at your crack. The good news is that most of these cracks can be fixed permanently using a low-pressure injection of polyurethane foam or epoxy. The epoxy takes longer to dry, but it is effective for structural repair. You can buy different concrete repair caulks at the home center, although you may still want to hire a professional contractor who is familiar with foundation repairs, especially for wider cracks.

PROBLEMS WITH GUTTERS AND DOWNSPOUTS
DIFFICULTY: 3+

If you don't have gutters on your home, *run*, don't walk, to your nearest home center and install them. When the rain comes beating down on your house, think of how many square feet the rain is hitting. All that rain is now going to come down around your home unless you have gutters. Gutters collect rain and channel it at a sloped angle toward and through the downspout and away from your house. If you have clogged gutters, the water will soon go right over your roof, landing next to the wall of the house and draining down into the ground and possibly into the basement.

Various gutter protection systems are easy to install and will protect the gutters from getting clogged with leaves, pine straw, and the like. Some clip on your gutters, while others slide onto the lip of the gutter. Always blow the debris off your roof so your gutters don't get clogged, even if they have covers.

IMPROPER INSTALLATION OF WINDOW WELLS
DIFFICULTY: 5

If your basement is half in the ground, you may have window wells to give you some light. If these window wells are leaking water, chances are good that the window wells were not installed with a proper drainage system. Basement window wells need to be drained to prevent water from flowing down the foundation and entering the basement.

Call a contractor to install a PVC pipeline from the bottom of the well, running away from the home.

Waterproofing

DIFFICULTY: 5

If your basement gets an enormous amount of water and you're tired of dealing with it, I would suggest hiring a contracting company to waterproof the walls. The basement can only be waterproofed by applying a membrane to the outside of the basement wall. I recommend this for those of you who live in a high water table area or have poor soil conditions. Of course, if you are not under new construction, you know what this means—you will need to remove the soil from around your home. Don't skimp by just "dampproofing" your home by painting that thick black goop that comes in a bucket on the outside of the foundation wall. Dampproofing will only retard moisture, making it water resistant but not waterproof.

When you hire a contractor, be sure he or she uses a waterproof system with an insulation board that will drain the water away from the basement walls.

DRAINAGE SYSTEMS
DIFFICULTY: 4 to 5

If you are going to go through all the trouble to excavate the ground around your home to waterproof the walls, you may want to install a drainage system while you're at it. First, know what kinds of pipes are available.

Drainage pipes come in different diameters and are either perforated or nonperforated. Perforated means that the pipe has holes in it to catch water in many areas and is then sloped to direct the water away from the house. The most popular, and the one I'd recommend, is the 4" diameter PVC pipe. Solid PVC pipe is effective in draining water away from one area and to the street. Corrugated black flex pipe can also be used. It looks like an accordion and is very flexible, making it ideal for bends and turns.

FRENCH DRAINS
DIFFICULTY: 4 to 5

French drains have been used all over the world for thousands of years. A French drain is a system that lays in a trench with gravel over it and is sloped to run water away from an area. This is a very popular system for dealing with water in the basement.

When water runs toward a home, landscapers will install a perforated pipe in the elevated level to catch the water and then divert it away from the house before it can run down to it. Other times, the perforated pipes are installed in a trench around a house near the foundation and then sloped running the water away from the home. It's important to wrap a weed barrier around the pipes so roots cannot grow into the perforations. Lay pea gravel over the pipes to allow the water to trickle down, seep into the pipes, and then be diverted away.

Basement Conversion

Everyone wants to have more space in their home, right? Now, I'm not suggesting that everyone who reads this book can take on the task of converting their basement, but those of you who feel confident with carpentry would be able to frame the walls, install furring strips to the outside walls, insulate, and finish with drywall. I will go over all the basic instructions. For those who don't feel confident to do such a task (yet), please read on so you can understand the basics of your home's renovation, which will help you better communicate with the contractor.

Well, converting your basement is easier than you may think, but there are some questions you need to consider. Is it dry? If it's not, you must deal with the water or moisture problems first. Next, you need to figure out if you have enough height. You will need at least seven feet of standing space from finished floor to finished ceiling. How about a bathroom? Plumbing for the bathroom can add good bit of cost to the renovation, although it will ultimately add value to your home. Heating and cooling need to be considered, but you may be able to tap into an existing duct. If not, then you can install an independent air conditioner or install a window unit through an exterior wall that is above ground. If you need to install heat, I would suggest baseboard heat if you can't tap into the ducts of central heat. Electricity will also need to be run in the walls for outlets.

After you have created your floor plan, you will need to make some decisions on the walls and ceilings. Your ceilings can be dropped acoustical or drywall. An acoustical dropped ceiling makes it very easy to get into the ceiling for any repairs to plumbing, duct work, or for running wires later on. A drywall ceiling will give the space a more finished look, but then you can't gain access to the ceiling after it's been installed, so you may also need to install some access panels. I strongly suggest insulating the entire space—including the ceiling.

Your walls can be framed out of wood or metal 2×4s. That's a personal choice. Because I've worked in commercial construction, I am partial to the ease and lightweight nature of metal studs.

METAL STUD FRAMING

DIFFICULTY: 4

TOOLS YOU MAY NEED: Drill with magnetic Phillips bit extension, yellow aviation snips, level, measuring tape, plumb bob, combination square, powder-actuated fastening gun, leather gloves, safety glasses

Fig 6.1- Framing a Door

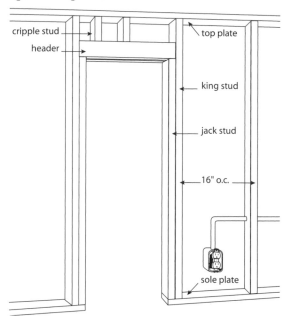

cripple stud
header
top plate
king stud
jack stud
16" o.c.
sole plate

MATERIALS YOU MAY NEED: 2×4 metal track and studs, corner bead, 1" drywall screws, power-driven fasteners, 1" common nails

Metal stud framing is resistant to fire and decay, it's cost competetive, and it's easy to install. A metal stud framing system has metal tracks and metal studs in a U shape. The track is screwed into the ceiling joists above and nailed into the concrete floor below with a powder-actuated nail gun. The studs are cut to fit in between the two tracks with aviation snips. A ⁷⁄₁₆" pan head framing screw, also called a "zippy" in the trade, is screwed through the track and into the stud on each side, top, and bottom to hold the stud in place after it is plumbed straight up and down.

Be sure you wear leather gloves when you're working with metal because the metal can have little slivers that can cut *you* after you cut *it*.

Layout: Lay out your rooms on the floor similar to the blueprint. Using a chalk line, snap a line where the track will go. To get the position of the track above, you must use a plumb bob. A plumb bob looks like a metal top (the kind you spin) that's attached to a string. When you hold a plumb bob from the ceiling to the floor, position it until it is directly over the line of the track. You will need to hold it over the layout line at two points from the ceiling so you can snap the chalk line across the ceiling joists. If there is a corner, always hold the plumb bob at the corner.

Remember to allow for the width of the door + the jamb + another ¾" to allow for shimming the jamb to the studs, which would give you enough wiggle room to shim the jamb plumb on each side.

Securing the tracks: The track above is attached to the ceiling joists. If you have drywall already in place, you will need to find the joists with a stud finder. Using drywall screws, which are black in color and have a flat head, screw the track to the ceiling joists. To secure the track to the floor, I suggest renting a powder-actuated nail gun. These are fantastic (and fast) for nailing the track into concrete! You can rent these for the day, but remember to wear ear and eye protection, because the discharge and noise are similar to a gun. The charge that is used is actual gun powder, which drives the nail into the concrete. You shouldn't have to buy a nail larger than 1" to go through the metal track and into the concrete slab. Follow the manufacturer's directions that come with the tool.

Cutting the track and the studs: Use yellow aviation snips to cut the track and the studs. When you know the length to cut, mark it on the track/stud and use a combination square to square the line around. Then using your aviation snips, cut both flanges (shallow sides), bend the track backward, and continue to cut the widest part of the track/stud. I like to cut my studs ¼" smaller than needed just so I am sure they fit in between the tracks.

Installing the studs: Position the studs into place at 16" o.c. (on center) from each other. I like to start in the corner and mark on the track where my studs will go with a Magic Marker. Remember that when you install your drywall, you need to have the drywall edge end in the center of a 16" stud. You will only have ¾" of stud to screw into at the end because you're sharing it with the other piece of drywall. So plan how your drywall is going to lay out.

Slide the studs to the top track at an angle to allow it to get into the bottom track, position in place, and then twist them so they lock in place. A nice feature on metal studs is the knockouts or holes in the studs that make it easy to run electrical wiring and plumbing through. Align all the studs so the knockouts all line up with each other and are all facing in the same direction. When you get the layout correct, attach the track to the studs using the ⁷⁄₁₆" pan head framing screws or "zippy" or by using a "crimper." A crimper does away with the need for screws. It looks similar to a staple gun except, when you squeeze the handles together, it drives a metal shank into the track and studs, making a hole with the metal pieces flaring out the back. It's this flaring of the metal that holds them together. I like the zippy because the crimper starts to hurt my hand. The trick to using a zippy is to apply a lot of force when screwing it into the track. In either case, you will need to screw or crimp on both sides, top, and bottom.

Doorways and windows: You will need to have some wood 2×4s for the studs and headers around the doors and window with the wood facing all around the rough opening. This will give you something solid to nail or screw the window to. Give yourself room for adjustments when installing your windows and doors. The rough opening for both should be ½" taller and ¾" to 1" wider than the door or window you are installing.

The studs: For the studs around the door or window, cut the wood 2×4s the same length as the metal stud, and screw the flat part of the metal stud to the wood stud. Screw this metal and wood stud to the top and bottom track with the wood side facing the rough opening. This gives you the blocking to nail your door jamb and moldings around the door and window.

The header: Because this is not a load-bearing wall, you will not have to make a heavy-duty header. For the header, use two 2×4s (or two 2×6s) with a ½" piece of plywood cut at the same width in between them. You will screw the two 2×4s and plywood in the middle together. Because the header is put in with the smaller edge facing down to give it more strength, the ½" in between the 2×4s make the width of the header equal to the width of the track. You can screw in a piece of track on the top of the header for the "cripple studs" to fit between the track on the ceiling and the track you screwed to the top of your header. Screw the cripple studs to the ceiling track and to the header.

If you are installing a window in an interior room, it too will not be load bearing. You can follow the same steps as the door header, but you will need to use two wood 2×4s laying flat for the sill and then cripple studs between the sill and the floor track.

Insulation: Be sure you install insulation between your studs. An R-value of 11 is recommended between walls. Batt fiberglass insulation is precut to fit between the 16" o.c. studs with a paper facing that you can staple to the studs. This will also help keep sound from traveling from room to room.

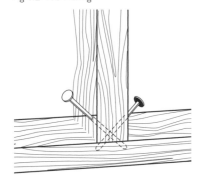

Fig 6.2- Toe-Nailing

For information on the R-value of insulation in your area, go to the Department of Energy's website: www.eere.energy. gov/consumerinfo/energy_savers/r-value_map.html.

WOOD STUDS

Basically the layout of wood studs is the same as metal studs except that instead of track, you have a top plate and a sole plate made of wood 2×4s. The studs are screwed into both plates by screwing/nailing in at an angle (toe screwing/nailing).

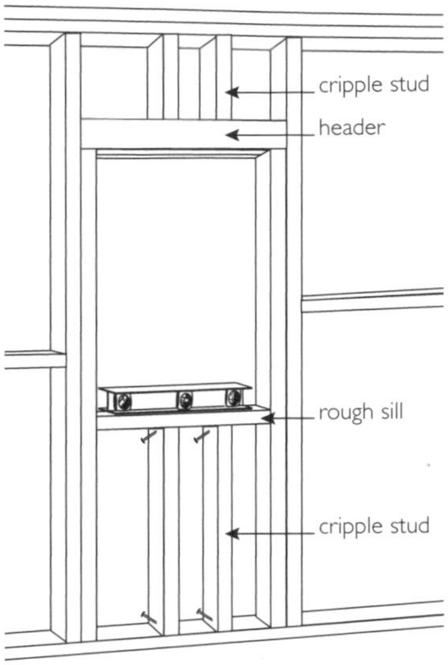

Doorways and windows: The rough opening around a door requires a "king stud" and a "jack stud" on each side of the opening and a "header" above it. The king stud goes from the sole plate (bottom) to the top plate. Next to the king stud and screwed or nailed to it, is the jack stud, which only goes from the floor to the top of the rough opening. The jack stud is what the header sits on. The length of the header is the width of the opening. The header is made of two 2×4s or 2×6s sandwiching a ½" piece of plywood to make up the width of the 2×4 studs. The header is screwed or nailed into the king and jack studs with 3" drywall screws or 10p common nails. The cripple studs are cut to fit between the header and the top plate.

Fig 6.3- Window Framing

cripple stud

header

rough sill

cripple stud

Doors come "prehung," meaning that the door is already mounted to the frame by the hinges. This takes out the step of making your own door frame, also known as a "jamb." Be sure you level and plumb the door.

Again, the rough opening for the window is the same except you need to make a rough sill plate made of two 2×4s nailed together and screwed or nailed to the jack studs. The rough sill plate does not need to be on its edge, so you will not need the ½" plywood between it, but you will need to be sure it is level. Then cut cripple studs and screw them to the bottom of the rough sill and the sole plate.

Drywall: Check with the local codes in your area, but most times you can put up ½" drywall and pass code. One half inch is a good bit lighter to work with than ⅝" drywall. Drywall comes in standard 4 × 8 foot lengths or 4 × 10 foot lengths. The "proper" way to install drywall is by "railroading" it, or laying it sideways or horizontally and staggering the joints. That's how I learned how to do it at the Union Carpenter's School—but guess what? I've never seen it installed like that. Every job I worked on had the drywall standing vertical, and to this day, that is how I've always installed it. Just be sure the joints don't fall in the same place on each side of the wall. Installing drywall like this makes taping the joints a lot easier, too! Use 1¼" drywall screws for ½" drywall 8 inches apart and drive them in with a drill or a drywall gun. Be sure the screw

If It Were My House:

I am a big believer in using screws instead of nails. I like the control of the screws. It is much easier to take out a screw than it is to take out a nail. I would use screws to frame my home, and if I was going to use wood 2×4s, I would still use metal track that the wood 2×4 studs fit into easily. It makes framing very fast!

Fig 6.4- Corner Bead

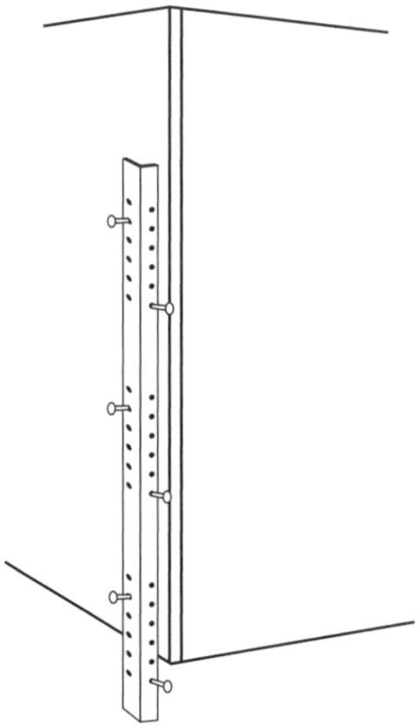

heads dimple the paper so you can hide them with joint compound later. Don't screw the heads too deep as to rip through the paper, because it won't hold the drywall.

Corner bead: Corner bead is needed on every outside corner for protection of the drywall except where you will have a door. Position the corner bead on the outside corners and use a level to plumb it straight up and down. Then nail it into place using 1¼" common nails (wallboard nails) 8 inches apart.

Taping the joints and corner: You will need to tape the joints of the drywall. I prefer mesh tape, because it sticks directly to the drywall and doesn't require a layer of joint compound like the paper tape. You will need to tape the corners, too, which gets a little tricky so take your time.

Using joint compound and a 6" taping knife (blade), apply a thin coat of joint compound over the screw heads, taped joints, and the inside and outside corners. Let dry overnight, and sand lightly with 100-grit sandpaper. Apply a second coat with an 8" or 10" taping knife to smooth the joints and corners. Let dry and sand. The third coat is the beauty coat, and you will need a 12" taping knife to make the joints and corners look flush to the wall. Let dry and sand with 120-grit sandpaper.

For more information on taping joints, please refer to "Walls: Patching a Hole: Tape the Joints" in "The Interior" chapter and "Carpentry: Walls" in the bathroom chapter.

Insulating Basement Foundation Walls

DIFFICULTY: 4

TOOLS YOU MAY NEED: Drill with magnetic Phillips bit extension, level, measuring tape, plumb bob, powder-actuated fastening gun, safety glasses

MATERIALS YOU MAY NEED: Furring strips, panel adhesive, 1" or 1¼" drywall screws, masonry nails or powder-driven fasteners

The question is, how insulated do you want your basement wall? If you nail furring strips to the wall, you will have to use rigid foam usually with an R-value of 4. For many, this is enough if the basement is used as a recreation room, but if you are planning to move a family member into the basement, you will need more insulation. You will need to frame out a wall next to the perimeter wall of your basement allowing for the thicker R-11 or higher fiberglass insulation to fit. If you decide on framing the wall, go back to the beginning of this chapter under "Metal Stud Framing" (page 249) or "Wood Studs."

If you do not need as much insulation, you can nail furring strips to your concrete or cinderblock walls, which will act as the studs to screw your drywall to. You will need four furring strips per a 4 × 8 foot sheet of drywall.

Caulking and sealing the wall: It's always a good idea to use a silicone caulk around any window or door opening where there are gaps or holes. Painting a sealer on the cement block is a good idea, too; however, the sealer isn't as necessary as the caulking.

Plumbing and shimming the furring strips: Furring strips are called 1×2s in the trade. They are really 3¼" × 1½" in size and are typically made of pine. Starting in

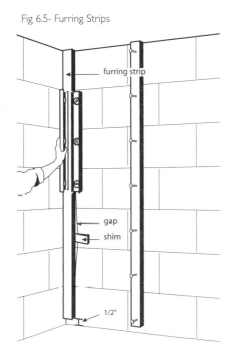

Fig 6.5- Furring Strips

furring strip

gap

shim

1/2"

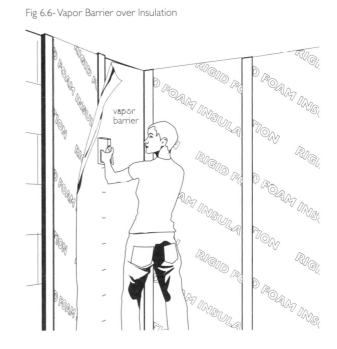

Fig 6.6- Vapor Barrier over Insulation

vapor barrier

the corner, attach the furring strips to the concrete or cinderblock wall with masonry "cut" nails or "fluted" nails. Cut nails are crude looking, square, and tapered. Fluted masonry nails are fluted with lines down the shank of the nail with a big, flat, common nail head. Both are good. If you can nail the furring strips in between the joints of the cinderblock, you will notice that they will drive in much easier. You can also rent a powder-actuated nail gun that will make this process a lot faster. See "Metal Studs: Securing the Track (page 250)."

Measure and cut the furring strips so they are ½" above the ground. When attaching the furring strips, put your level vertical against them and, where needed, shim it out to keep it plumb.

Rigid foam board insulation: Lay the rigid foam board insulation between the furring strips. Apply panel adhesive on the back of the rigid foam board to stick it to the wall. Keeping it ½" above the ground, use a utility knife to cut and a keyhole drywall saw to cut around receptacles.

Vapor barrier: Staple a 6-mil polyethylene sheet across the furring strips. The 6-mil refers to the thickness of the plastic sheet, which will act as a vapor barrier between the outside wall and your living space. Overlap the sheets, and tape along the seam with duct tape.

Drywall: Install ½" drywall over the furring strips with drywall screws. You may need to screw the 1¼" screws in at a slight angle because the length of the screws are the thickness of the furring strips and drywall.

Taping the joints: You will need to finish the drywall by taping the joints, applying three coats of joint compound and sanding. For more information on drywall and taping joints, please refer to "Walls: Patching a Hole: Tape the Joints" in The Interior chapter (page 33) and "Carpentry: Walls" in the Bathroom Chapter.

Basement Floors

If you want to convert your basement, you will definitely want to finish the floors. Depending on what you will be doing in the basement will determine on what floor you will want. It also depends if you have moisture coming from the concrete or not. If you do, you will need to address the moisture before proceeding.

CHECKING YOUR FLOOR FOR MOISTURE
DIFFICULTY: 1

See if your concrete floor can be sealed by taking a 2' × 2' square piece of plastic and duct taping it down to your concrete floor on all four sides so no air can get in. Wait twenty-four hours, and pull up the plastic. If the concrete is damp, you have a moisture problem. See "Moisture Problems." If it is dry, you can paint it. If the plastic has moisture on the outside, this indicates condensation and you need a dehumidifier in the room.

PAINTING A FLOOR
DIFFICULTY: 2

I suggest using a garage floor paint, which is epoxy based, seals the concrete, and will give you a nice finish. When it comes to painting a floor, there are all sorts of ways to do it. You can sponge it with many different colors or make it look like faux tile. Faux tile is labor intensive, because it takes a good bit of thin blue painter's tape for the faux grout lines. I recommend picking up one of the many books at the paint store for techniques. See "Painting" in The Interior chapter.

CONCRETE STAIN
DIFFICULTY: 2

Before you paint your floors, you may want to investigate concrete stain. Concrete stain has become very popular, comes in many water-based colors, and can be sprayed in different layers and then sealed with a few layers of sealer.

SOLID HARDWOOD FLOOR
DIFFICULTY: 5

This is an expensive and labor-intensive job. Do yourself a favor and hire out this job. This is why: first you will need to lay down a 6-mil or 8-mil polyethylene plastic vapor barrier and fasten "sleepers" to the concrete floor. Sleepers are the treated wood framework that is leveled and then fastened to the floor. The leveling process is a job unto itself! Then the solid hardwood floor is nailed into this framework.

FLOATING FLOOR
DIFFICULTY: 4

For those of you who would like to have a wood floor but don't want to go to the hassle of laying in supports for a solid oak floor, you may want to install a laminated floating floor. These floor systems are set on 6-mil polyethylene plastic vapor barrier and a thin layer of foam underneath to make it more comfortable to walk on and provide a bit of insulation. See "Floors" in "The Interior" chapter (page 77).

FLOOR TILE
DIFFICULTY: 4

This is another idea you may want to consider if you are flooring over concrete. See "Floors" in the kitchen and bathroom chapters.

CARPET
DIFFICULTY: 5

You may want to break up your living space with carpet. Carpet will give the space a very cozy feel. See "Floors" in "The Interior" chapter (page 79).

RADIANT HEAT
DIFFICULTY: 4 to 5

If It Were My House:
If I was going to install radiant floor heat on all the floors in my house, I would definitely go with the water system over the electric.

Because this is the basement and is usually the coolest place in the house, you may want to consider installing radiant heat. Radiant baseboards are very popular in the basement. There are two types of radiant heat systems: electric and water (hydronic). Because of moisture in the basement, I would go with the hydronic system.

A radiant floor is an excellent choice if you are planning on using your basement as a bedroom or living area. A radiant flooring system has electric or water coils that are laid on the cement floor with a thermometer on the wall and are covered with your choice of flooring.

The electric system is less expensive to install but may be more expensive in the long run, because electricity can be fairly expensive. Again, because basements are susceptible to water leaking in, I would not suggest an electric system in the basement. A water, or hydronic, system uses hot water traveling in small tubes. The hydronic system can be more expensive to install but less expensive in the long run.

Fig 6.7- Water Heater

Appliances

WATER HEATER:

If you live in a home, you will have a water heater. Homes with basements usually have the water heater in the basement. The cold water goes to the water heater, the water is heated, and your hot water pipes are born to feed your kitchens and sinks.

There are two types of water heaters: gas and electric. They are both similar in construction except for the way they are heated. A gas heater will have a gas burner on the bottom of the inside of the tank to heat the water. An electric heater has two heating elements jutting in from the side to heat the water.

Both gas and electric heaters have these components:

- **Outer case** that we see
- **Insulation** inside and around the tank
- **Heavy-duty inner steel tank** that holds the hot water and typically has a glass liner bonded to the inside to keep rust out of the water
- **Dip tube** lets in the cold water down deep in the tank
- **Hot water pipe** lets out the hot water
- **Thermostat or control valve** controls the temperature or the burner (gas)
- **Drain valve** allows the tank to be drained so you can move the tank or replace the elements

- **Pressure relief valve** keeps the tank from exploding if it were to ever get too hot (very important!)
- **Sacrificial anode rod** helps keep the steel tank from corroding

The differences are minimal:

Electric: Heating elements that heat the water in the upper and lower areas of the tank. Each has its own thermostat. The upper element heats the top of the water and then the thermostat transfers the power to the lower thermostat to turn on the lower element.

Gas: Burner that goes on by a pilot light and a **vent** for the fumes of the combustion of gas to exit your home.

MAINTENANCE OF ELECTRIC AND GAS WATER HEATERS
DIFFICULTY: 2+

Twice a year, remove about 5 gallons of water from the drain valve into a bucket to remove any sediment from the bottom of the heater until the water is clear.

Once a year, test the pressure relief valve in a bucket to be sure it works properly.

You may need to replace the sacrificial anode, which is a rod that is inserted from the top of the tank that helps prevent corrosion of the metal tank. Instead of the electrolysis eating away at the steel tank, it will eat up this rod, hence the name "sacrificial."

TROUBLESHOOTING FOR AN ELECTRIC WATER HEATER:
DIFFICULTY: 2 or 3

No hot water: Check the power to be sure that all connections are secure and then check the circuit breaker. Check the thermostat to be sure it did not get bumped and lowered. The heating element(s) may need to be replaced.

Rusty water: Check to see if the sacrificial anode rod screwed into the water tank from the top needs to be replaced. This rod gets eaten by a process called electrolysis and is sacrificed instead of the steel tank. After this rod has been eaten away, you will start to see the rust in your water. Unscrew the anode rode from the top. If it is badly pitted, replace it.

Replace the heating elements: Turn off the power at the circuit breaker or fuse box. Remove the panel to your electric heater and, using a multimeter set to RX1000, touch one probe to the element mounting bolt and the other probe to each element terminal screw. If the tester displays anything but infinity, the element needs to be replaced. Do this on the lower element, too. Drain the water out of the heater with the power *off* (which will also remove the sediment from the water heater) and remove the element(s). If testing with the multimeter gets you cockeyed, just drain the water out through the water heater and remove the elements by unscrewing the mounting bolts. Usually you can tell by looking if they need to be replaced because the loop will be broken. Bring it to your hardware store to replace with the same.

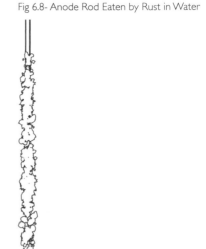
Fig 6.8- Anode Rod Eaten by Rust in Water

Always check your water heater's manual for proper removal and testing with a multimeter. A multimeter is a test instrument for measuring voltage, current, and resistance. You can pick up one at your hardware store.

TROUBLESHOOTING FOR A GAS WATER HEATER
DIFFICULTY: 2 to 5

Smell gas: If you smell gas, open all the windows and doors and let your house air out. Call the gas company immediately.

No hot water: Check to see if the pilot light is lit. If not, light it following the manufacturer's directions on the panel. Check to see if a draft keeps blowing it out. You could have a clog in the line. If it lights but doesn't stay lit, it could be a problem with the thermocouple connection to the control valve of the burner. In either case, call your gas company.

If the pilot light is lit but the burner doesn't go on, check to be sure your control valve is set to "ON" and not "PILOT." If it is on, you may have a faulty thermostat or control valve. Call a professional.

Not hot enough: Check the thermostat or control valve, and set it at a higher setting. The dip tube may have broken off and the cold water is not getting to the bottom of the tank and going straight into the hot water pipe. Turn the valve off to the dip tube and turn down the temperature. Remove the dip tube, and replace it the same day.

Leaking tank: Replace the water heater.

CENTRAL AIR

If something goes wrong with your central air conditioner, call an appliance repair-person immediately. Every year before the summer, a professional technician should be called for an annual maintenance visit. They will clean the evaporator coils and check out your unit. There are a few maintenance tasks that you can do yourself.

MAINTENANCE
DIFFICULTY: 2

- Keep any leaves and debris clear of the condensing unit outside, and be sure to prune back any shrubs or hedges.
- Change the air conditioner filter every one or two months, depending on your environment's conditions. In homes undergoing dusty renovations or with more than one pet, change the filter once a month. In the summer months, check to see if the condensation drain is removing excess moisture. On most central air appliances, the condensation drain is located underneath the evaporator coil on the inside of the house at the furnace/air conditioner unit. If the water has been standing stagnant for a year, it may have algae or fungus buildup that could clog the drain or hose leading the water out. Check your unit's manual for placement and troubleshooting.

FORCED AIR HEAT

This system pulls the air from the rooms into the cold air returns, through the duct through a filter, and back into the furnace. The air is heated and then flows back to the rooms through the warm air ducts and registers. You can maintain your heater to keep it working properly. First check your owner's manual for further information on the following:

MAINTENANCE
DIFFICULTY: 2

- Replace or clean the filter every month during the heating season.
- Clean the blower blades at the start of each season
- Check for belt alignment and tension if the furnace is belt-driven.
- Seal any leaks in the duct with duct tape.

Steam Heat: This system requires a boiler that needs a little maintenance.

MAINTENANCE

DIFFICULTY: 2 to 5

- Check the safety valve once a month during heating season by depressing the handle of the valve. Be sure you stand clear, and wear gloves and a jacket. If steam does *not* come out, call a professional to replace the valve.
- Check the pressure on the gauge to be sure the steam in the boiler is within 2 to 10 pounds per square inch (PSI). If not, call a professional.
- Check the water level, which should be in the middle of the sight glass. If you can't see it, shut off the boiler, let it cool, and open the fill valve. Call a professional if it has an automatic fill valve.

Gas heat: This is a very popular system to heat the air in your home. If you smell gas in your home, open all your doors and windows and leave. Call the gas company immediately.

TROUBLESHOOTING

DIFFICULTY: 2

- Read the owner's manual to relight your pilot light. Always light the pilot according the instructions, and use extreme caution.
- Before adjusting the pilot light, turn down the thermostat and adjust the pilot so it is blue in color covering the thermocouple.
- Clean the gas burners with a wire brush at the start of a heating season to be sure they don't clog. Be sure the unit is *off* when doing this.
- Heaters that are fueled with natural gas should burn a bright blue flame with a blue-green interior. No yellow tips. Check your owner's manual for proper adjustment.

A Frozen Pipe

Because water expands when frozen, the water that is sitting in your pipes in areas that are exposed to the cold will expand beyond the containment of the pipe, causing it to burst, and causing you to reach in your pocket and pay for the repair.

A Burst Pipe: First things first, shut off the *main water supply* and call your plumber. Do not turn on any lights or use any electrical switches or appliances if there is standing water.

TO PREVENT A FROZEN PIPE
DIFFICULTY: 2

- **Insulate** the pipes with pipe insulation. Pipe insulation comes in long tubes and slips over the pipes. Use duct tape to seal the seam.
- **Use heat tape or heated cables** around the pipe and plug into an outlet to keep the pipes warm. This is for those areas of the country that get quite cold.
- **Seal** any openings around the pipes that may let in cold air. Use expandable insulating foam or silicone caulk.
- **Drain or disconnect** any garden hoses. If you have a shut-off valve on the inside of your home or basement leading to the garden hose, be sure you shut off the valve.

THAWING A FROZEN PIPE
DIFFICULTY: 1

You can thaw a pipe with a hair dryer, a propane torch, or a heat lamp. Open the faucet and work from the faucet to the frozen area to keep the steam from being trapped and bursting the pipe. You will be able to see when the ice melts by seeing it drip out the faucet. (You will probably need someone to go outside as you are thawing to keep an eye out for the drip.)

Difficulty Key:
1 Beginner
2 Confident
  beginner
3 Intermediate
4 Advanced
5 Professional

Chapter Seven

The Attic

If you have bought a newer home, you may not have an attic. This is because trusses have become very popular for building roofs. Two of the most popular options for framing a roof are the rafter system and the truss roof.

A rafter system connects the rafters, which can be 2×6s, to the ridge beam. This system allows a house to have an attic if there are ceiling joists, which act as floor joists for the attic. Without the ceiling joists, your home would have a cathedral ceiling.

A truss system can span a lot farther, creating larger spaces below. A truss roof is

Fig 7.1 - A Truss System

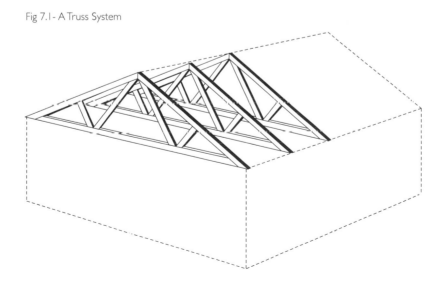

faster to erect, because they arrive to the site preassembled. A truss looks like a triangle with lumber webbing to provide its strength. It's the crisscross of these supports that don't allow for an attic.

Any time you need to work in the attic, you need to work safely and have a large piece of ½" or ¾" plywood to sit on. Without this, if you were to lose your balance on the joists, you might fall right through the drywall or plaster and land in the room below. The plywood needs to be long enough to cover a few spans of the joists and may have to be cut in 24" lengths to get them through the attic drop downstairs.

Proper Ventilation

Did you know that it is important for your home to breathe properly? Proper air circulation is essential to a healthy roof and soffit system (the area that hangs over the side of the house). If you don't have proper ventilation, you risk mildew, water damage from trapped moisture, and a higher energy bill in the summer.

You need to have a balanced circulation system with equal distribution of intake through the soffit vents and outtake through the roof or gable vents.

Check your soffit vents by going outside and looking underneath the overhang of the roof. This overhang is called the soffit. You can always install more soffit vents. Soffit vents come in continuous vents, too. You may want to hire out this work.

Gable vent: If you need to get more air out of the attic, you may want to install a gable vent, which is less conspicuous than a roof vent. When you're inside the attic, look to see if you have a gable vent. It would be located underneath the peak of your roof at one or both ends.

Roof vent: This vent sits right on top of your roof. The nice thing about this vent is that you can install one that has a powered fan, which will increase the circulation and ventilation without installing more fans.

Continuous ridge vent: Ridge vents can span the entire length of your home. They provide a consistent ventilation, because the hot air goes to the top part of your home and out the vent. Usually these are installed during the construction of your home, but they can be retrofitted if you are getting a new roof.

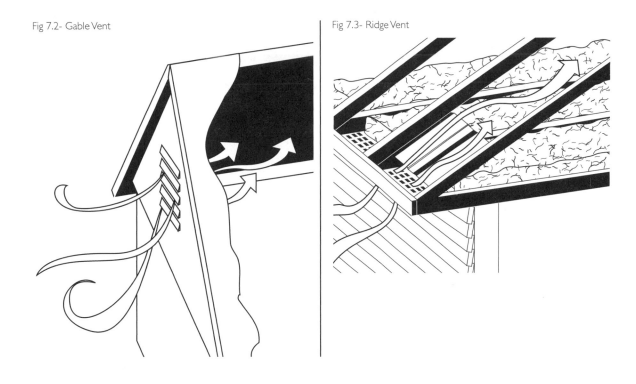

Fig 7.2- Gable Vent

Fig 7.3- Ridge Vent

ATTIC FAN
DIFFICULTY: 3+

In the summer your attic can become so hot that not only does it drive up your energy bill, but the heat can damage the roofing materials. An attic fan is an excellent way to cool the attic and is easy to install. You can mount an attic fan behind the gable vent, behind the gable louvers, or below the roof vent. If you mount the fan below the roof vent, you can buy an attic fan that will mount between the rafters. A fan behind a gable vent or louvers may need to be boxed in with 2×4 framing. You may want to hire an electrician to run power to the fan and install a switch in the wall below.

Insulation

It is important to be sure your attic is insulated properly. Just think—if the attic isn't insulated properly, in the summer you will have a very hot attic, which will make your energy bill rise in the summer. In the winter, it will take more money to heat your home. But before you install insulation in the attic, it's important to install a circulation system with baffles.

BAFFLES
DIFFICULTY: 2

Baffles are made of lightweight polystyrene material that are molded to make an unobstructed path for air flow and are about 4 feet in length. They are sized to fit in between the rafters and can be stapled into place with a staple gun. You just need to put one in between every rafter above a soffit vent, but not all the way up to the ceiling. Push the baffle down to the soffit vent or as far as it will go. They are needed to keep the airflow going into the attic. Otherwise, the insulation will clog up the soffit vents and not allow the proper flow.

R-Value: "R-value" is the measurement of heat resistance. The higher the number, the more resistant. If you live in a very cold climate, you many want to have an R-value of R-49. Check the building codes or a local lumber store for this information. For information on the R-value of insulation in your area, go to the Department of Energy's website: www.eere.energy.gov/consumer info/energysavers/r-value map.html.

INSULATION
DIFFICULTY: 2

Now that the baffles are in place, you can install the insulation right up to the baffles, but not over the soffit vent. Find out the R-value for attic insulation for your area. Most homes in the United States are between R-22 and R-49.

Blown-in, batt insulation, or sprayed-in foam: You have a few choices: blown-in insulation, which can be fast and easy but also fairly dusty; sprayed-in foam insulation is sprayed in between the joists by a professional and sets up hard; or you can use batt insulation. You've seen batt insulation; it is usually pink or yellow and comes in big rolls. Although it looks and feels soft and fluffy, it is made primarily of fiberglass. Some have paper or foil on one side, and others have nothing. If you're going to blow in the insulation, I suggest hiring out that job. If you want to lay in the batt insulation, you can do it yourself!

BATT INSULATION
DIFFICULTY: 2

Once you determine the proper R-value for your attic, measure how much you will need. Count how many sections are needed between the ceiling joists below, and multiply that by the length of the attic. This will give you the linear footage to buy. Also, measure between the joists, and buy that width of batt insulation.

If you have insulation already in place and want to add on, buy the insulation without paper or foil. The paper or foil act like a moisture barrier, and you won't need it if you are going to stack it on existing insulation. If your home calls for an R-value of 38 and you only have R-19 in your attic, you can stack another R-19 over it to create an R-value of 38. If the existing batt insulation is covered on both sides with paper or foil, use your utility knife to make slices through that top paper before laying the new insulation above it. This will let the insulation breathe and not trap moisture between the two batts of insulation.

If you don't have any insulation in between the joists, buy batts with the paper or foil. The paper or foil side needs to face down toward the floor below.

Proper clothing: Because you're dealing with fiberglass, you don't want to get it on your skin—it can really be itchy. Wear safety goggles, a dust mask, a long-sleeve shirt (a turtleneck is good), long pants, cloth or leather gloves, high socks, and boots or sneakers. I even like to tape the gloves to the bottom of my sleeves. Because this is the attic and heat rises, try doing this on a cool day!

Installing the batt insulation: The only thing you need to know about installation is to lay the insulation between the joists with the paper or foil facing down. This is the moisture barrier and needs to be closest to the living space below. Use your utility knife to cut the insulation. It will cut easily but may take a few passes to cut through it. When cutting the insulation, use a level or piece of wood to compress the insulation down to act as a guide for your utility knife. You do not need to tape it or staple it down to the joists.

Fig 7.4- Batt Insulation

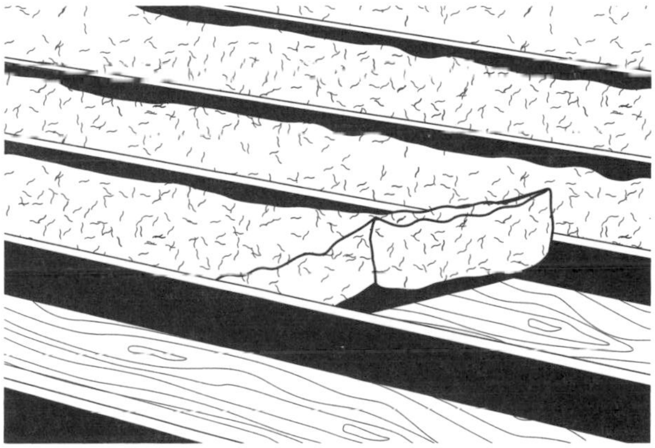

If you already have insulation between the joists and are adding more, use nonpapered insulation (without the moisture barrier) and lay the new insulation perpendicular to the joists so it crosses over the existing insulation.

When I was an Apprentice:

When I was an apprentice carpenter, I worked with all men who like to "break my chops," so to speak. I remember the first day I had to work with fiberglass insulation. They told me to be sure to go home and take a real hot shower after work. Well, that was the *last* time I ever did that, because a hot shower will open your pores, allowing the fiberglass to go deeper into your skin.

If you have a floor in your attic, you will need to remove the floor to install the insulation or have holes drilled to blow insulation in between the joists.

Take a cold shower: After you have finished insulating your attic, go outside and brush off your clothing. Then remove them and put them in the wash. Hopefully, you've stepped back inside to do this.

As soon as you've finished, be sure you take a *cold* shower. A cold shower helps close your pores to the fibers of fiberglass. Using a soapy washcloth, scrub your body and rinse off well.

Chapter Eight

Childproofing

Every time I hold a baby, I'm fascinated by the ten little fingers and ten little toes! They're so small and adorable. Of course, these are the same little fingers and toes that can get them in trouble. A child's curiosity can be your nightmare if you haven't properly childproofed your home.

Many accidents that happen to children can be prevented by using safety devices that are presently on the market. A few years ago, I got wind of a few companies that will come and install these safety features in your home. You can save yourself a bundle of money by installing these features yourself. Most are very simple and use common sense. Be sure to show older children (and spouses) how to use these safety features properly. Years ago, I stood in a bathroom for five minutes trying to figure out how to lift the toilet lid. How could I tell my host that I, the union carpenter, couldn't figure out how to lift the lid? When I figured it out, I felt like a dope and couldn't believe how easy it was.

I always suggest to parents that they get on all fours and look at their home from their toddler's perspective. Just remember, toddlers want to pull themselves up to stand and will grab onto anything; therefore, a wobbly table could become a hazard. When you're on all fours, look at everything with the thought that your child will probably want to put his or her mouth on it. It may not look tasty for you, but a child who is teething will see things differently. Pay attention to details. You may even want to buy toothpaste that has the cap attached to the tube so the cap won't have a chance to fall and get lost on the floor for little fingers to pick up.

The Outlets: Go around your house and count the outlets. That is the amount of outlet covers you will want to buy for your home. You can buy outlet covers and plates that will help prevent a child from poking his or her finger or small object in the slot of the outlet and getting electrocuted. When buying these, be sure they are large enough to prevent a child from choking on them.

Cabinets and Drawers: Your kitchen, bathroom, and other areas of the house may have medicine, cleaning fluids, etc., that have pretty colors, which may entice a child to swallow/lick them. Install safety latches and locks on cabinets and drawers that provide access to medicine, cleaning products, knives, and other sharp objects. These gadgets will come with full installation instructions.

Toilet: Children like to look in the toilet and can easily drown. Be sure you install a safety latch on the toilet lid so a child cannot pick up the lid.

Bathtub: As soon as you finish taking a bath, always let the water drain out. Set the temperature of your water at the water heater to 120 degrees Fahrenheit to help prevent scalding. If you feel comfortable with plumbing, install anti-scald devices on the bathtub faucet and the showerheads, or hire a plumber.

Corners and Edges: Hardware stores and baby stores sell edge and corner bumpers. These will help prevent injury if a child falls on or bangs his or her noggin on a sharp edge. They can also be used on fireplace hearths.

Doorknob Covers: Doorknob covers work really well on the inside of entrance doors to your home. These covers slip over the doorknob and require an adult hand to apply sufficient pressure all around the knob to open it.

Door Locks: Door locks are very important to restrict access to any hazardous rooms, such as a tool room. They need to be installed high enough that they are out of a child's reach.

Doorstops and Holders: Doorstops are easily attached to the baseboard to prevent a door from slamming into the wall and injuring fingers and hands. Doorstops and holders attached to door hinges can help prevent small fingers and hands from being crushed or pinched in doors.

Safety Gates: To prevent falls down stairs, install a safety gate at the top of the stairs and possibly at the bottom of the stairs—after all, what goes up, must come down!

The top of the stairs should have a gate screwed to the wall rather than a pressure gate that could be pushed over. Be sure the rungs on the gate are close enough together so a child cannot poke his or her head through.

Window Guards and Safety Netting: Window guards help prevent a child from falling out of the window. In many cities, it is now a law that households with children must have safety guards on the windows. The bars should be less than 4" apart. However, you need to allow one window in a room without guards for proper emergency escape if necessary. If you live in a high-rise building, be sure the window to the fire escape has a retractable window guard. Safety netting is important underneath balconies and decks to prevent falls. This is a project I would consider hiring a professional.

Be sure window treatment cords are up and out of the way of a child's reach. Cut all loops and install safety tassels on the ends to prevent possible strangulation.

Don't assume that because something is too high for your child to reach that he or she won't find a way to reach it. Toddlers are often stronger and possess more ingenuity than you may think. If there is a will, there is a way! Store stepstools or other such objects that can be dragged over to a high door latch safely away in a locked cabinet or storage closet.

CONCLUSION

Understanding the steps, materials, and tools is more than half the battle in home repair. The rest is practice, which will build confidence. If you're not accustomed to working with tools, give yourself some slack. It will come in time. You will have much practice, because a home is in constant need of repair and upkeep. Try not to cut corners. I have found out the hard way that by cutting corners and trying to save time, I have caused myself more work than if I had just had the patience to do it correctly in the first place. I've always felt that patience cannot be taught. It can only be learned.

INDEX